jacqueline lavenu.

Dedication

To Professor Ernst Weil for guidance and advice
that have served me well in my career.

First published in 2012 in softcover in the United States of America by Jacqueline Lavenu Studio & Gallery, 2400 Kettner Blvd #103, San Diego, California 92101.

www.lavenustudio.com

Library of Congress Catalog Card Number
2012940836

ISBN-10: 0615645062
ISBN-13: 978-0-615-64506-3

Photography by Hans E. Parge, PhD, San Diego, California.
Printed in China through Global Interprint.

Table of Contents

Introduction

Jacqueline Lavenu: Up Close and Personal

An intimate portrait by Hans E. Parge, PhD

"Plus les lignes et les formes sont simples, plus il y a de beauté et de force." – Ingres (1780-1867)

I met Jacqueline in Berlin in 1983. My first question when I saw her paintings was: "How can Jacqueline create such serenity in a world so full of commotion"?

In the intervening years frequent questioning and observations have increased my understanding of Jacqueline's creative and artistic process. I've learned that painting is about color. Colors express emotions and some, like red, Jacqueline rarely uses. Her intuitive way of mixing paints to get the color she needs is remarkable. It helps that Jacqueline can easily deconstruct any color into its constituent primary parts. Thus the paint is never used "raw" from the tube but always mixed resulting in a unique color palette.

As a young girl Jacqueline knew she wanted to make painting her life's work. This singular focus gained her acceptance into the Akademie der Bildenden Künste Nürnberg.

Learning any technical skill is hard work but harder still is finding and developing a unique artistic voice. Thus Jacqueline has always kept a studio to explore and follow her creative passions. Her body of work attests to this perseverance as each painting is instantly recognizable as "a Lavenu". Professor Weil gave Jacqueline invaluable advice: "Paint not with the idea in mind to sell – paint rather to make something good"; and "If you create 10 good paintings a year consider yourself successful".

People ask: where does Jacqueline get her inspiration? The answer of course is from everywhere. What is required is the ability to see. In Jacqueline's case her sight cuts through the clutter to extract the essence of her subject. In committing this essence to canvas the visible is not reproduced but the essentials are made visible. Once a landscape is filtered through Jacqueline's eye and put on canvas I will always see her rendition – even when I'm again in that same landscape.

For me, each piece in Jacqueline's, now over 300 strong, body of work is unique and a treasure. Especially so because there will be only one painting of each subject. The raw canvases are also prepared the traditional way. Five to seven days before a blank perfectly taut canvas is ready. Giclees, reprints or multiple versions are "verboten" in Jacqueline's continuing search for the "good" painting. Indeed the only danger to a painting comes from her sense of excellence – she often declares a work "bad" and paints over it.

Some visitors to the Studio & Gallery comment that Jacqueline's paintings look simple. I remember one local art student who remarked "this is simple, it's easy to do" only to come back a year later to declare that he tried to make it simple but found it very difficult. Indeed the hardest thing to do is to make things look easy and as good friend and artist Solomon Cohen once remarked; "Jacqueline's great gift is to make even simplicity simple."

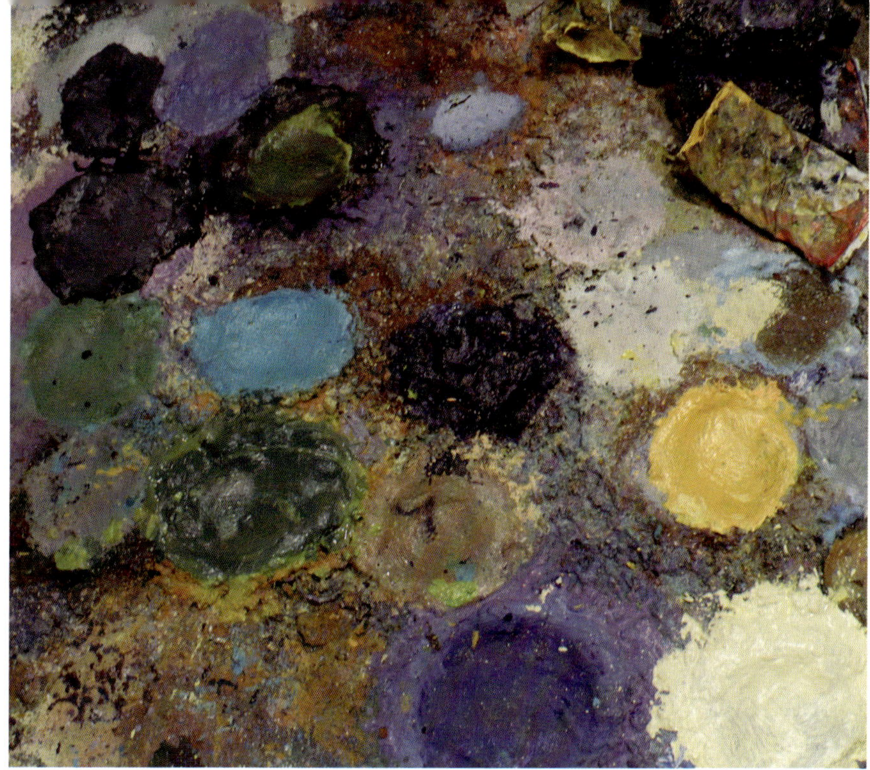

Palette of oil paint in Jacqueline's studio.

So how does Jacqueline do it? The foundations are sketches, sketches and more sketches. Her drawings are used to capture the feelings and emotions of, for example, a landscape we are driving through. I can never tell which landscape will trigger a sketch. However, I have learned that anything that looks like a postcard will not pass muster. She sets the same standards for her canvases; any rendition on canvas that does not capture the essence of the scene will be instantly changed or even discarded.

There are many recurring themes. Among them are nudes, women reading alone or with our cat, still lifes and our garden. Then there is Berlin and the Odenwald forests. Berlin is considered "home" and the many visits since leaving in 1986 for San Diego always inspire new works. Interestingly, though the move to San Diego had a profound effect on Jacqueline's color palette, there are many more paintings of Berlin than San Diego. However, California can take credit for replacing the industrial grey of northern Germany with an explosion of vibrant color. Indeed some of the early San Diego paintings have a unique and very "playful" palette.

No one lives in a vacuum and it is wonderful to overhear friends and visitors to the Studio & Gallery put Jacqueline in the company of familiar masters like Gauguin, Matisse, and Valadon. However, it is the German expressionists and the American Milton Avery that impress Jacqueline the most. The strong expression and colors of the German "Brücke" group showed Jacqueline that "Germans could also make very colorful paintings". In Avery, she found a kindred soul exploring the simple and essential.

Have I discovered the secret of her paintings' serenity? The answer must lie in Jacqueline's person and approach to painting and life. In the years we have shared I have found that there is an absence of pressure in the way she lives her life. Jacqueline has never chased money, clients, galleries or critical acclaim. Indeed her approach has always been to make good paintings and let the work speak for itself. Thus it is enormously gratifying to see her life's work culminating at the Jacqueline Lavenu Studio & Gallery. With this Gallery in San Diego's Little Italy, Jacqueline has an independent platform where she can share her aesthetics with those searching for the unique and authentic. I see it as proof that those who do what they love and love what they do are the most satisfied and successful among us.

Biography

Jacqueline Lavenu

Jacqueline was born in Cherbourg Normandy and demonstrated a talent for painting and color early in life. Leon Lavenu, Jacqueline's father, was an accomplished ebonist and teacher of woodwork at a Technical College. This exposure to fine furniture and design made a lasting impression and defined Jacqueline's life long passion for beauty in art and design. Throughout her early schooling, Jacqueline took additional painting classes, and the interior design publication "La Maison Française" became standard reading from age fifteen.

The culmination of Jacqueline's early education was an intense preparation for the entrance exam to the Ecole Duperré (Art & Design school). However, concerns about a young girl alone in Paris made her parents only support the safer alternative of a German language school in Heidelberg.

With a degree in German language in hand and her parent's wishes satisfied, Jacqueline headed directly to the Akademie der Bildenden Künste in Nürnberg. At the Akademie Jacqueline's talent and hard work was awarded with the distinction of Meisterschülerin. This recognition gave Jacqueline her own studio adjacent to her mentor, Prof. Ernst Weil, and started a trend that continued all her painting life – to always have, and constantly be working in, her own studio.

During the time at the Akademie Jacqueline participated in many group exhibitions. It was on the occasion of her first showing at the annual "Haus der Kunst" exhibit in Munich that Mr. Kahn (Contemporary Gallery) approached Jacqueline to represent her work in Dallas. This long and fruitful collaboration brought Jacqueline's paintings into many Dallas homes.

Jacqueline's move to Berlin with her Czech Architect friend, Peter Dosedla, immersed her into a city of great Art and Culture right in the central arena of the Cold War. The Wall surrounding West Berlin and the two superpowers in a tense standoff produced the most "real place" to live on the planet. Günter Grass maintained that in those years, Berlin was the center of the world, because if all hell were to erupt, it would do so first in Berlin.

This "realpolitik" also selected for a particular kind of person, and not surprisingly these included a fair contingent of creative people, many of whom were Jacqueline's friends. During this Berlin period extensive travels through Italy, France, Spain, Greece, and Turkey as far as the Syrian border informed her subject matter, though the grey light of Berlin defined her colors.

The grey immediately vanished with Jacqueline's first painting in San Diego. Thankfully her work did not reflect the culture shock that moving to San Diego represented. Renting apartments all over San Diego, was a first hand and treasured experience of living "the American dream". The location of Jacqueline's studios map this "dream" beautifully, i.e, Hillcrest, Sherman Heights/Barrio Logan, Golden Hills, Mission Hills to the current location of Jacqueline Lavenu Studio & Gallery in the Kettner Arts and Design building of Little Italy.

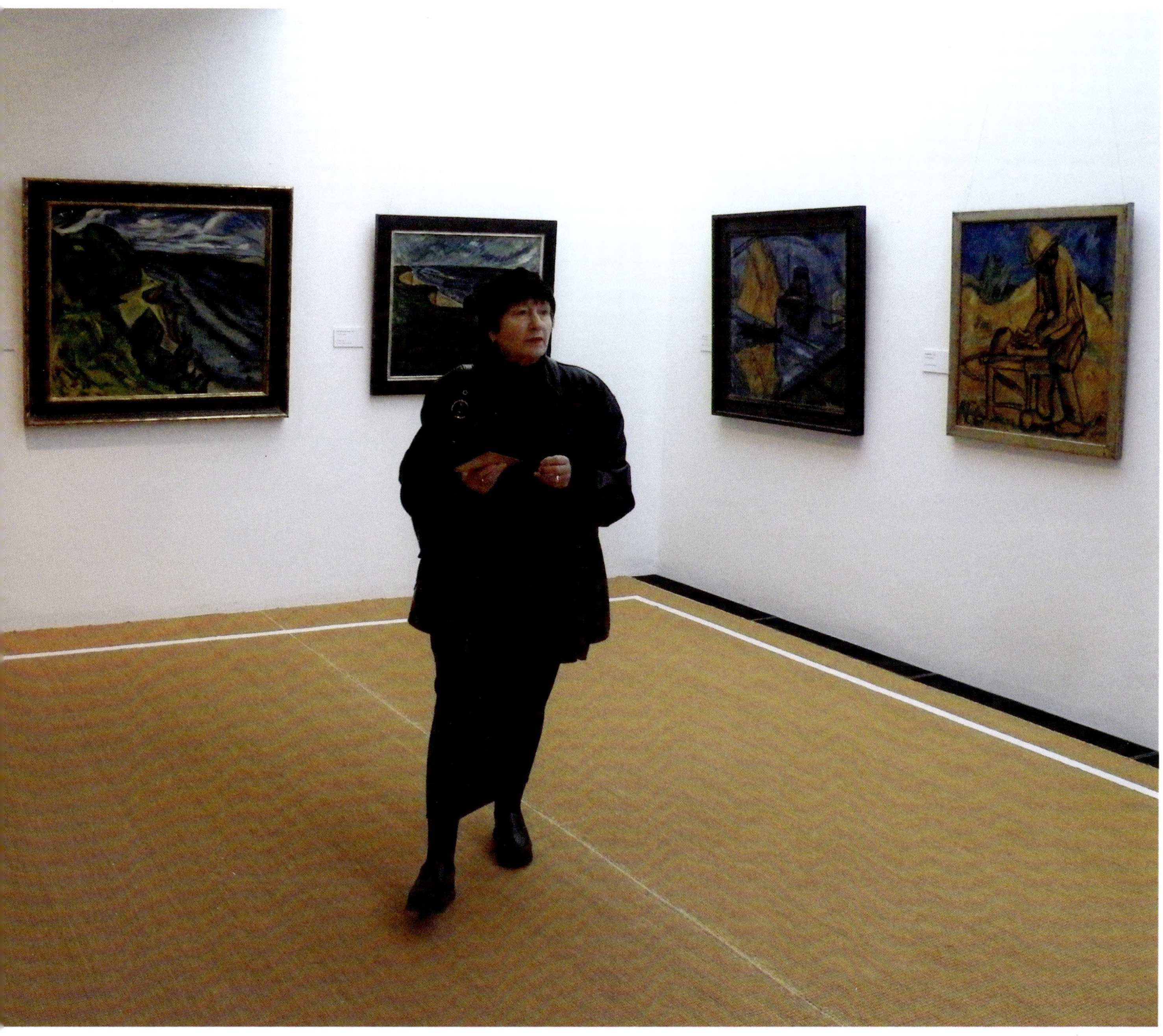

"The Brücke museum is my favorite. I visit every time I am in Berlin."

NÜRNBERG

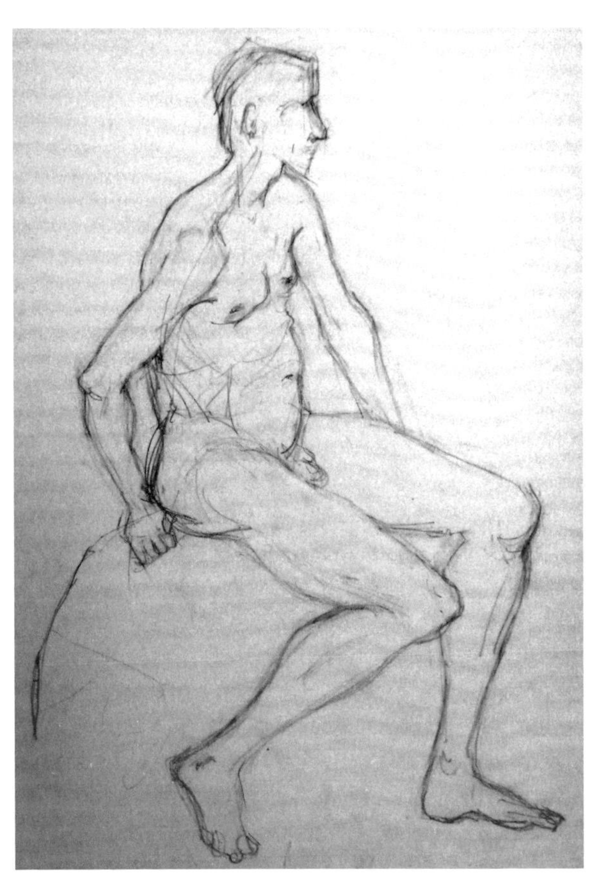

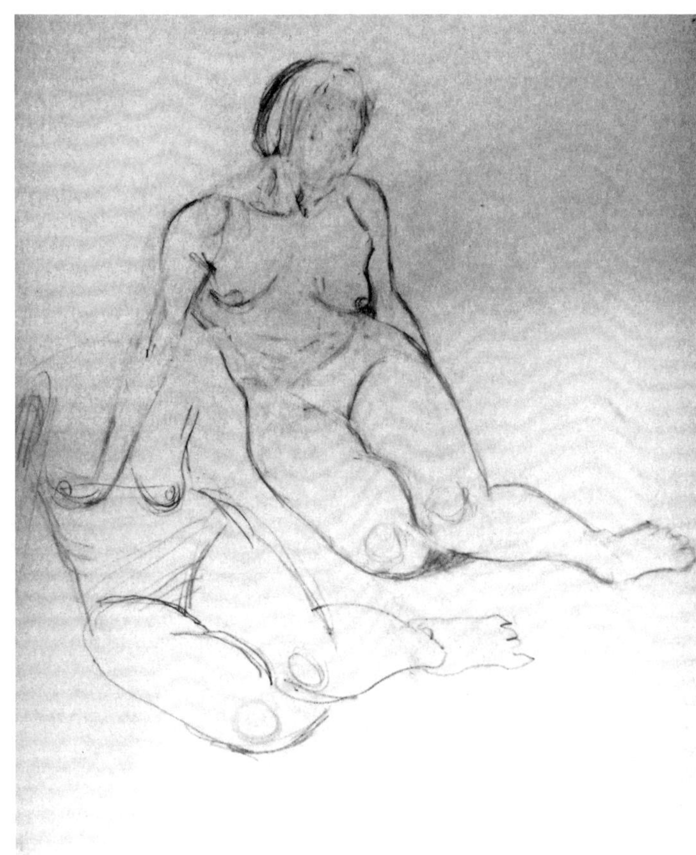

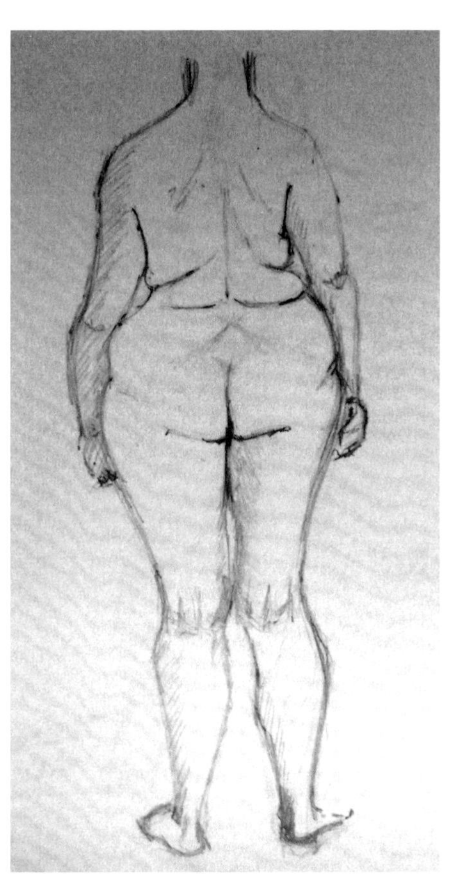

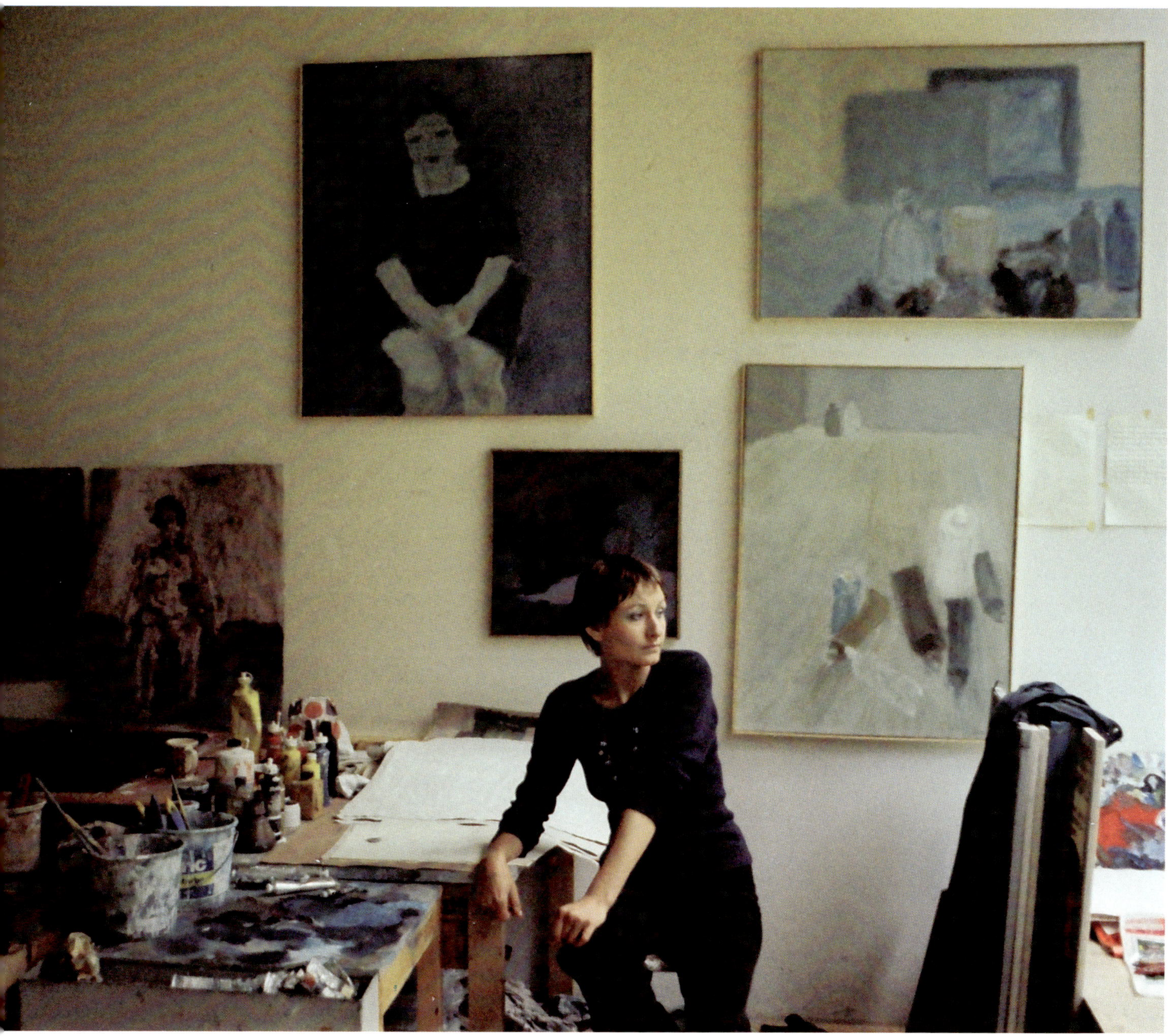

"As Meisterschülerin at the Akademie der Bildenden Künste Nürnberg I was privileged to have this studio next door to Professor Weil."

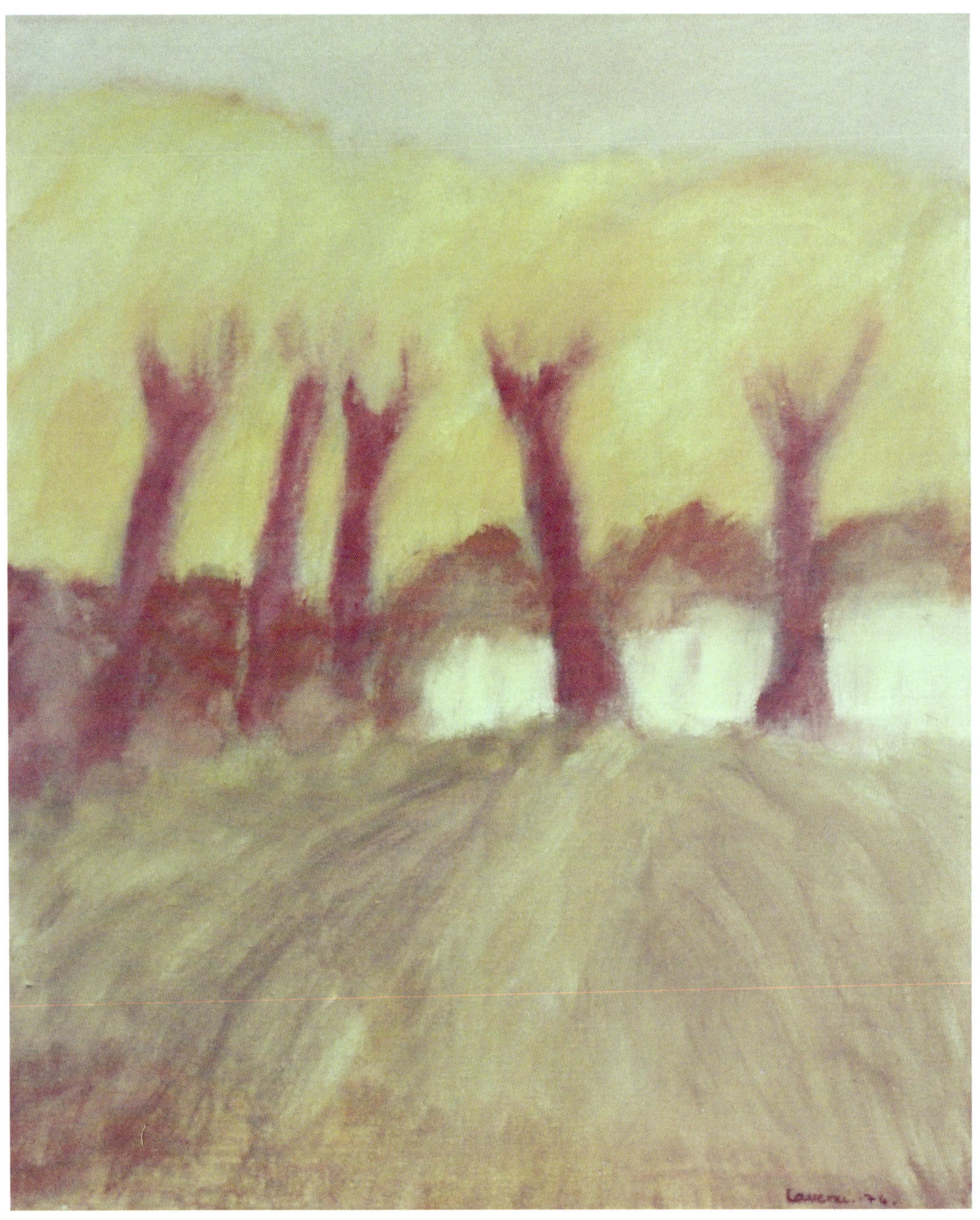

Automne, oil on canvas, 100x81 cm, 1974. Private collection.

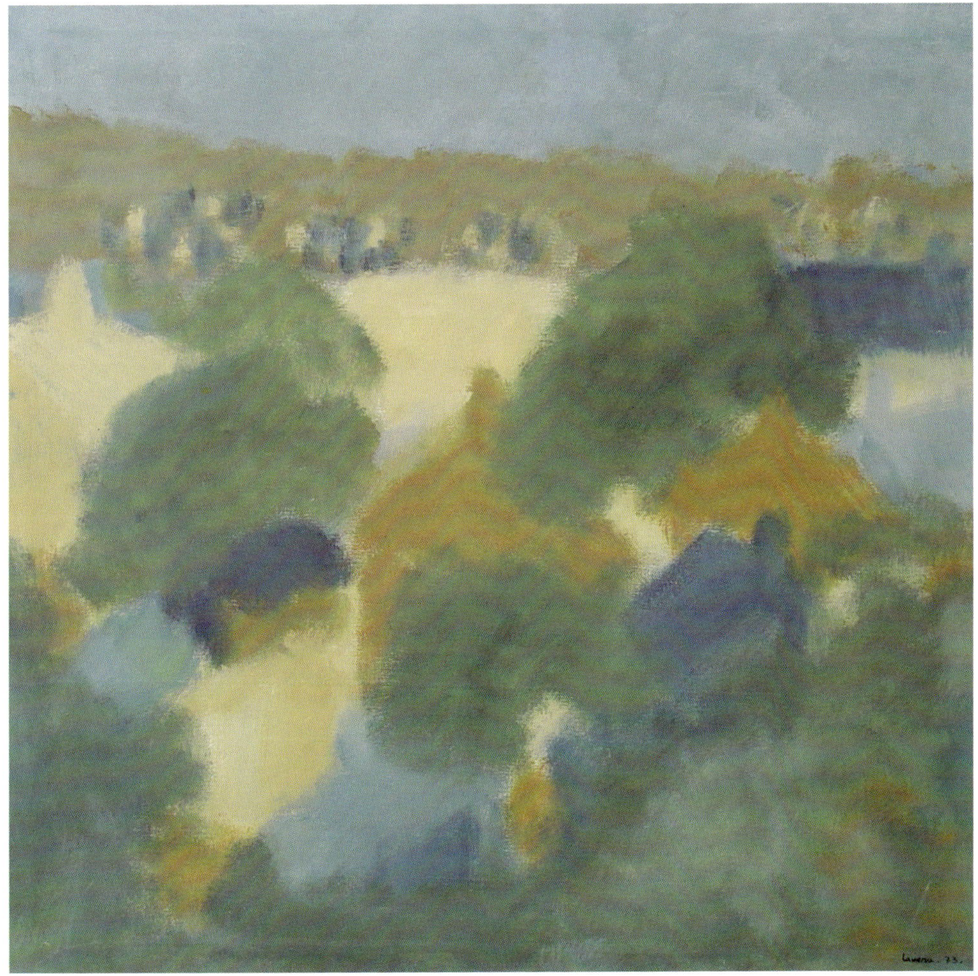

Daecher (Roofs), oil on canvas, 90x90 cm, 1973. Private collection.

As a long time collector of art, and a frequent visitor to museums in the United States as well as Europe, I've been exposed to the works of many artists and diverse styles.

Jacqueline's work embodies what good art is all about. She has a great sense of composition and color and the works seem to draw the viewer into the canvas.

It has been a pleasure to be introduced to her paintings and a privilege to be able to see each new work as it is completed.

Martin Breslauer
Experienced Art Collector

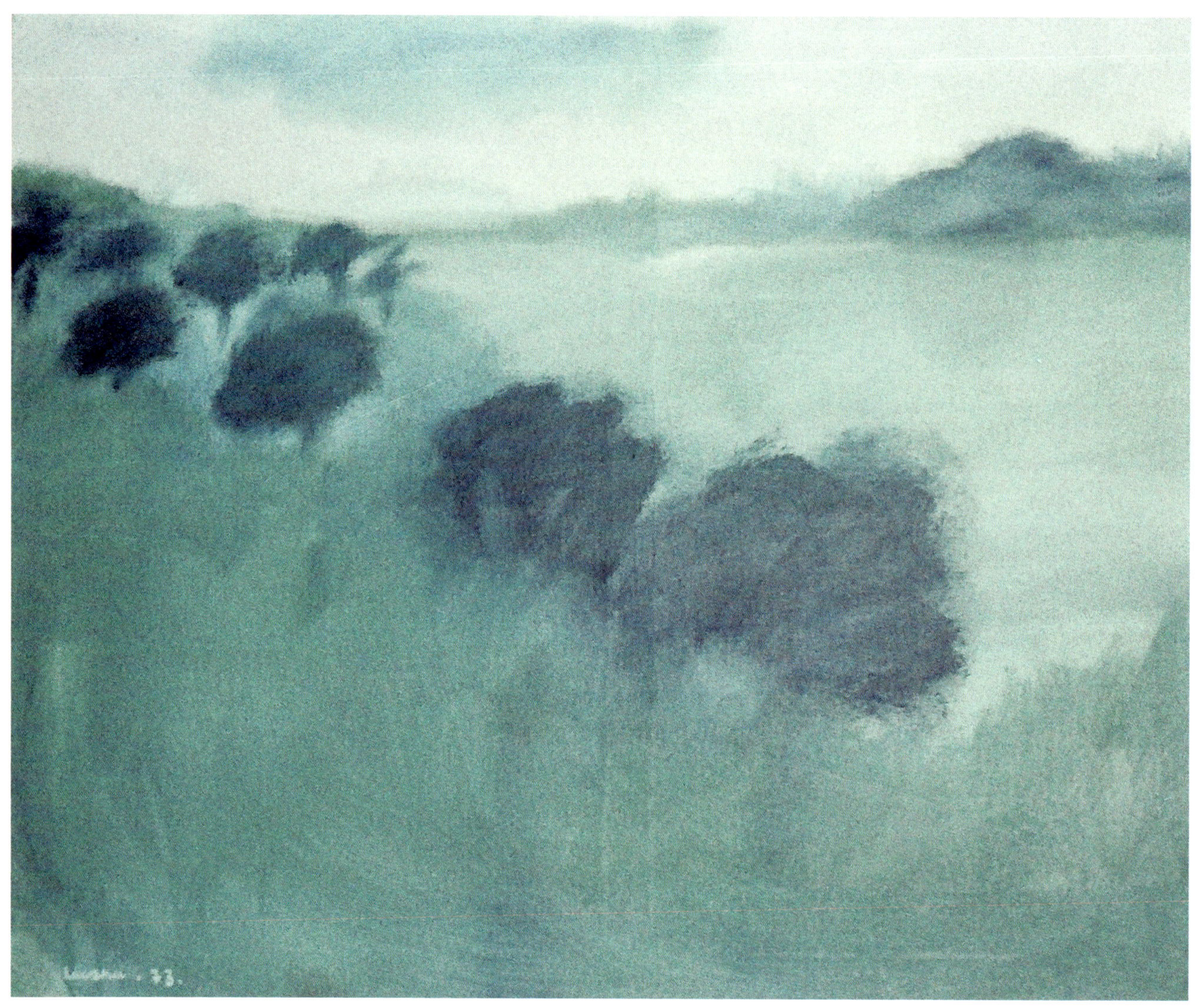

Nebel (Fog), Oil on canvas, 70x85 cm, 1973. Private collection.

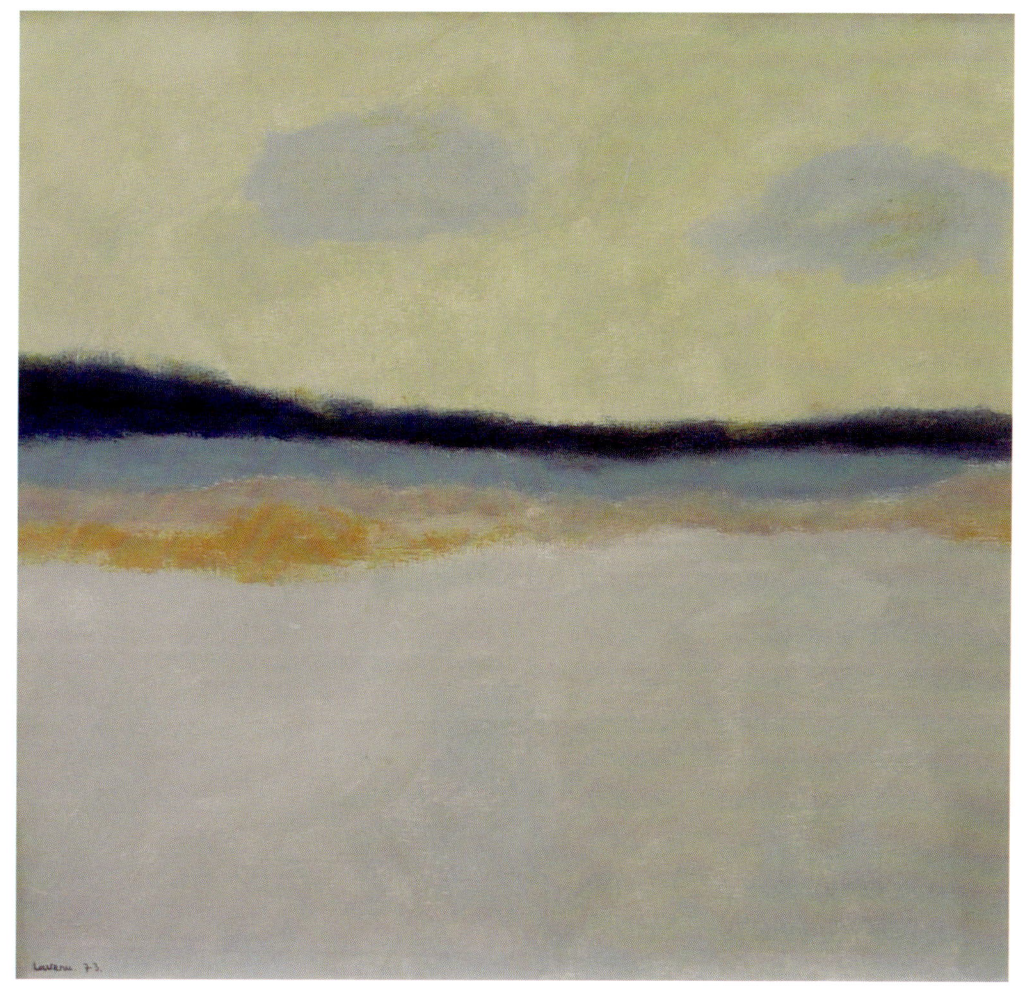

Plage, Oil on canvas, 80x90 cm, 1973

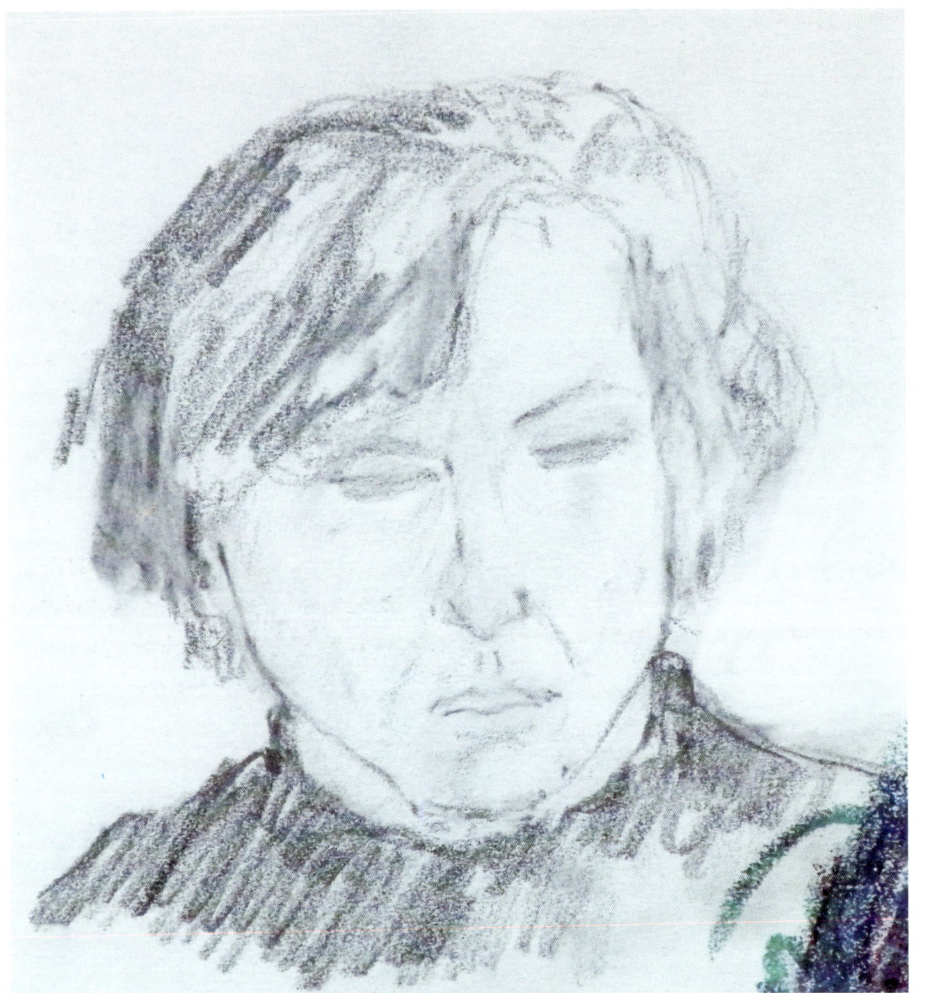

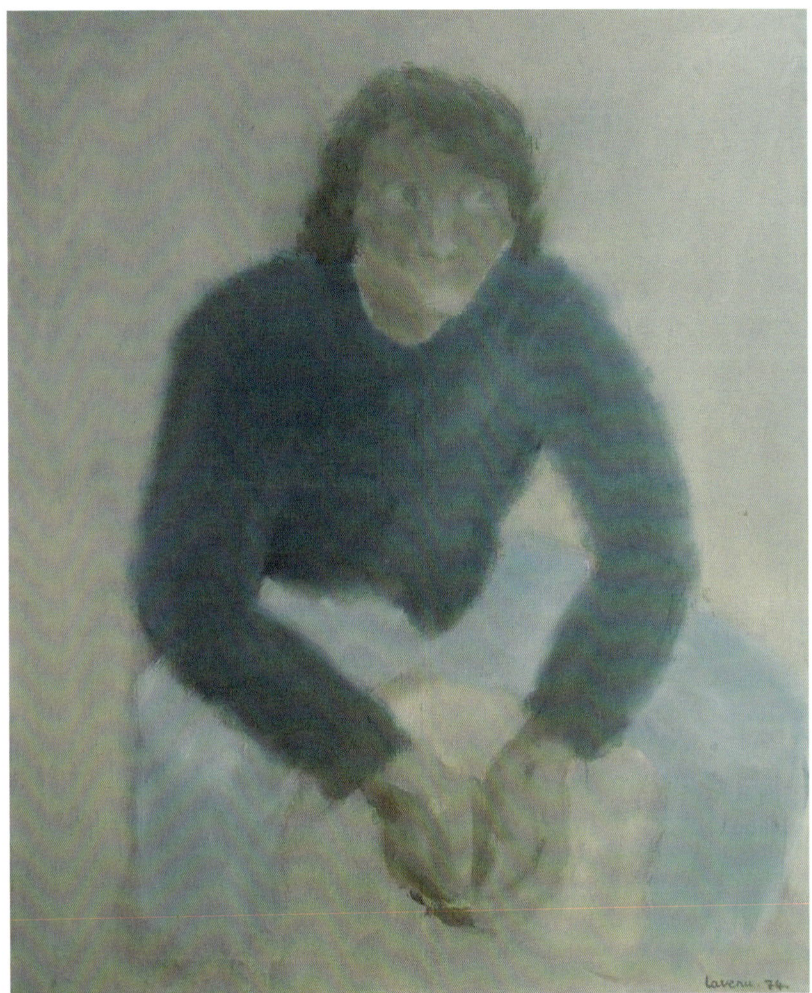

Peter Dosedla, oil on canvas, 100x81 cm, 1974.

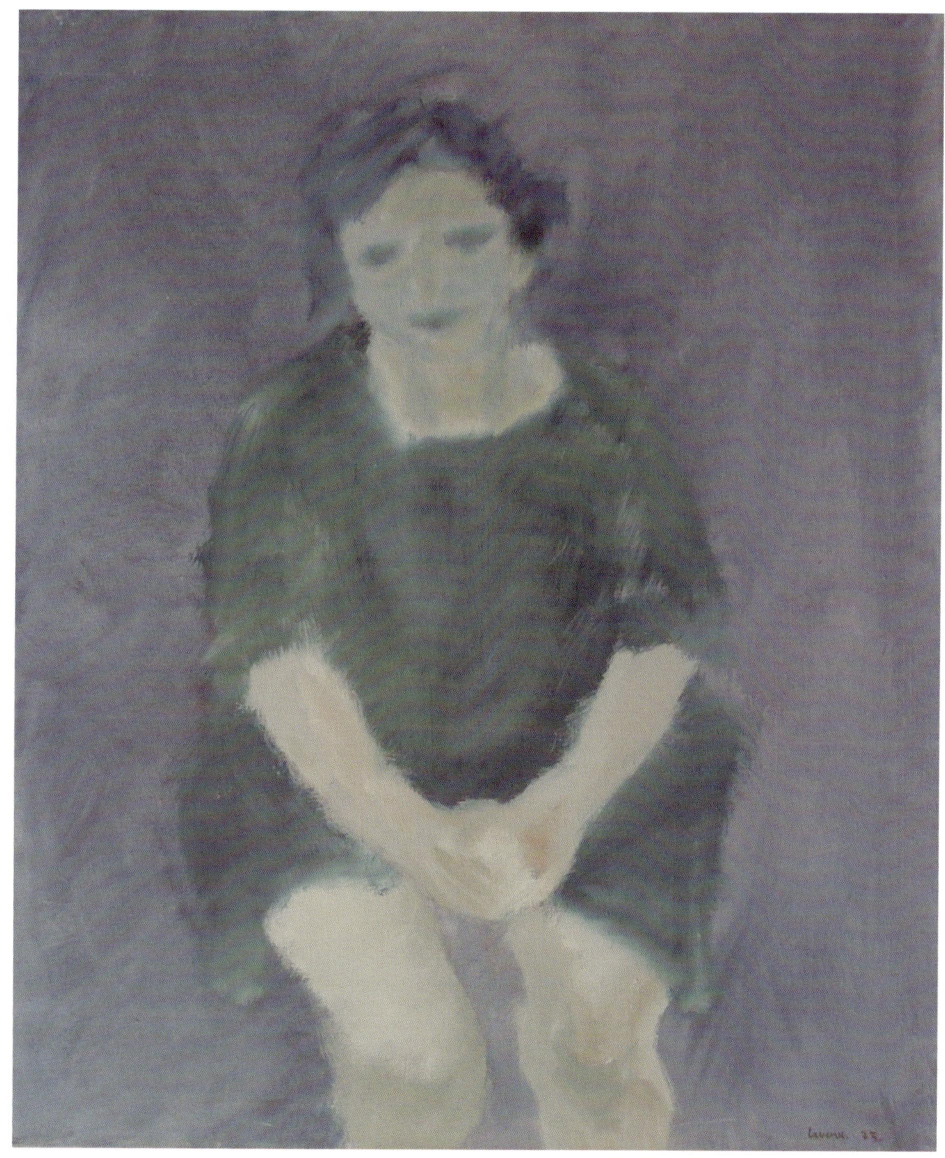

Evelyne, oil on canvas, 100x81 cm, 1973.

"The unfinished oil portrait of Peter Dosedla and this one of my sister Evelyne show my approach to painting; namely minimalize, simplify and capture the subject in large expanses of color.

Peter Dosedla, a Czech born architect, still lives and works in Berlin. We studied at the Akademie in Nürnberg and lived together for many years in Berlin."

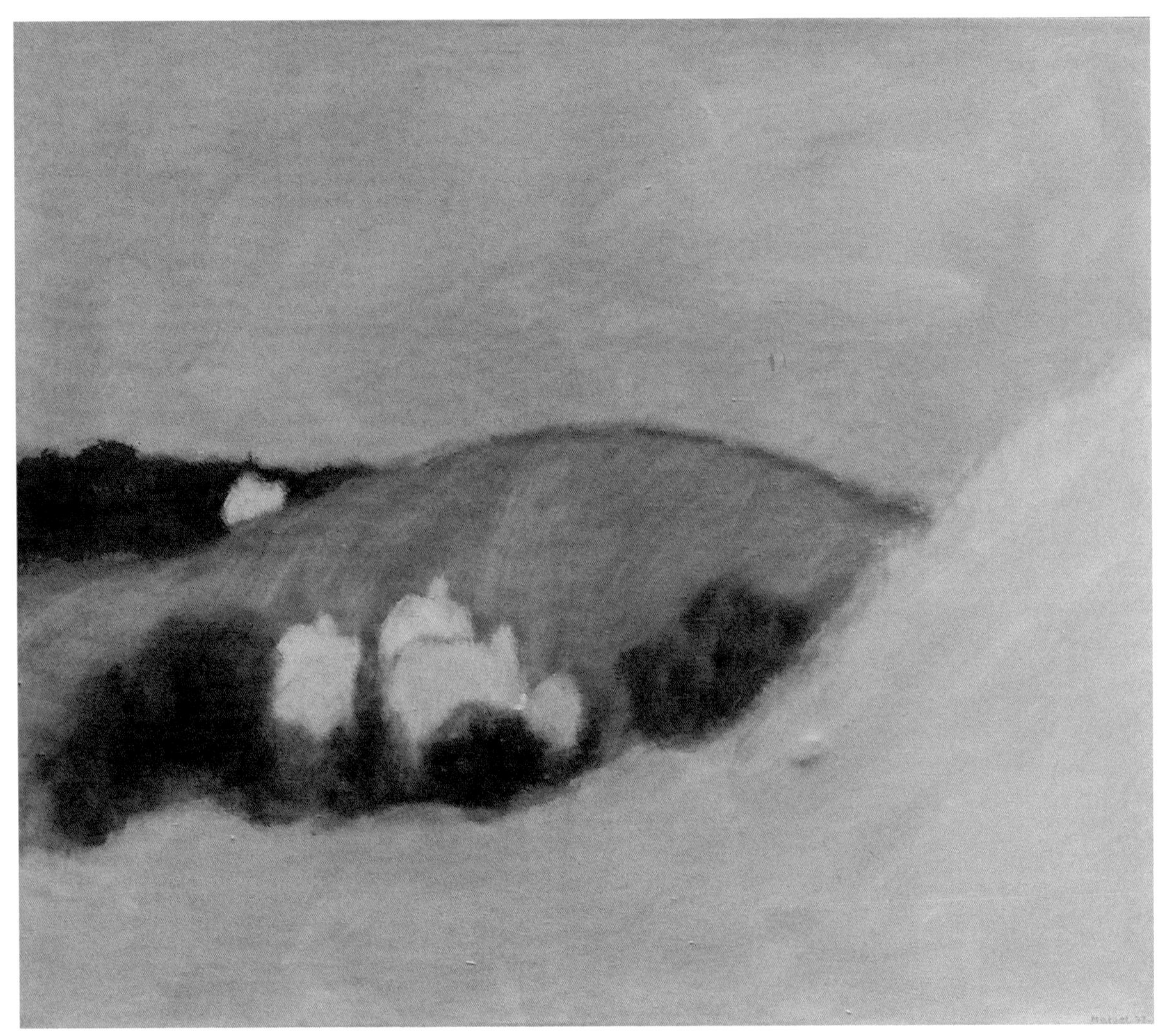

Paysage de Bretagne, oil on canvas, 85x90 cm, 1973. Private collection.

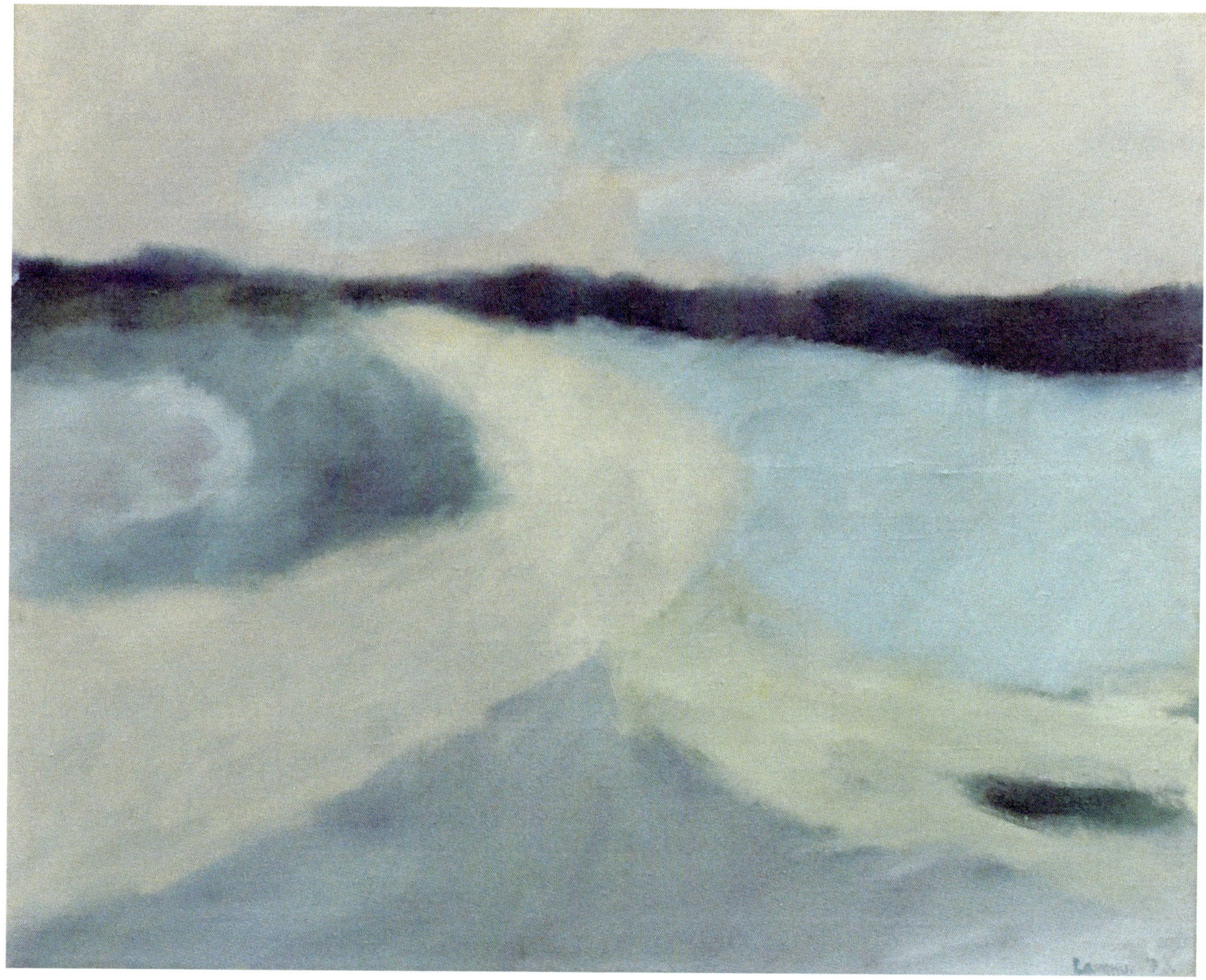

Feld (Field), oil on canvas, 70x85 cm, 1973. Private collection.

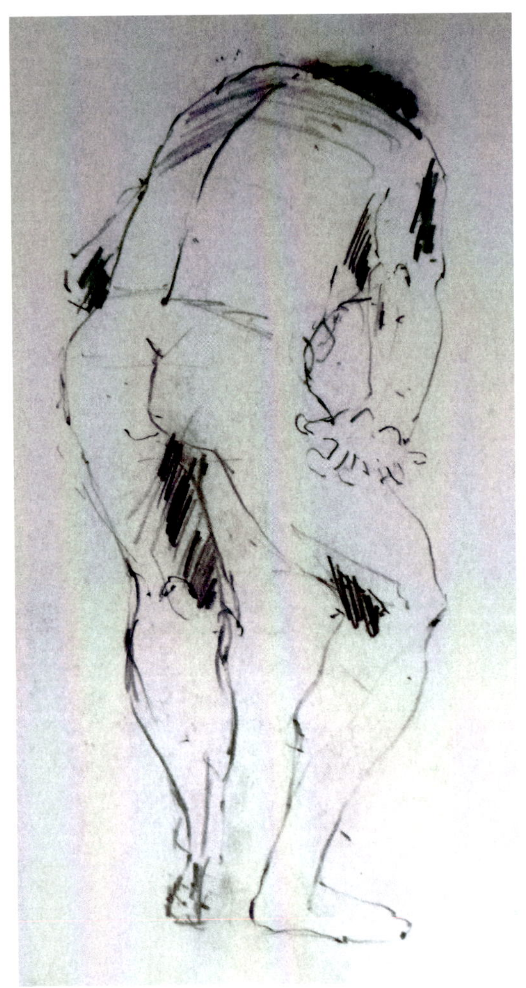

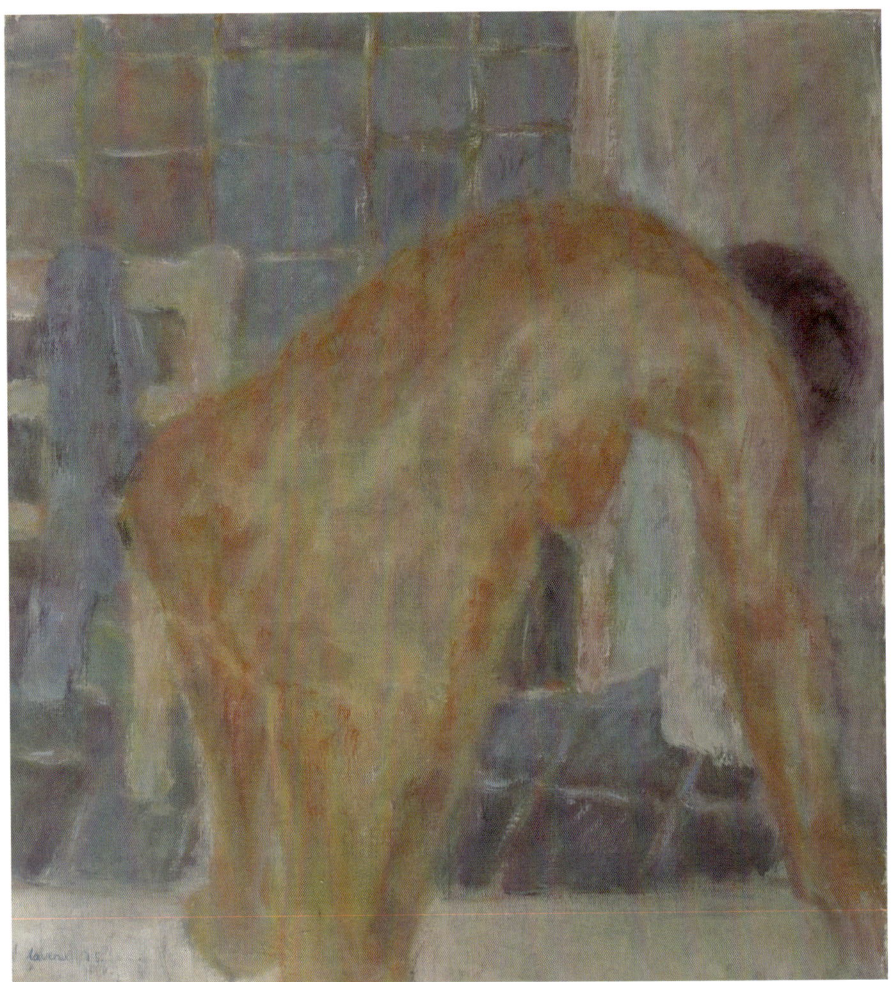

In the bathroom, oil on canvas, 100x90 cm, 1975. Private collection.

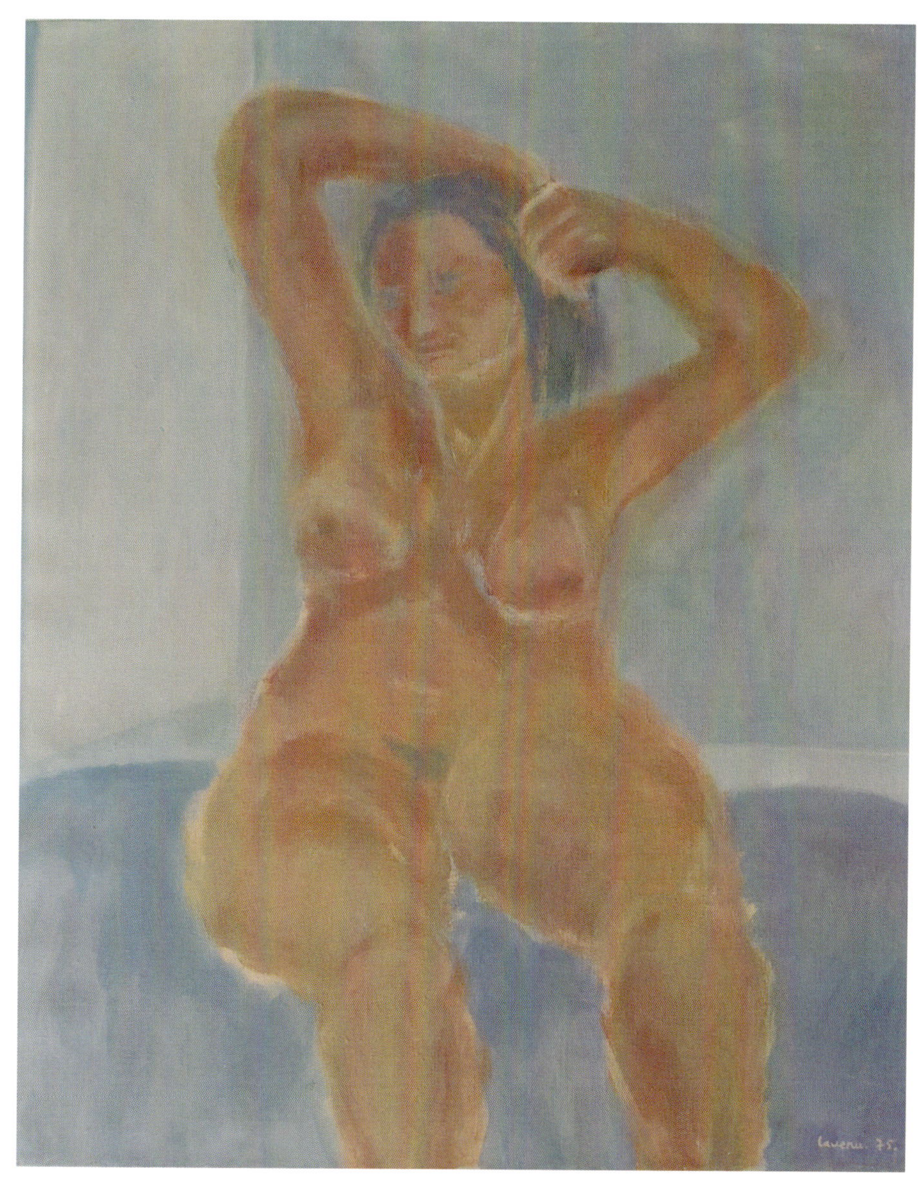

Femme se coiffant, oil on canvas, 100x81 cm, 1975.
Akademie competition 1975, 2nd Prize.

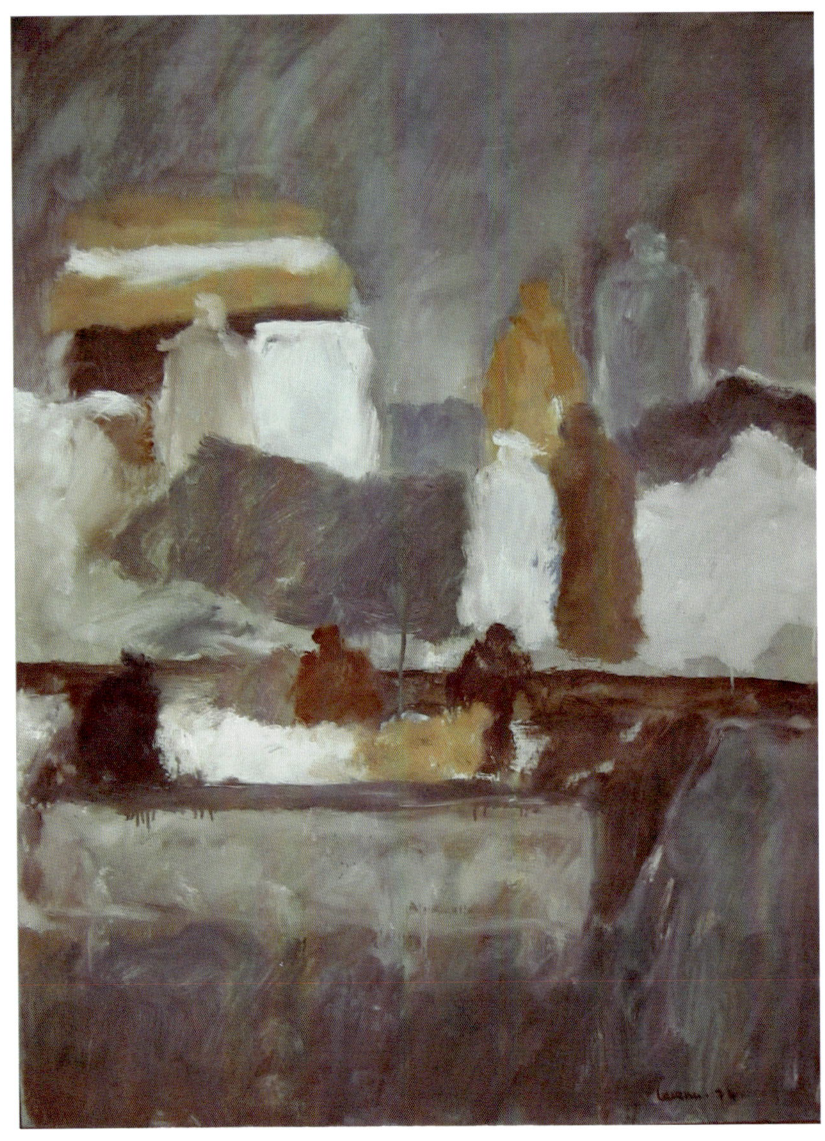

Still life in atelier, oil on canvas, 100x73 cm, 1974. Private collection.

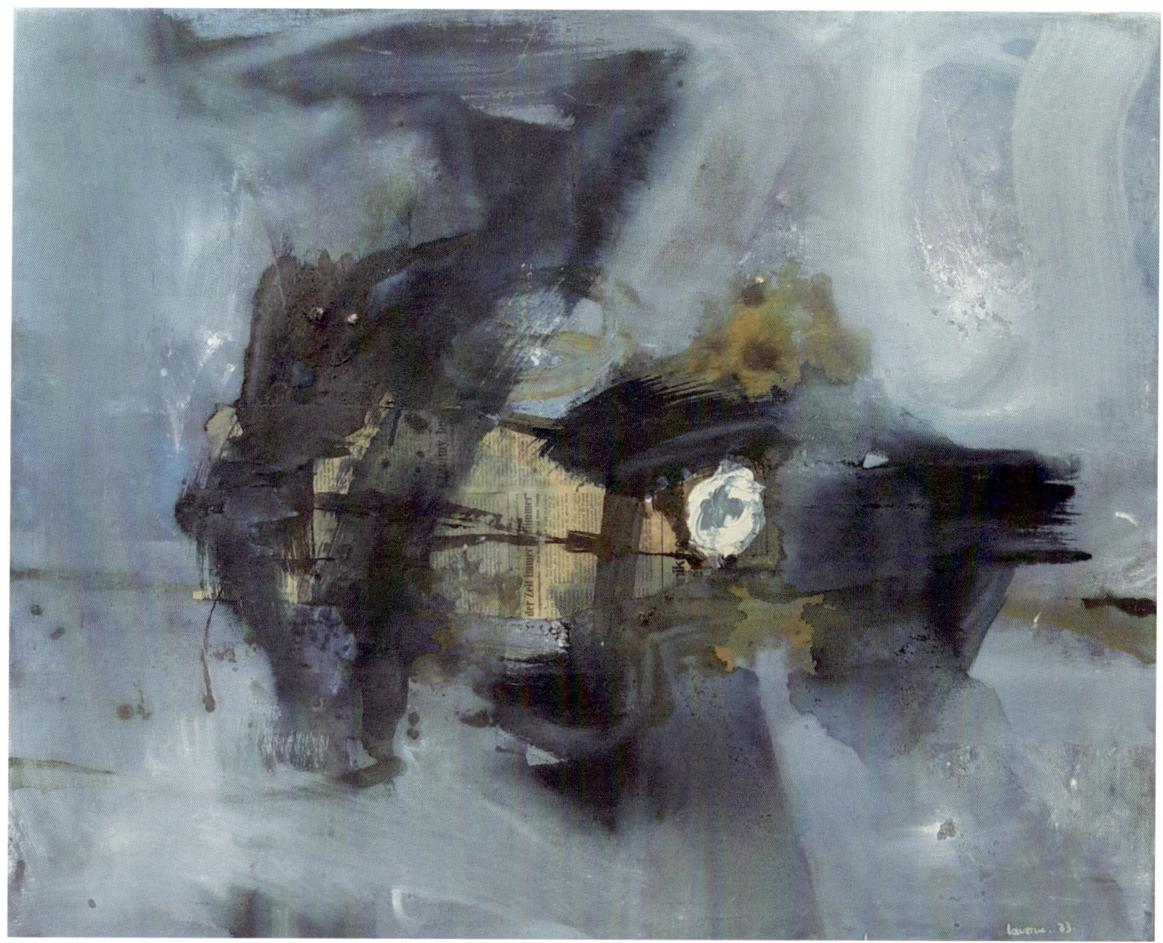

Blaue Flecken, mixed media/oil on canvas, 70x85 cm, 1973.

"After seeing the Wols (Wolfgang Schulze) exhibit in the Nationalgalerie, Berlin, 1973, I experimented in abstract painting. This mixed media example is the only one that survived."

BERLIN

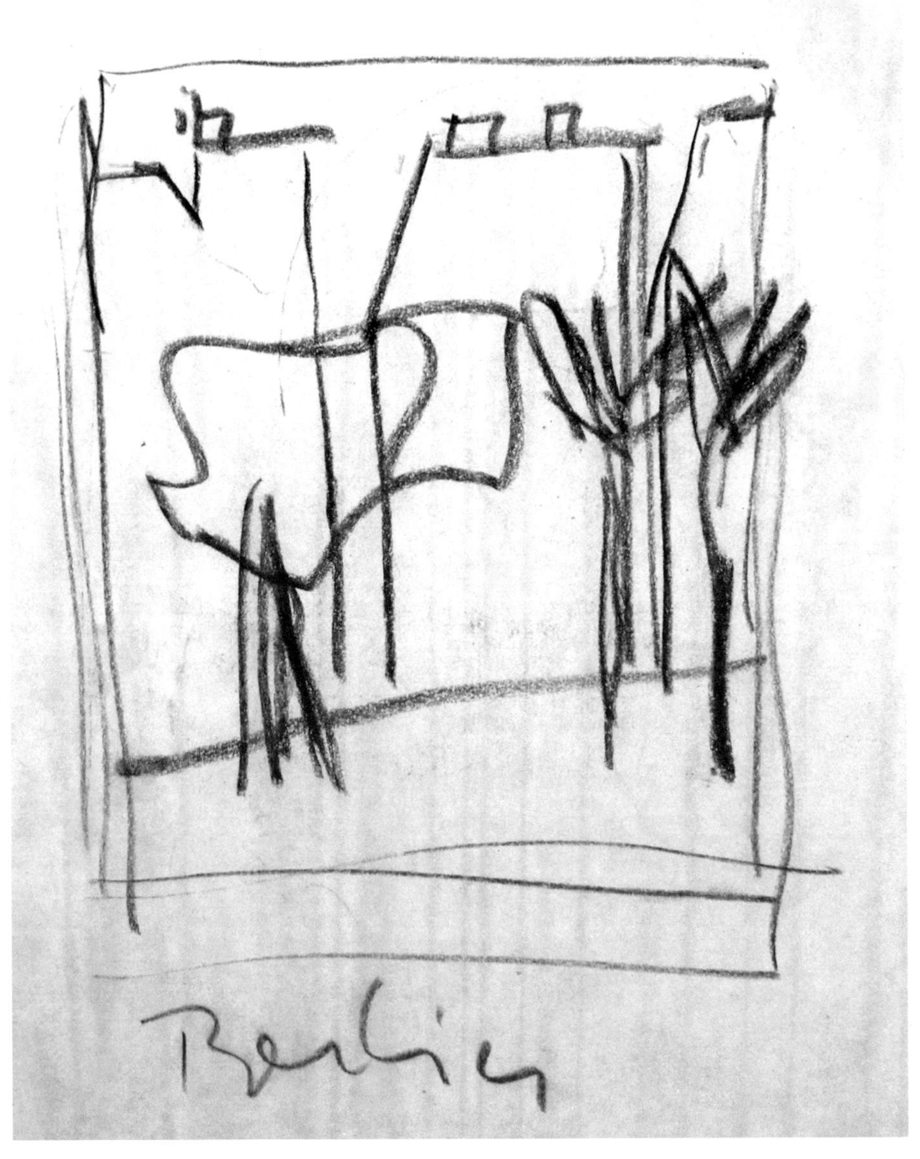

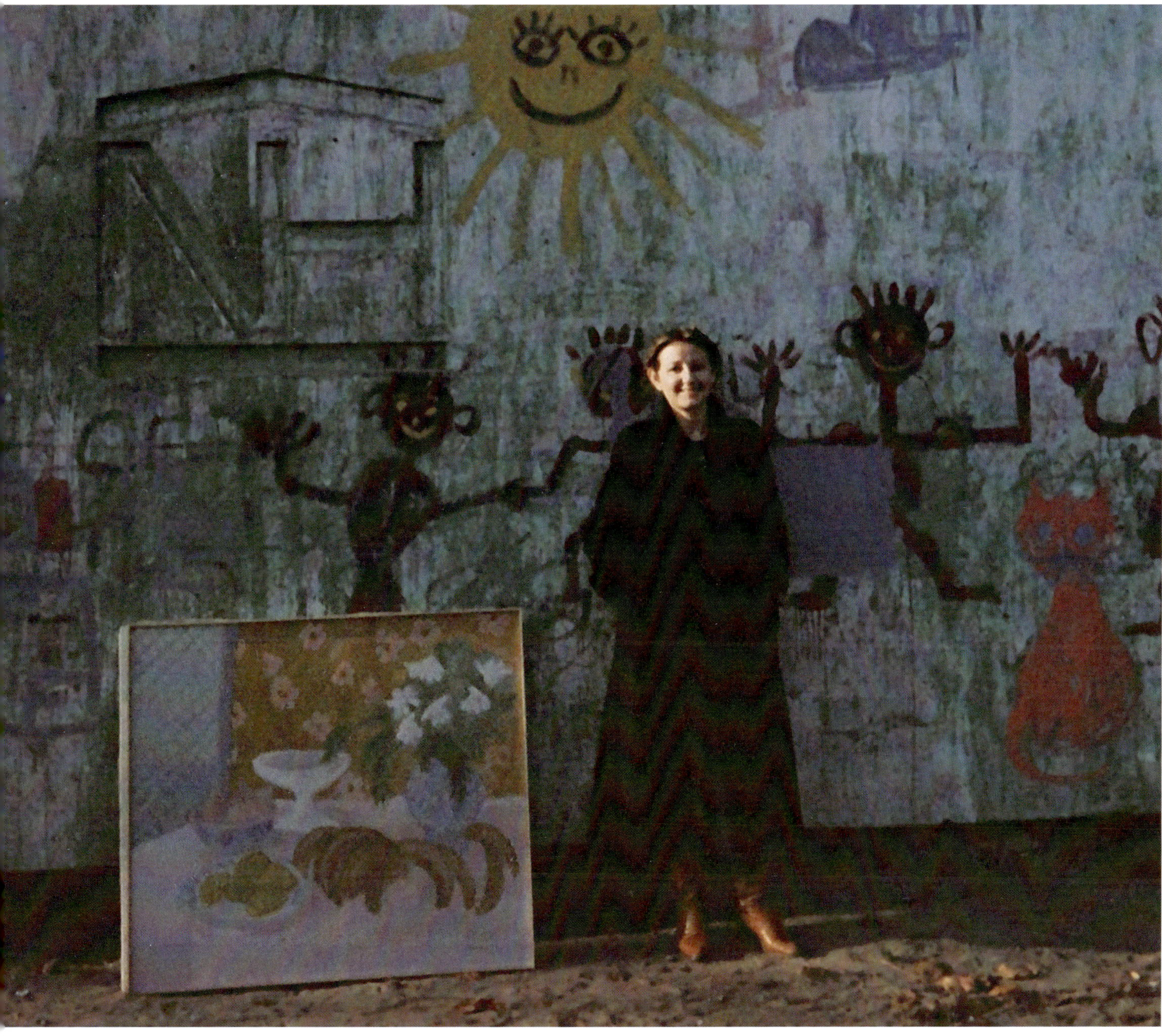

"Berlin holds a very special place in my heart and continues, even after so many years, to provide inspiration for my work."

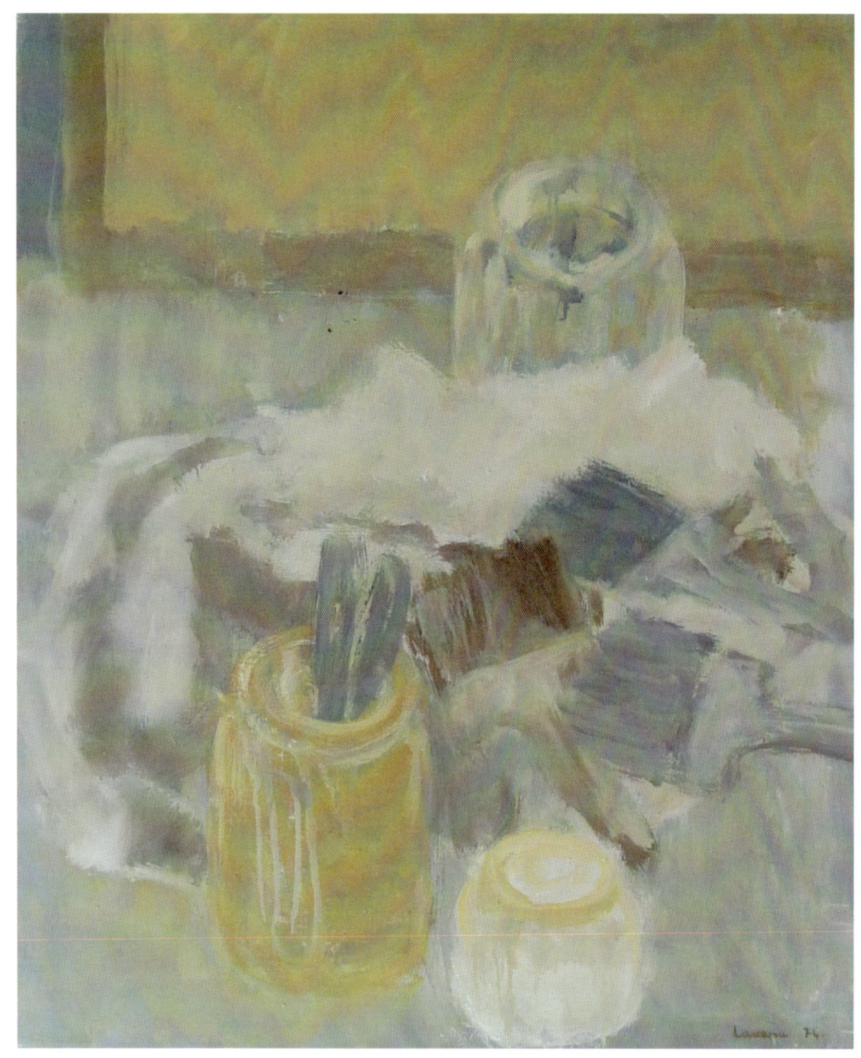

Still life in atelier, oil on canvas, 85x70 cm, 1974.

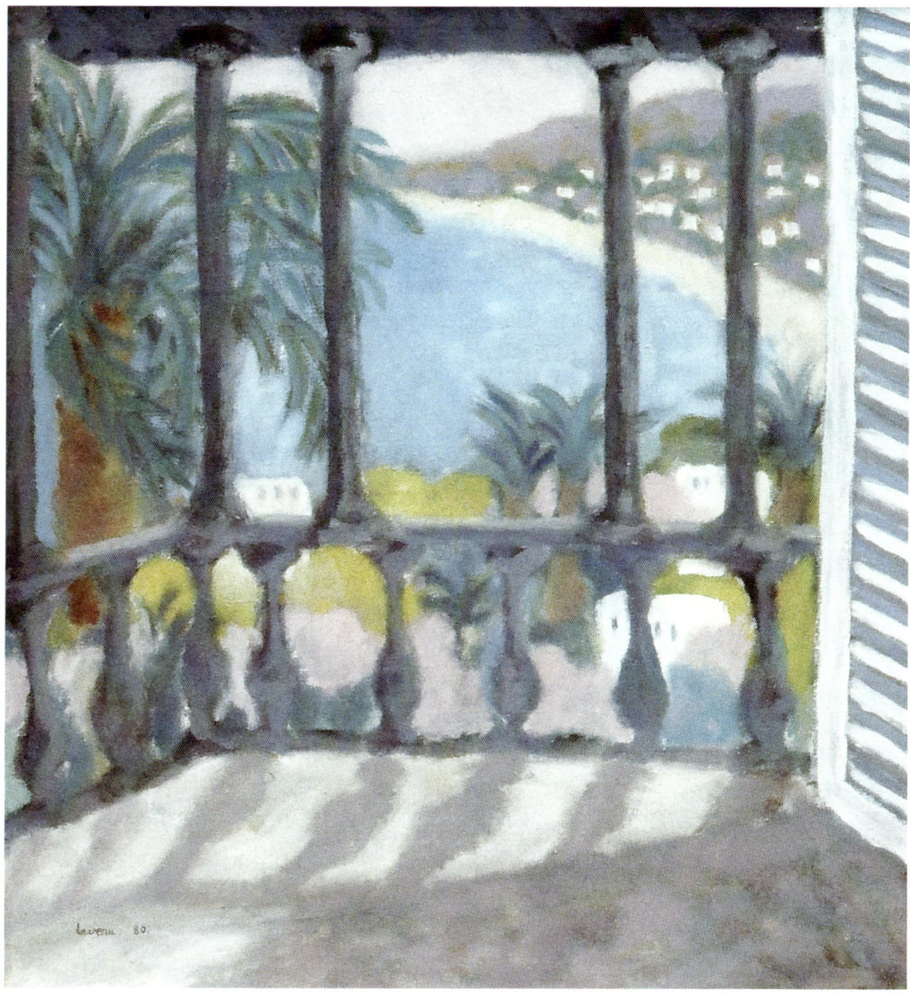

Balcon en Italie, oil on canvas, 100x90 cm, 1980. Private collection.

She feathered the mundane, the universal, with gentleness marked by sophisticated minimalist, prompting the extraordinary – through a color palette that is at times so contradictory that it takes your breath away. A tonality that defies nature and yet resonates a proclamation and invitation into the unseen, the mystical.

Defined only by her mind's eye, she flickers and gives life to natures own, veiling trunks in blue violet, inanimate objects in slate gray and olive green, figures ordained in royal blue and mauve. Roads and forests in yellow-gold and deep pink, bottomless azure turquoise skies brimming with masterful, impetuous strokes. The color wheel upside down, and yet, it is all sublime and fused befitting a broader soul, prompting like the Fauves, a wild and unruly creativity.

She is a modern artist whose works emphasize painterly traits and powerful color over the emblematic or pragmatic principles retained by academia. Like her predecessors, Cézanne, Gauguin, Matisse and André Derain the centurions of revolution, the guardians of the unknown, she soars like a bird into new infinite varieties, unhindered, liberated, like her work, like her imagination.

Solomon Cohen
Fine Art Restorer and Dealer

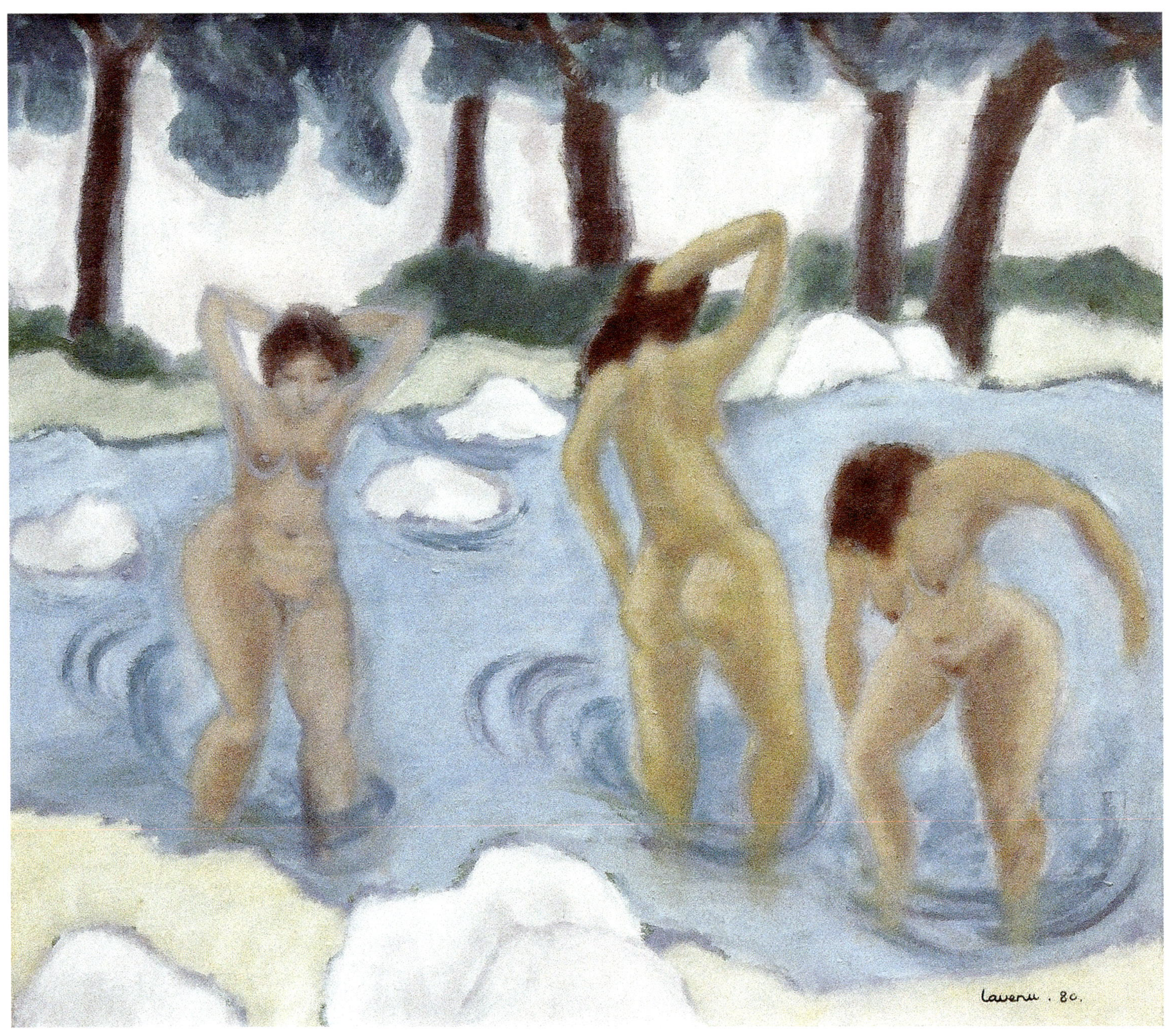

Baigneuses, oil on canvas, 85x100 cm, 1980. Private collection.

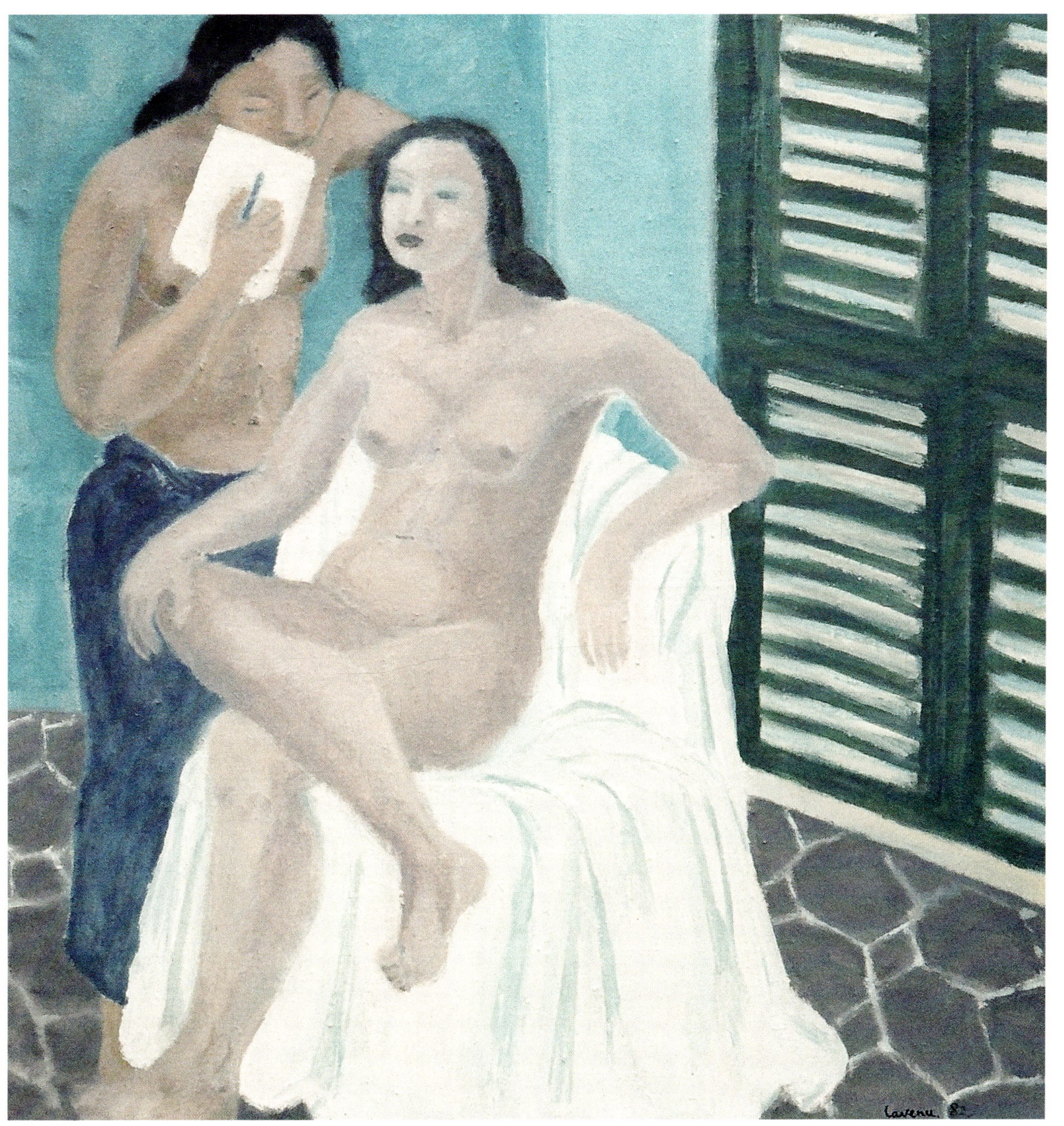

Toilette, oil on canvas, 100x90 cm, 1982. Private collection.

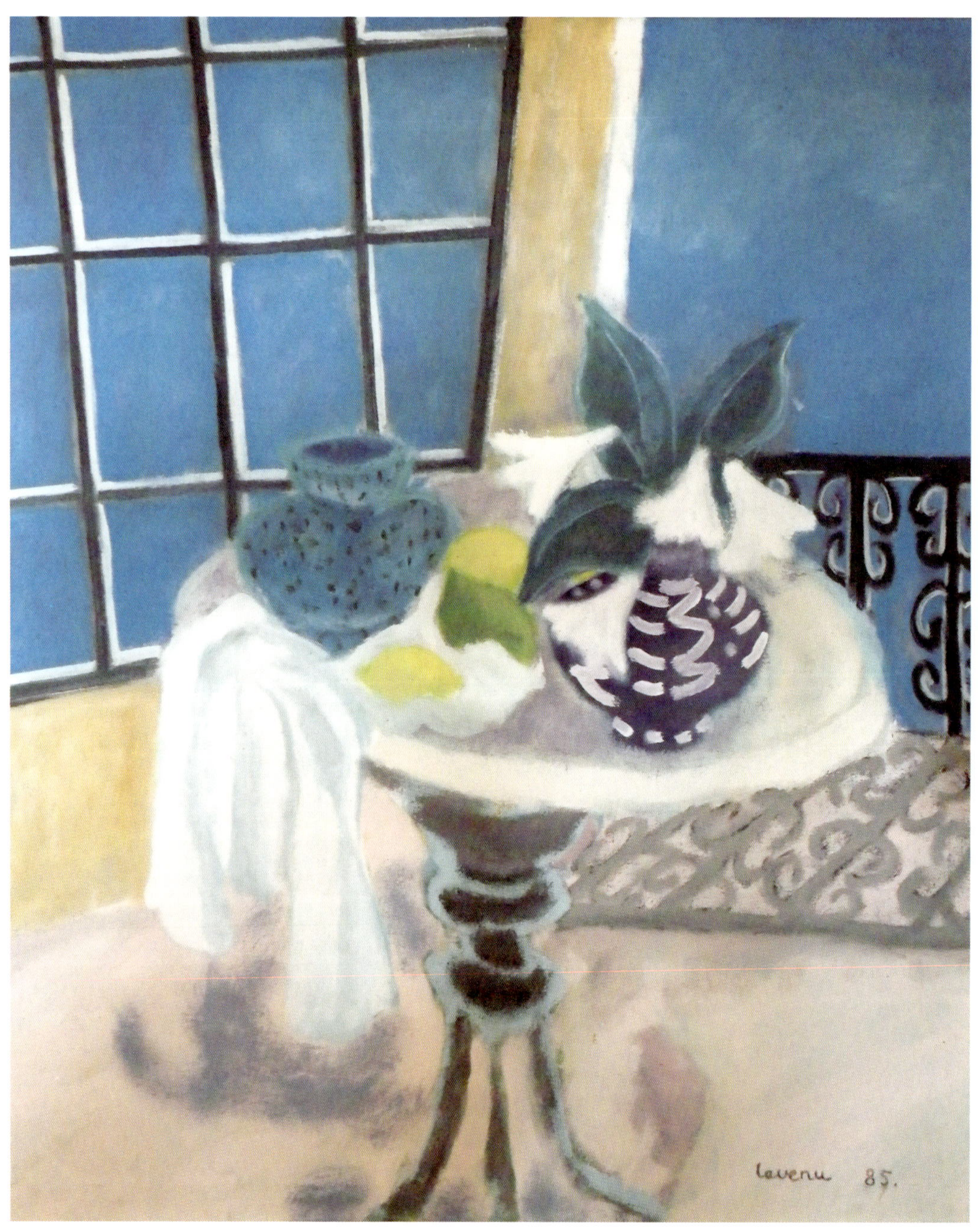

Nature morte au balcon, oil on canvas, 116x97 cm, 1985. Private collection.

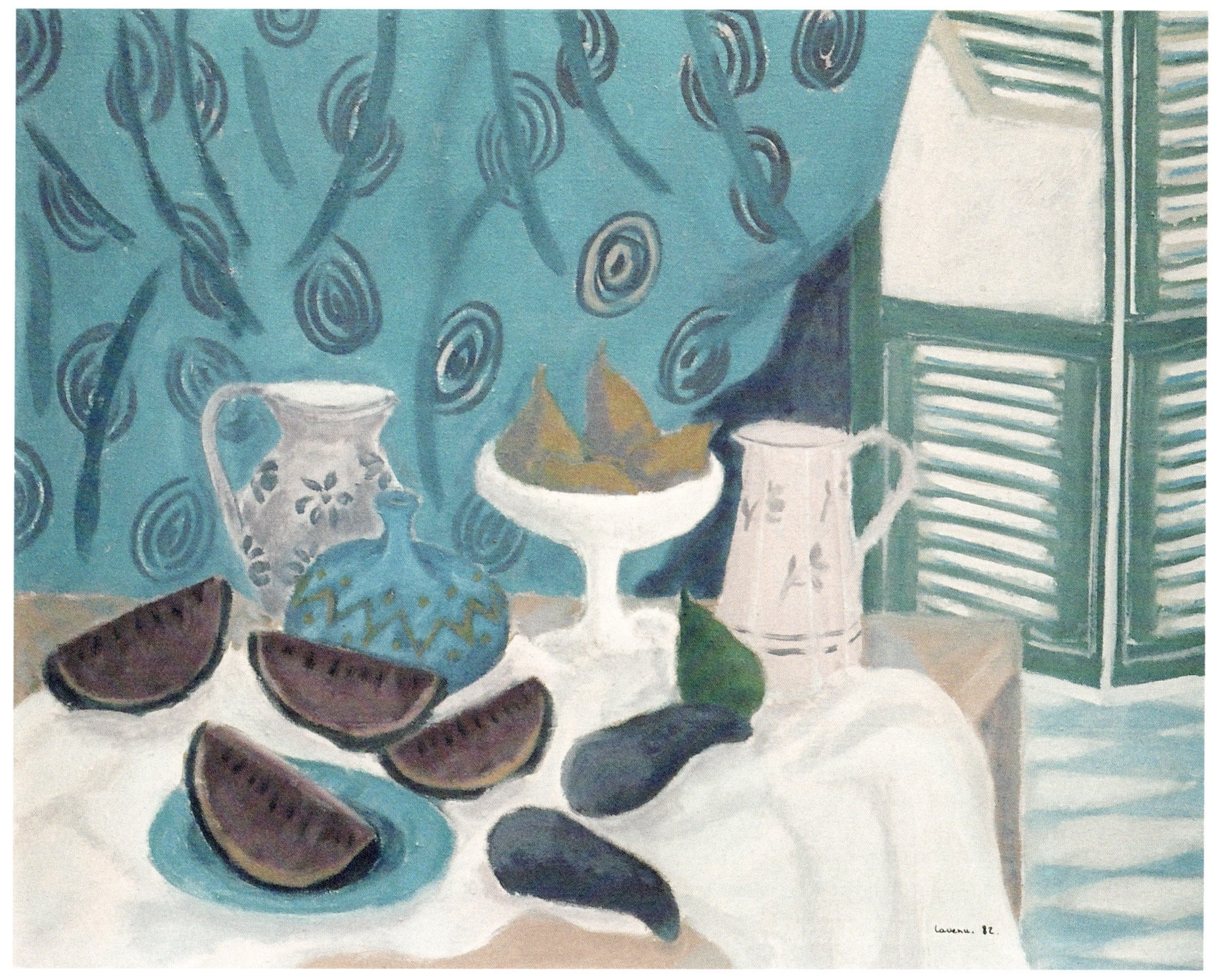

Nature morte et pastèques, oil on canvas, 97x116 cm, 1982. Private collection.

" On the ferry ride to Crete three American girls were stretched out in their sleeping bags. I sketched the scene on my boat ticket which later inspired this work."

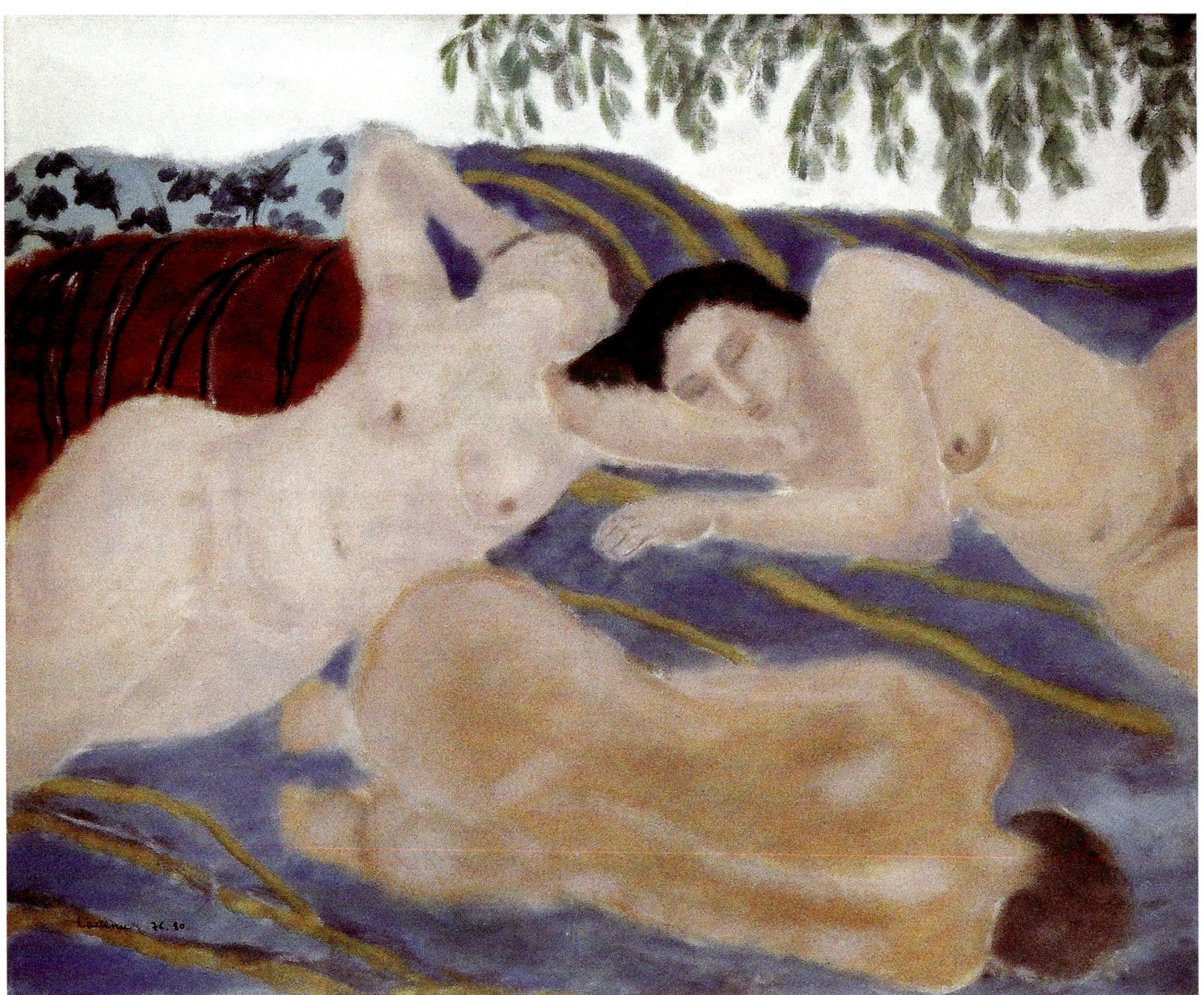

Siesta, oil on canvas, 97x116 cm, 1976-1980. Private collection.

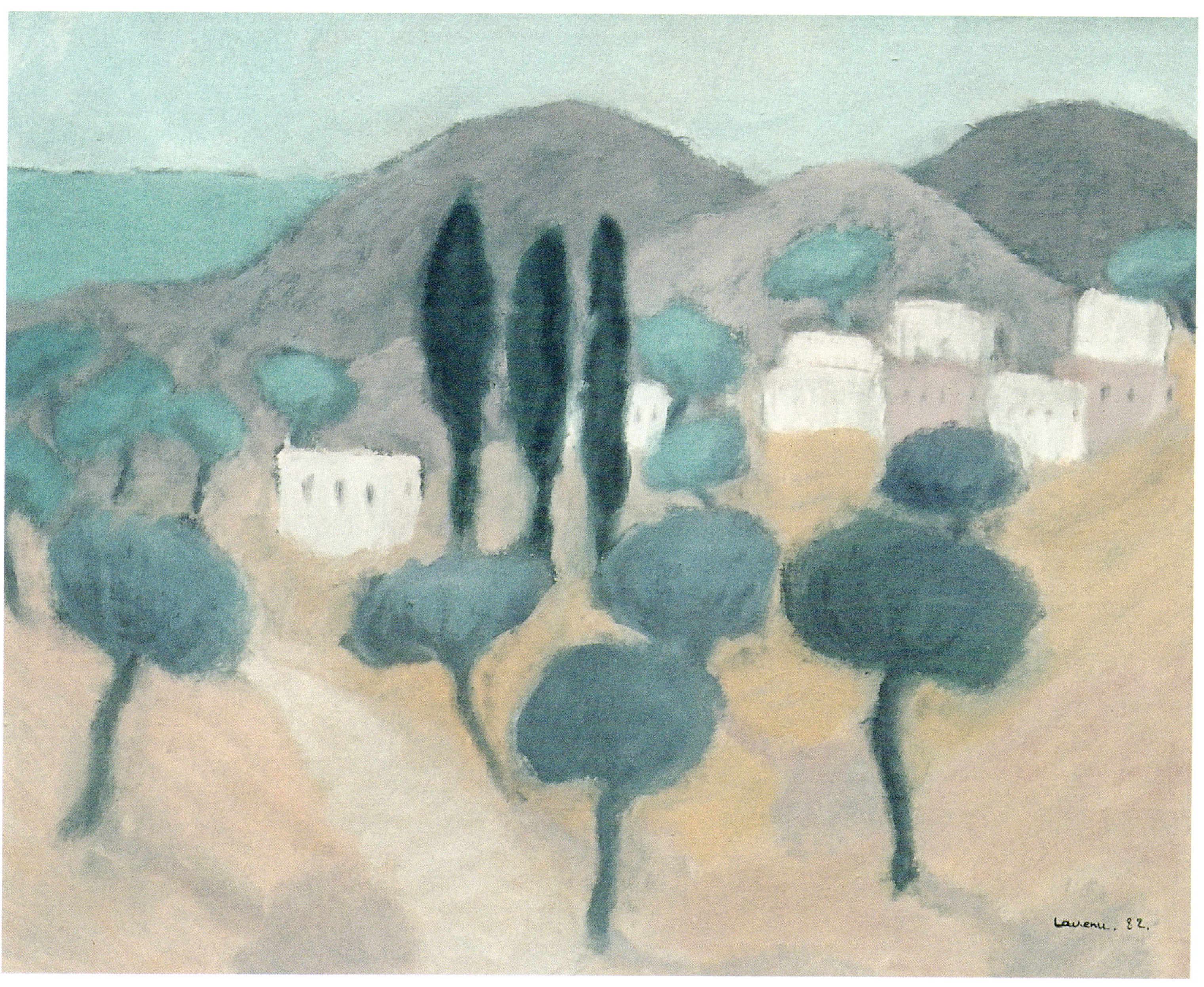

Paysage du sud, oil on canvas, 70x85 cm, 1982. Private collection.

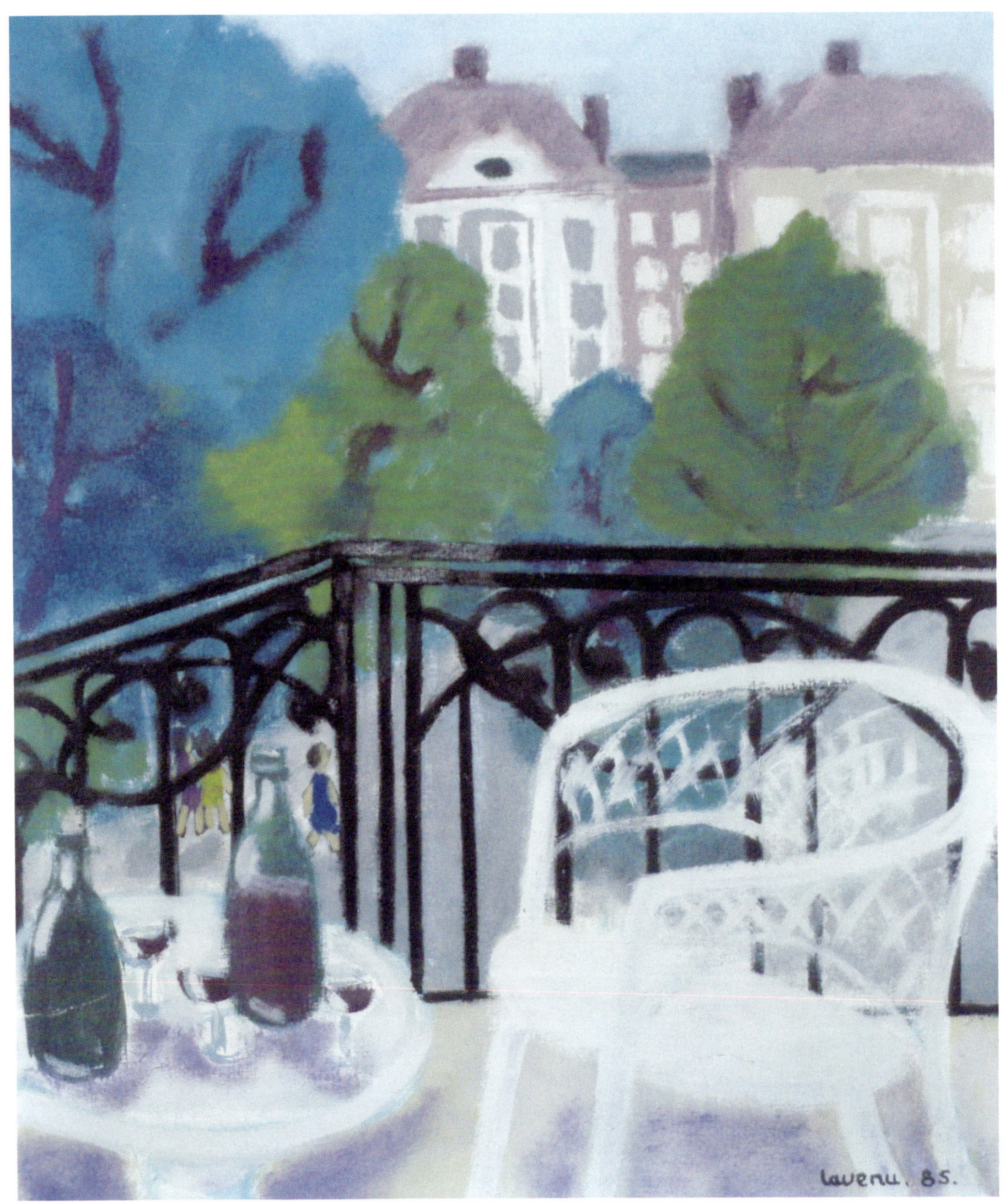

Atelier balcon, Berlin, oil on canvas, 85x70 cm, 1985. Private collection.

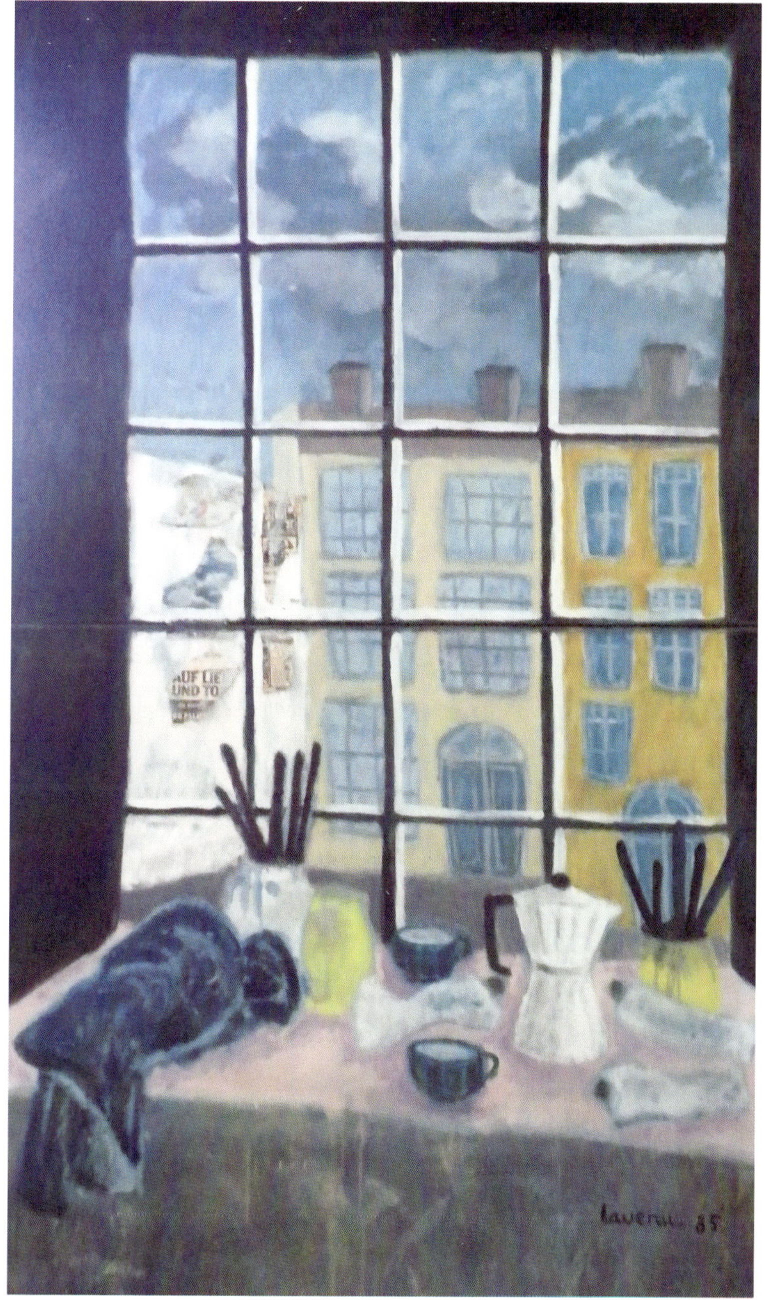

Atelier Berlin, oil on canvas, 171x100 cm, 1985. Private collection.

"I met Hans Parge while he was working at the Freie Universitat Berlin. His position at The Scripps Research Institute in La Jolla was responsible for our move to California."

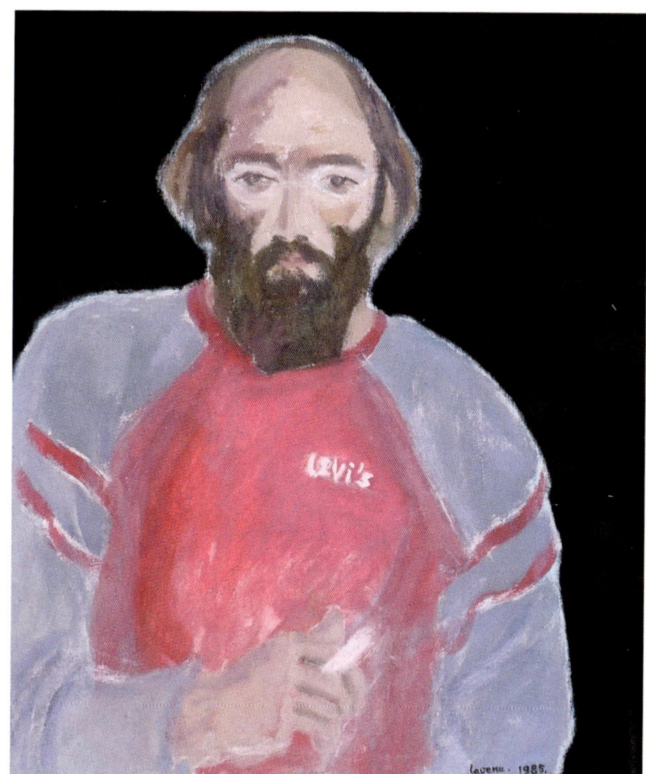

Hans, oil on canvas, 85x70 cm, 1985.

CALIFORNIA

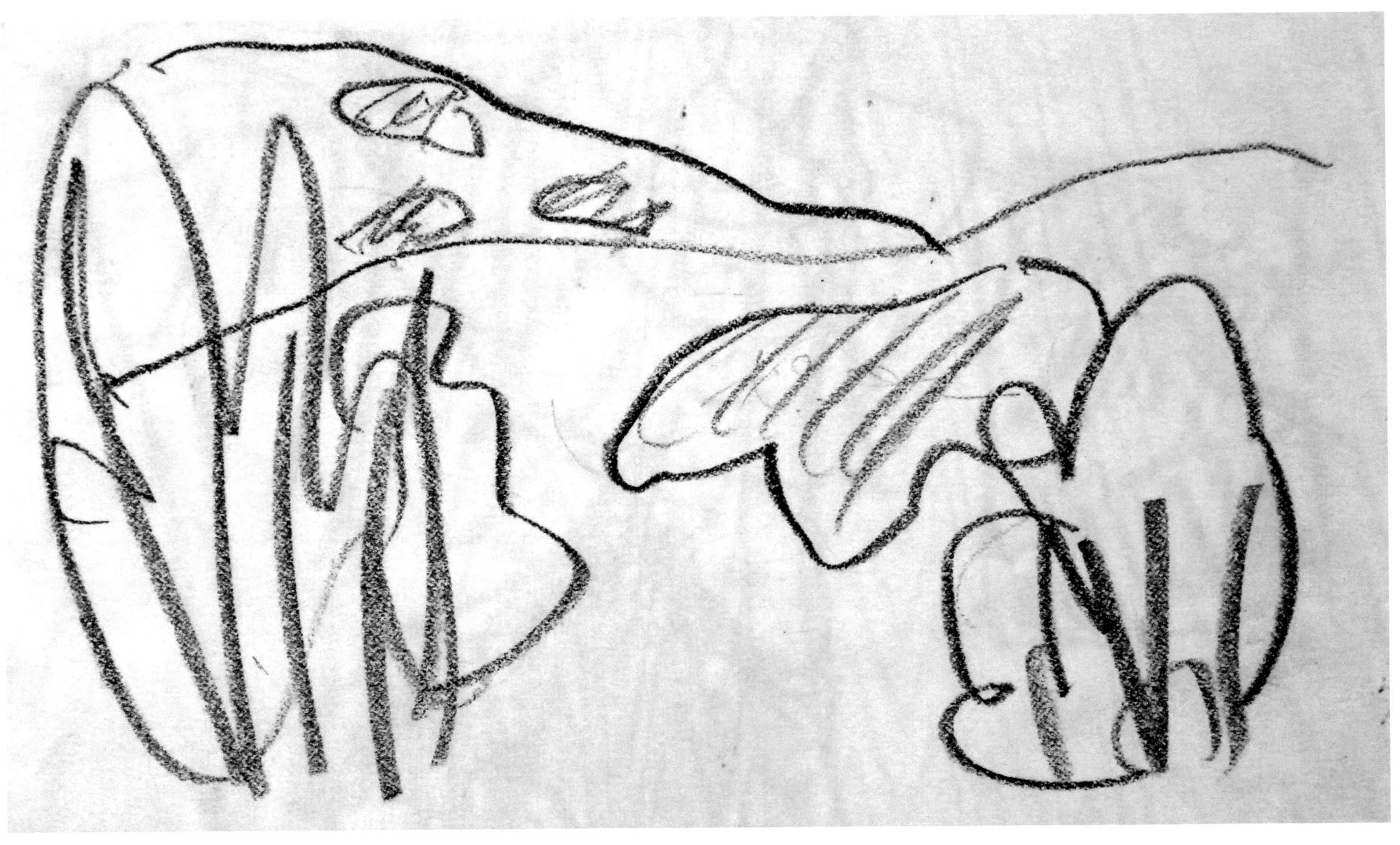

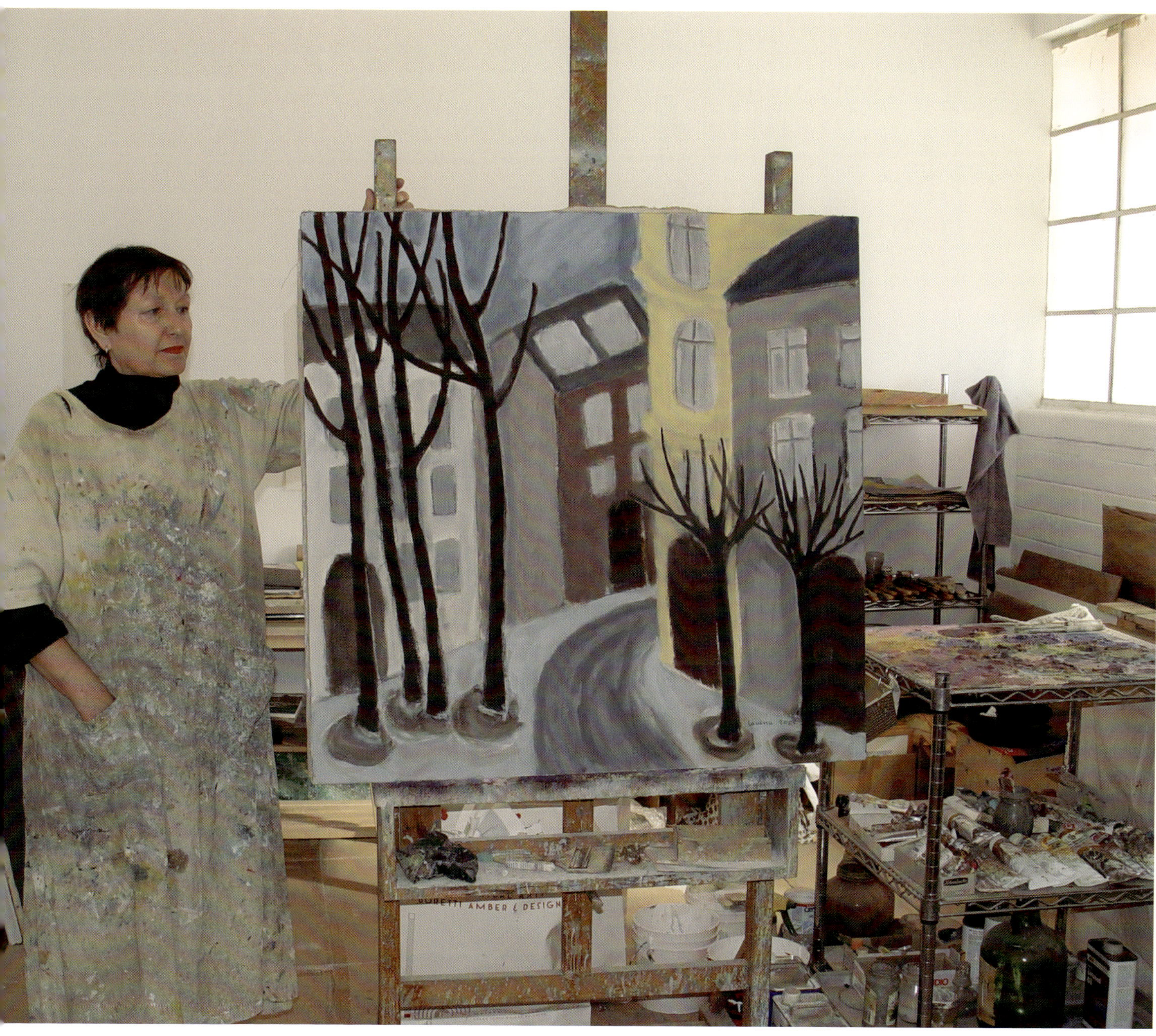

"I spent many productive years in this largest and brightest of my ateliers in San Diego before moving to the Kettner Arts and Design building."

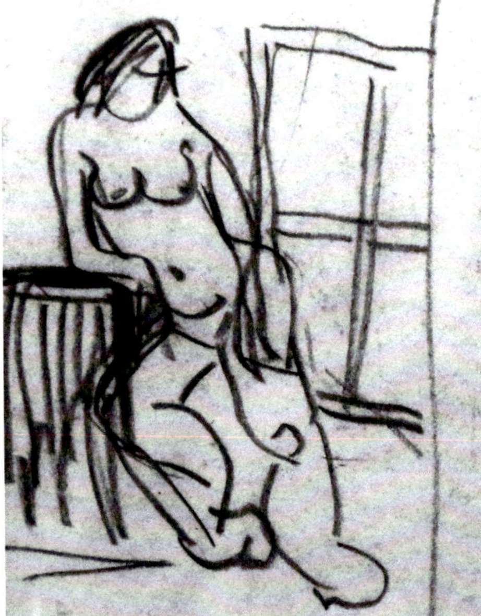

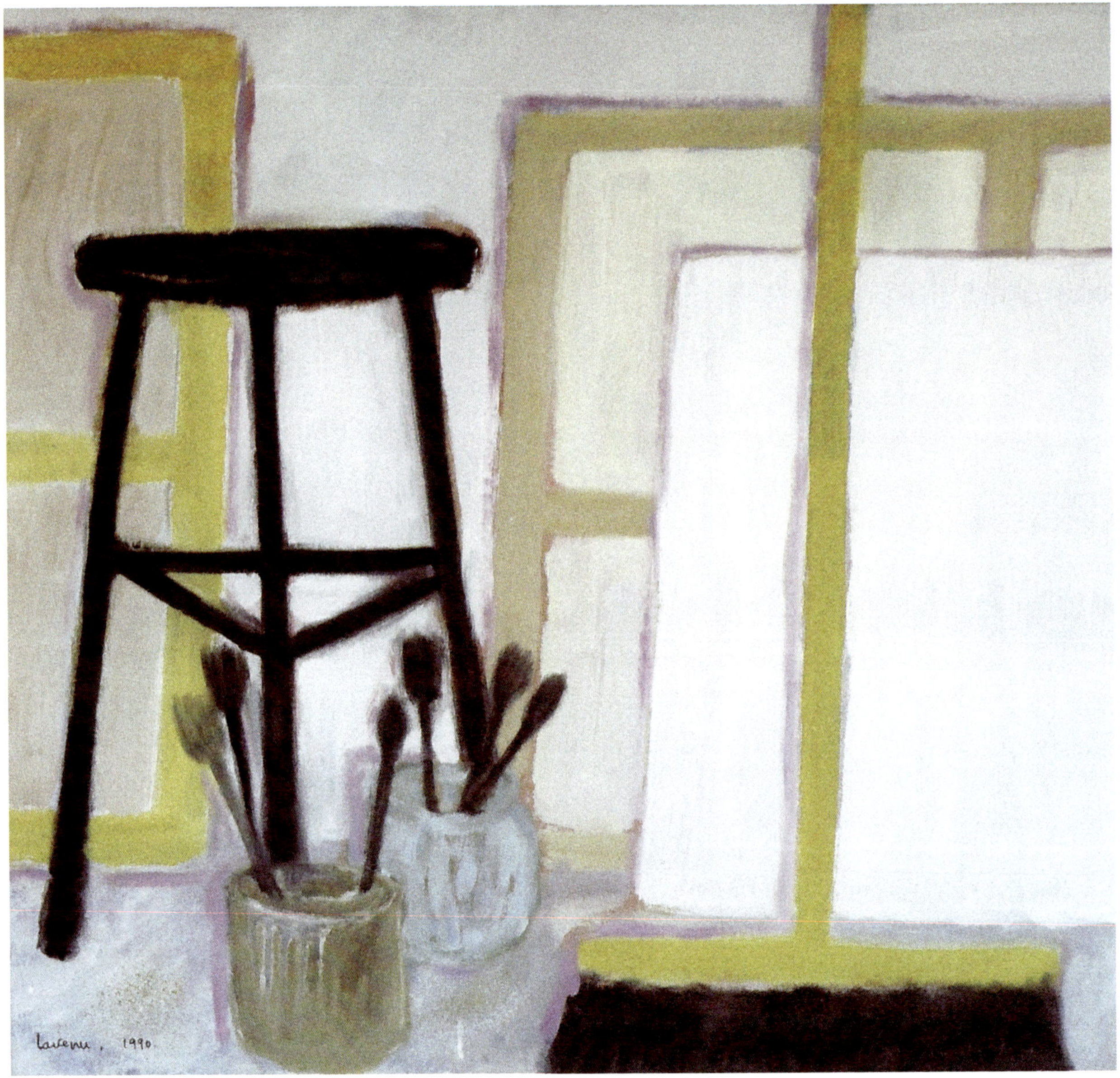

Atelier San Diego, oil on canvas, 81x85 cm, 1990. Private collection.

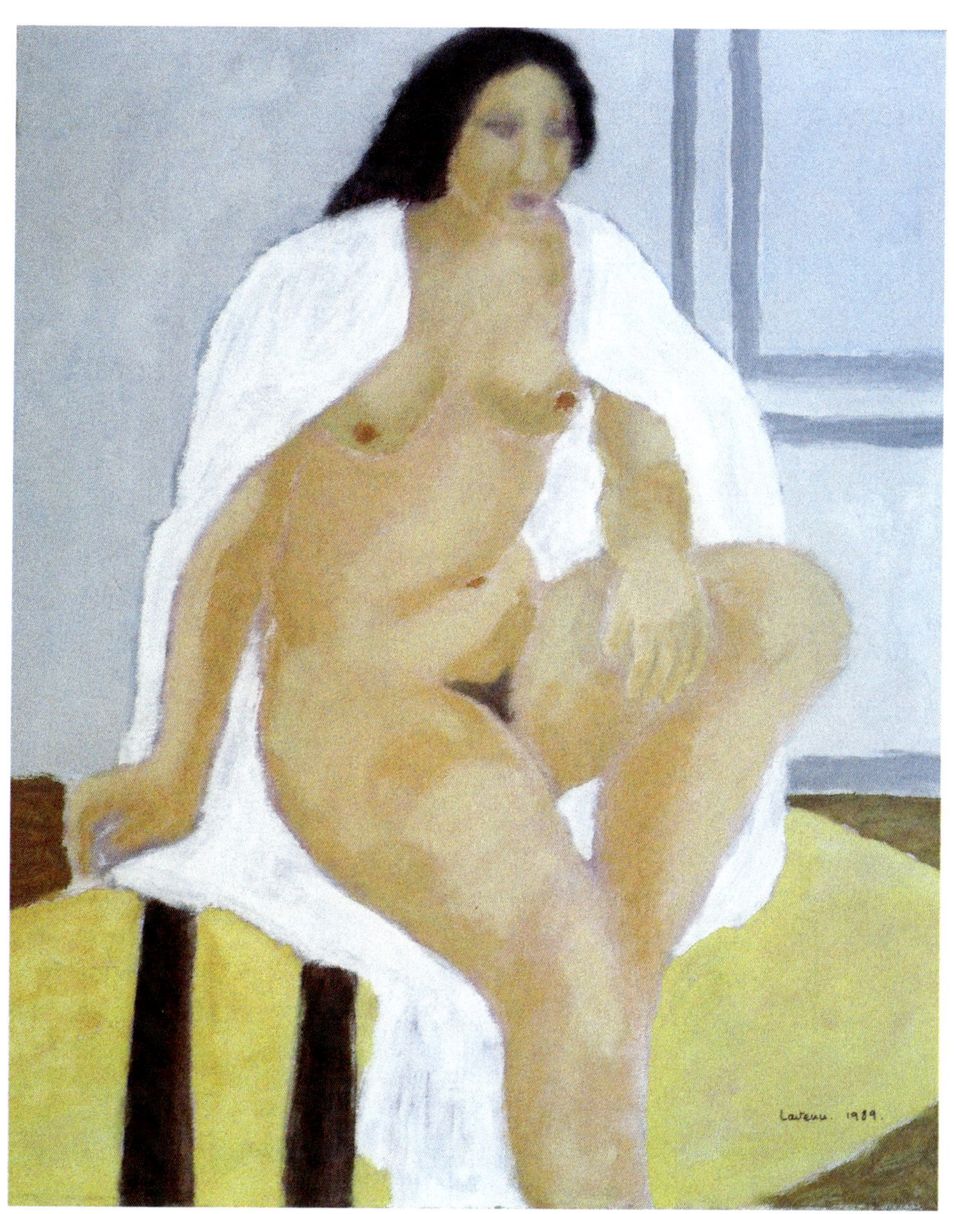

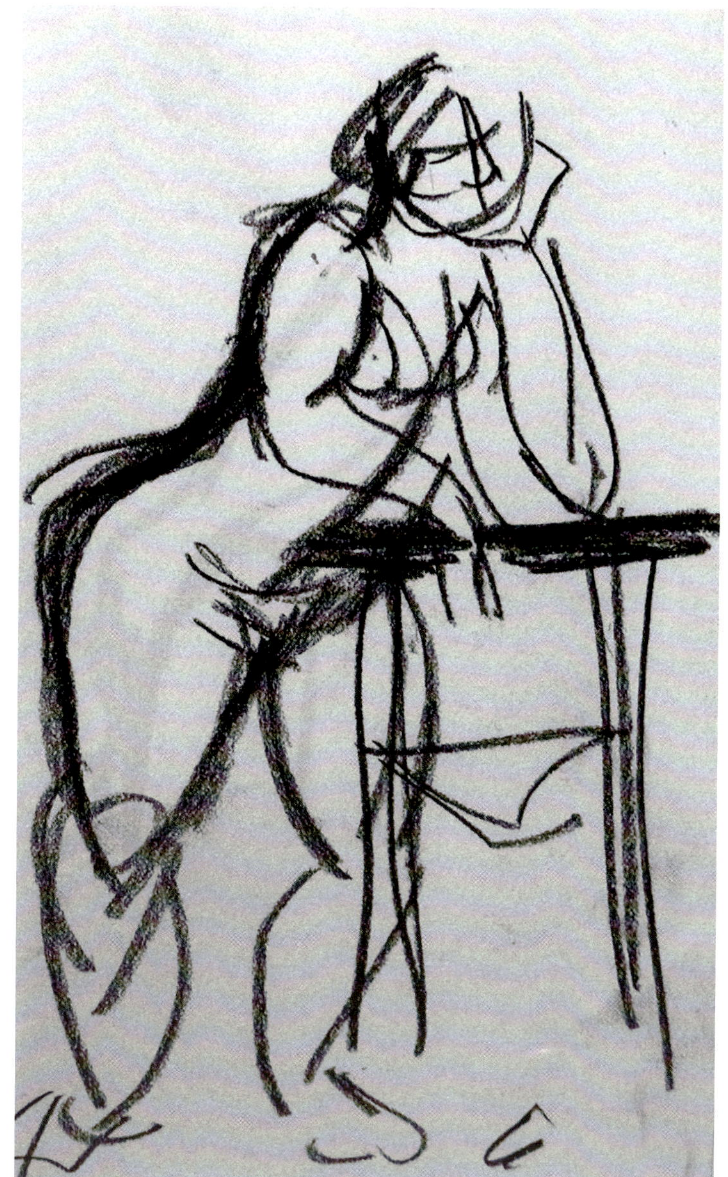

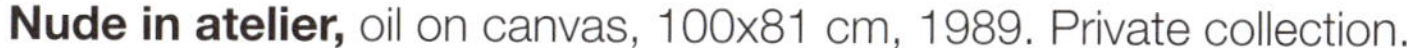

Nude in atelier, oil on canvas, 100x81 cm, 1989. Private collection.

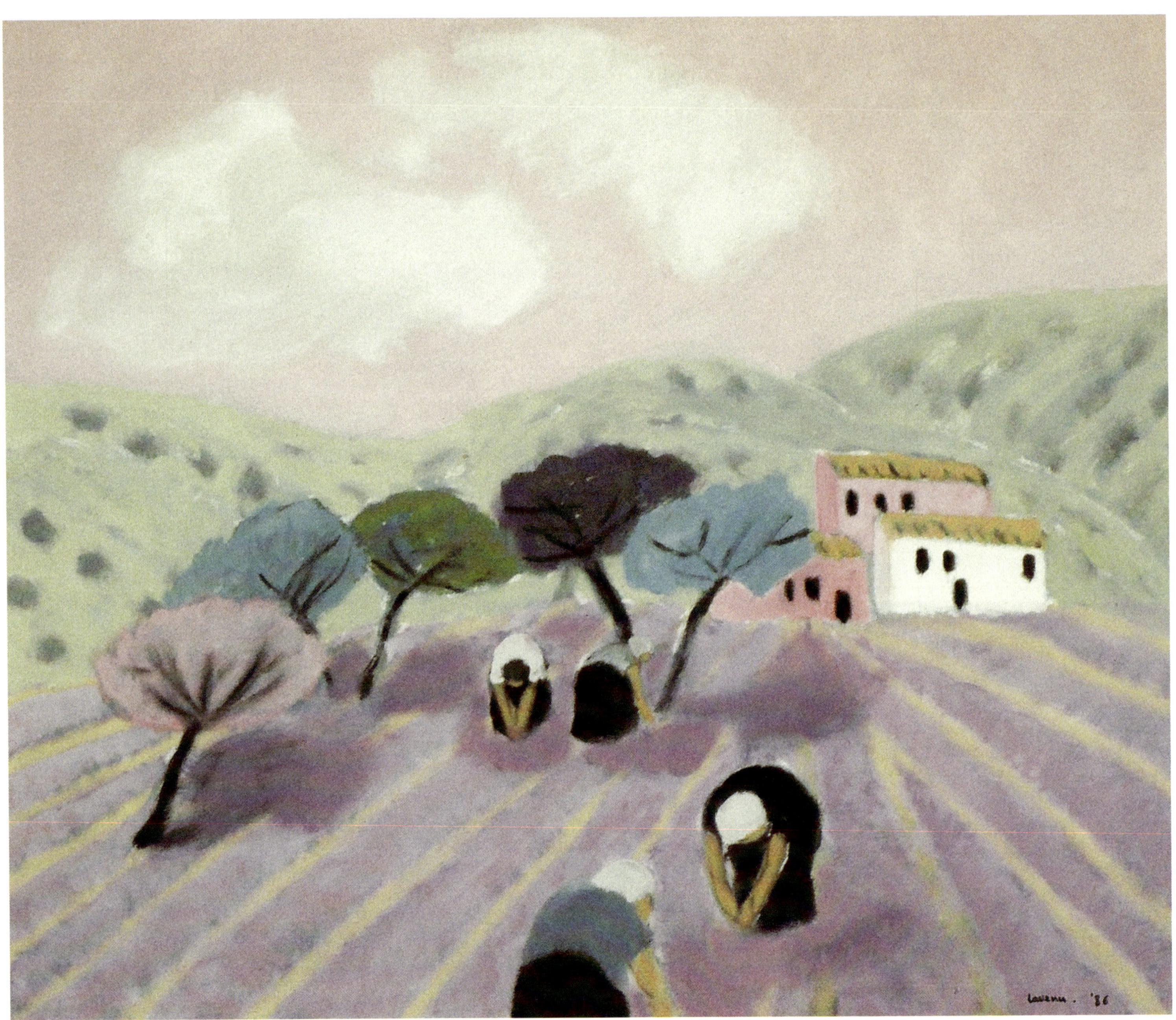

Lavande en Provence, oil on canvas, 122x138 cm, 1986. Private collection.

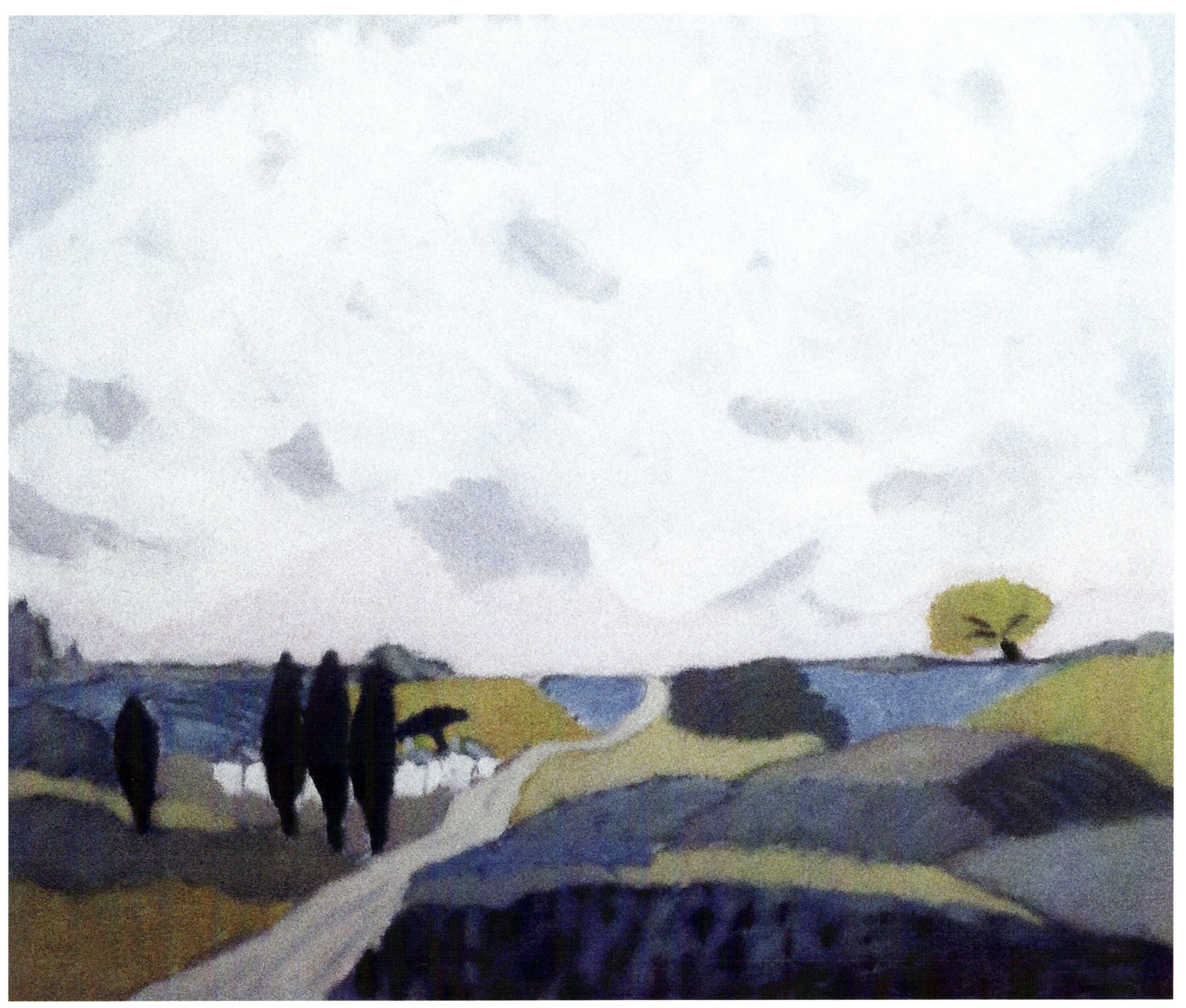

Champigny-sur-Veude, oil on canvas, 122x138 cm, 1986. Private collection.

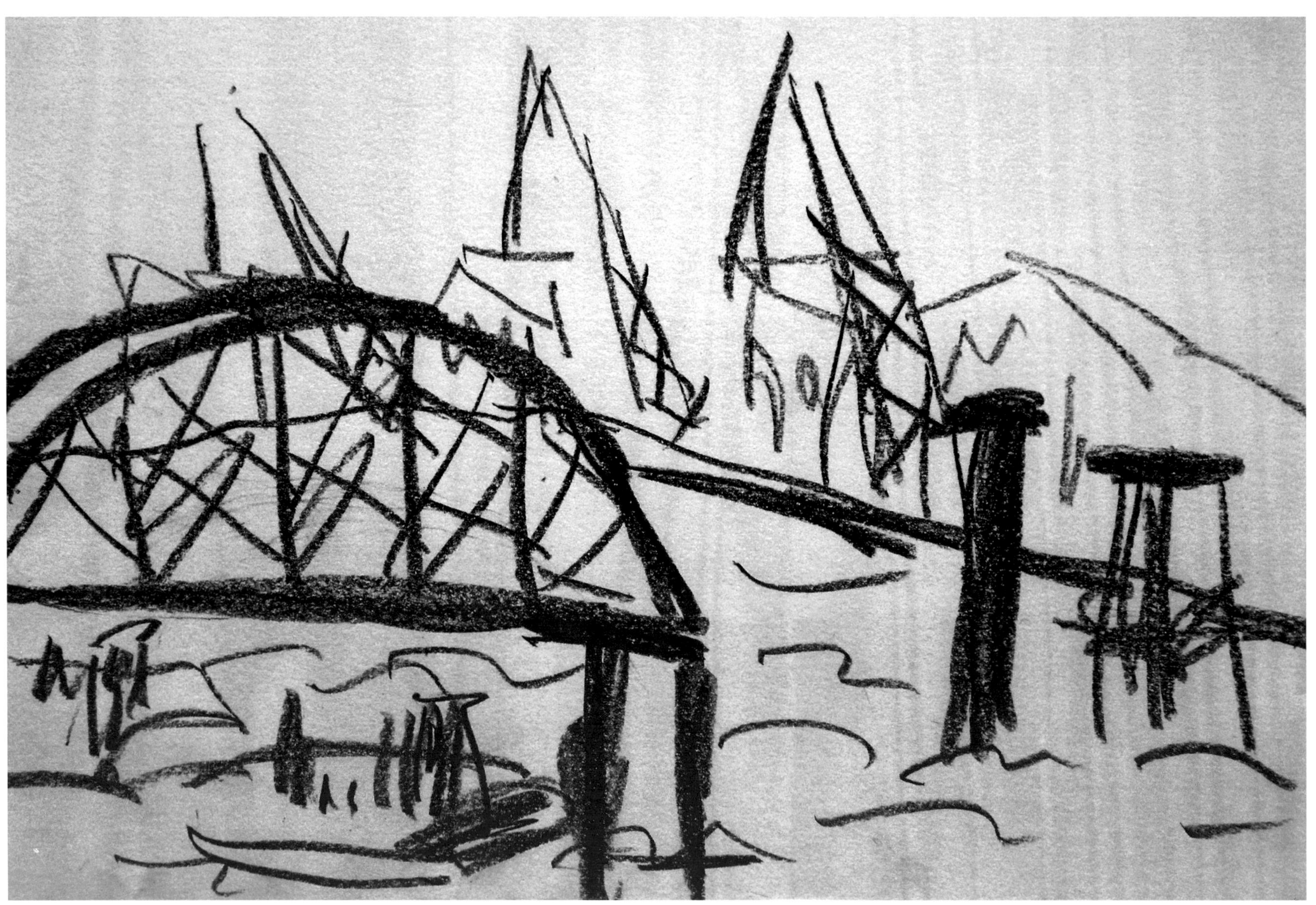

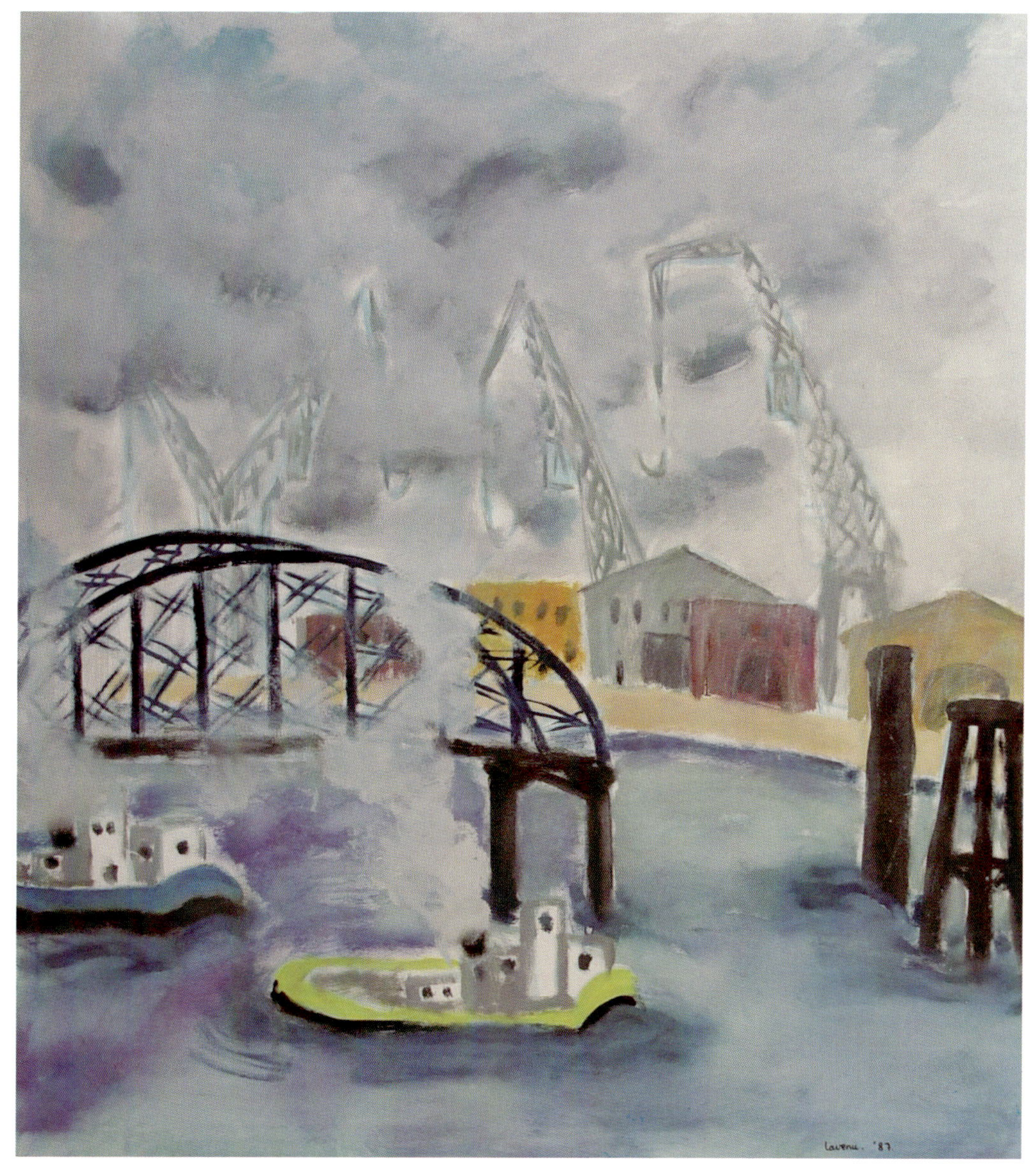

Hamburg harbor, oil on canvas, 138x122 cm, 1987.

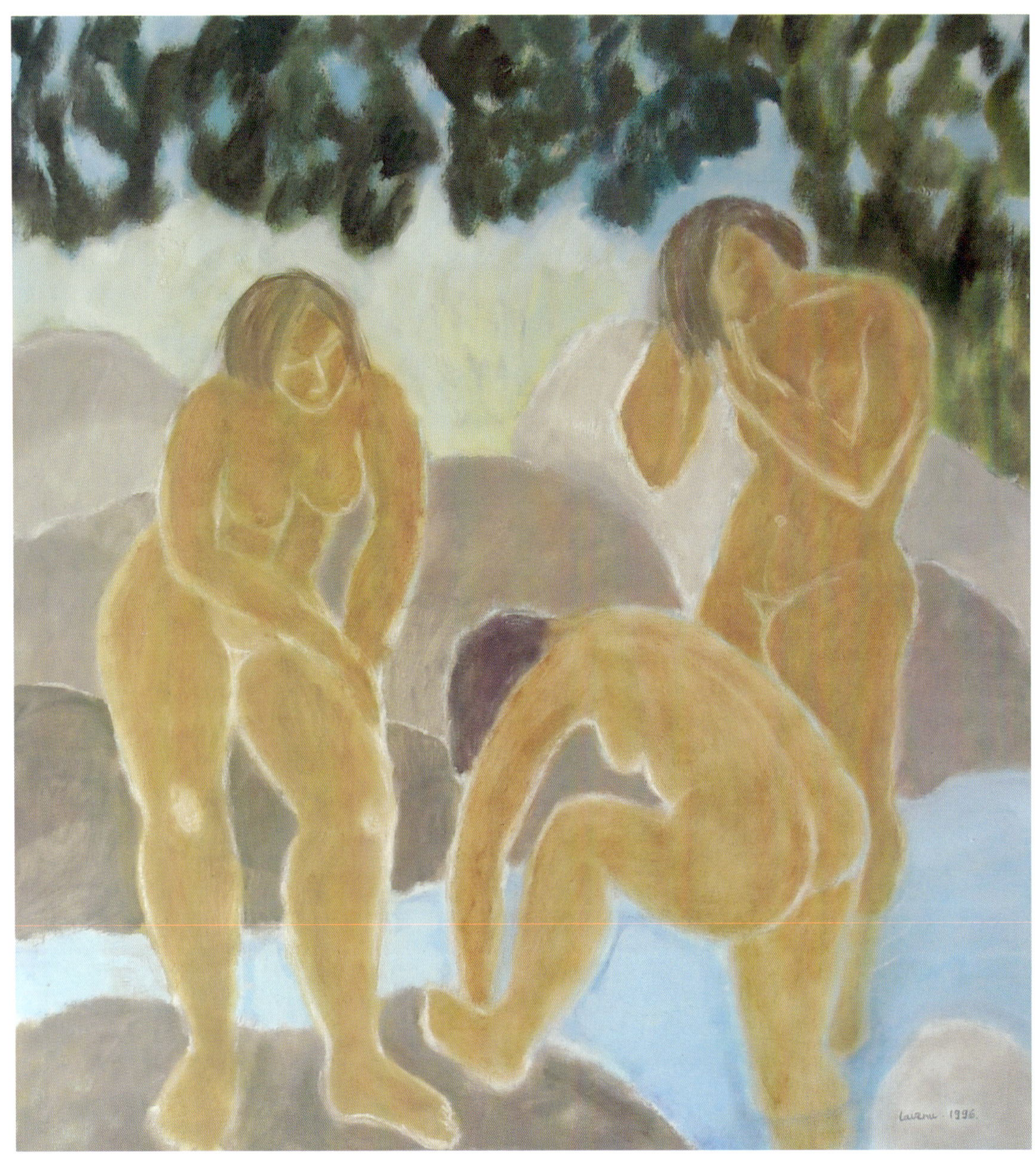

Trois baigneuses, oil on canvas, 138x122 cm, 1996. Private collection.

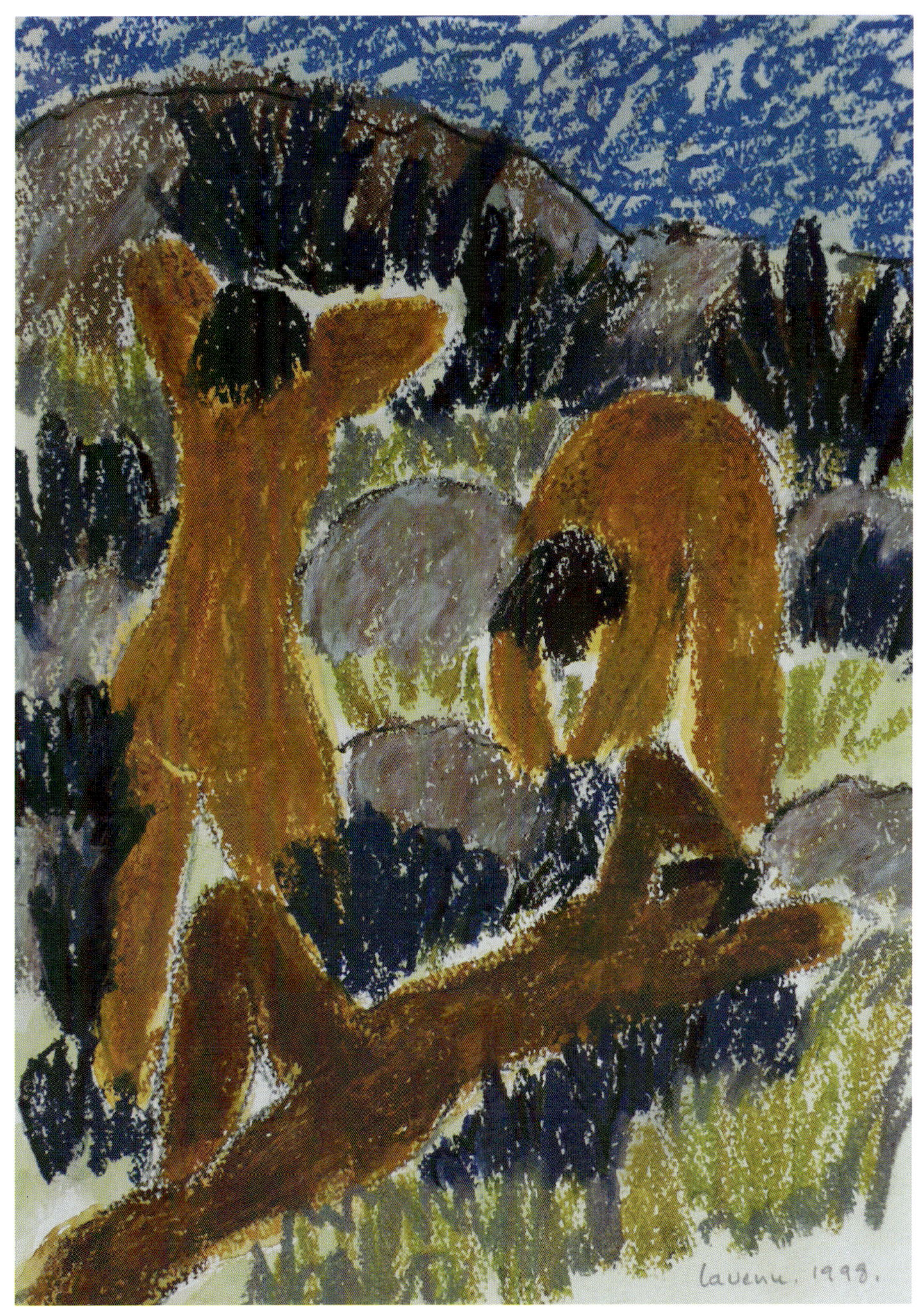

Baigneuses dans les rochers, oil pastel, 40x30 cm, 1998.

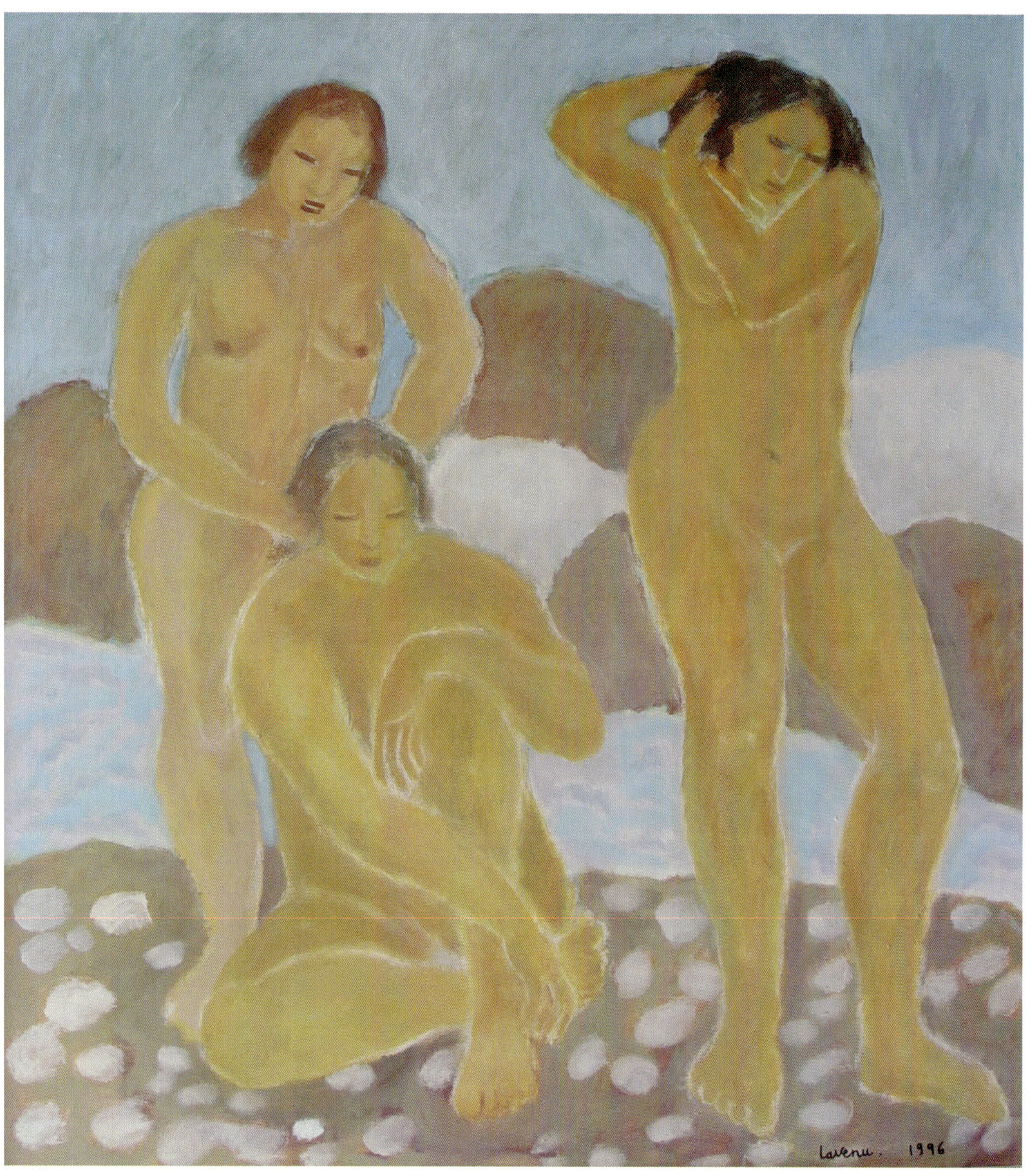

Beach in Greece, oil on canvas, 138x122 cm, 1996.

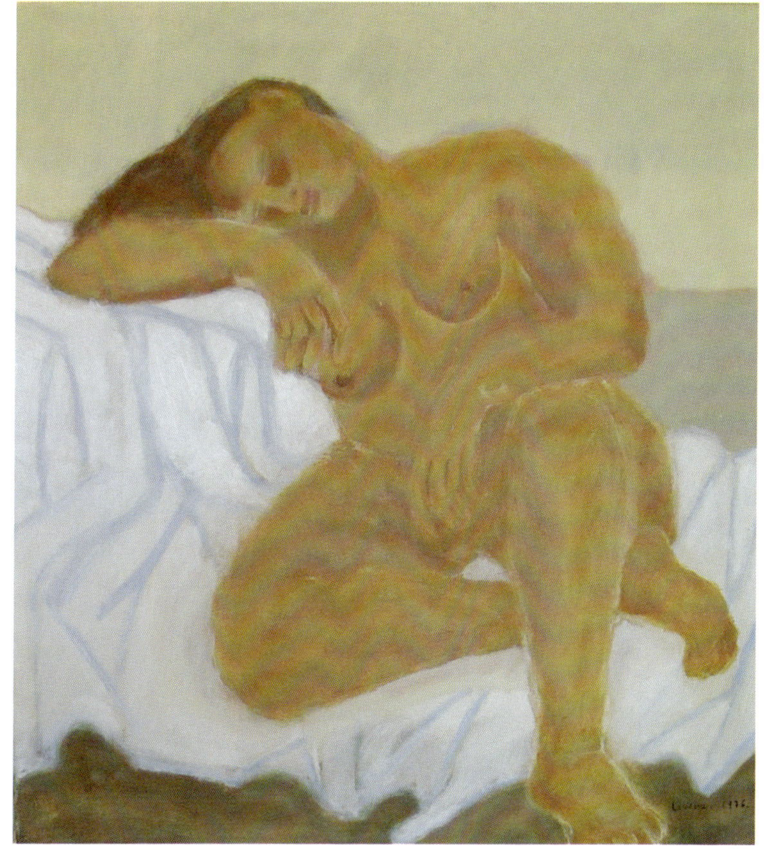

Sleeping nude, oil on canvas, 100x90 cm, 1976-1997.

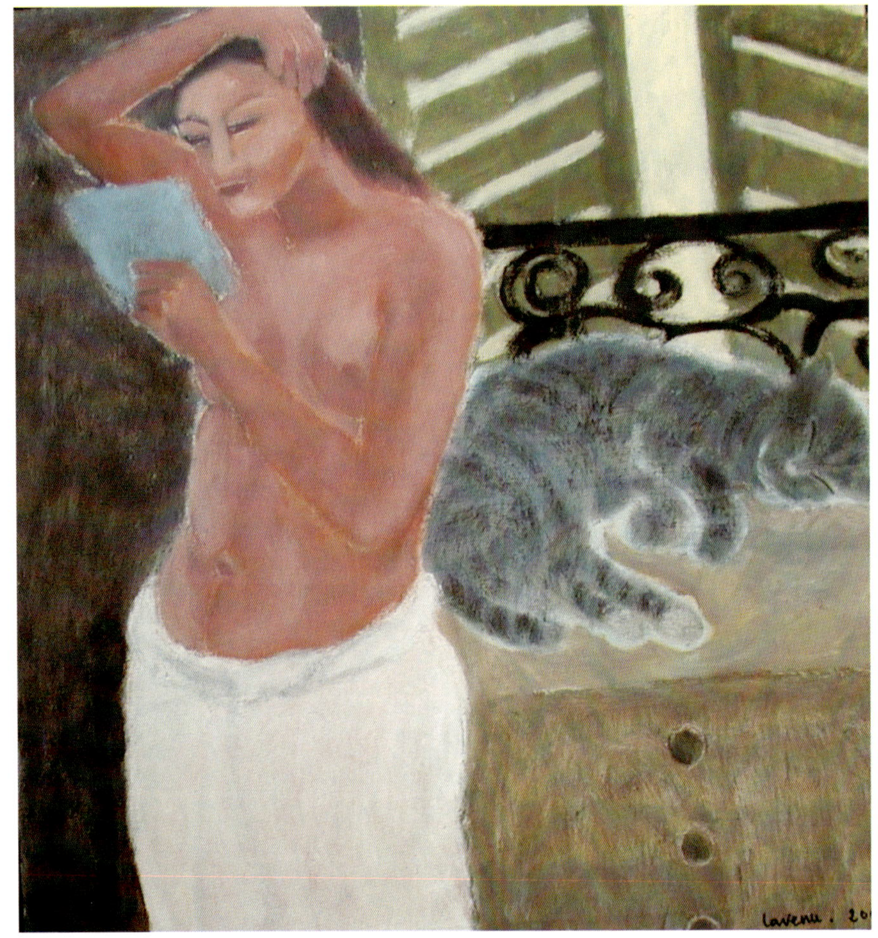

Femme et chat, oil on canvas, 100x90 cm, 2000. Private collection.

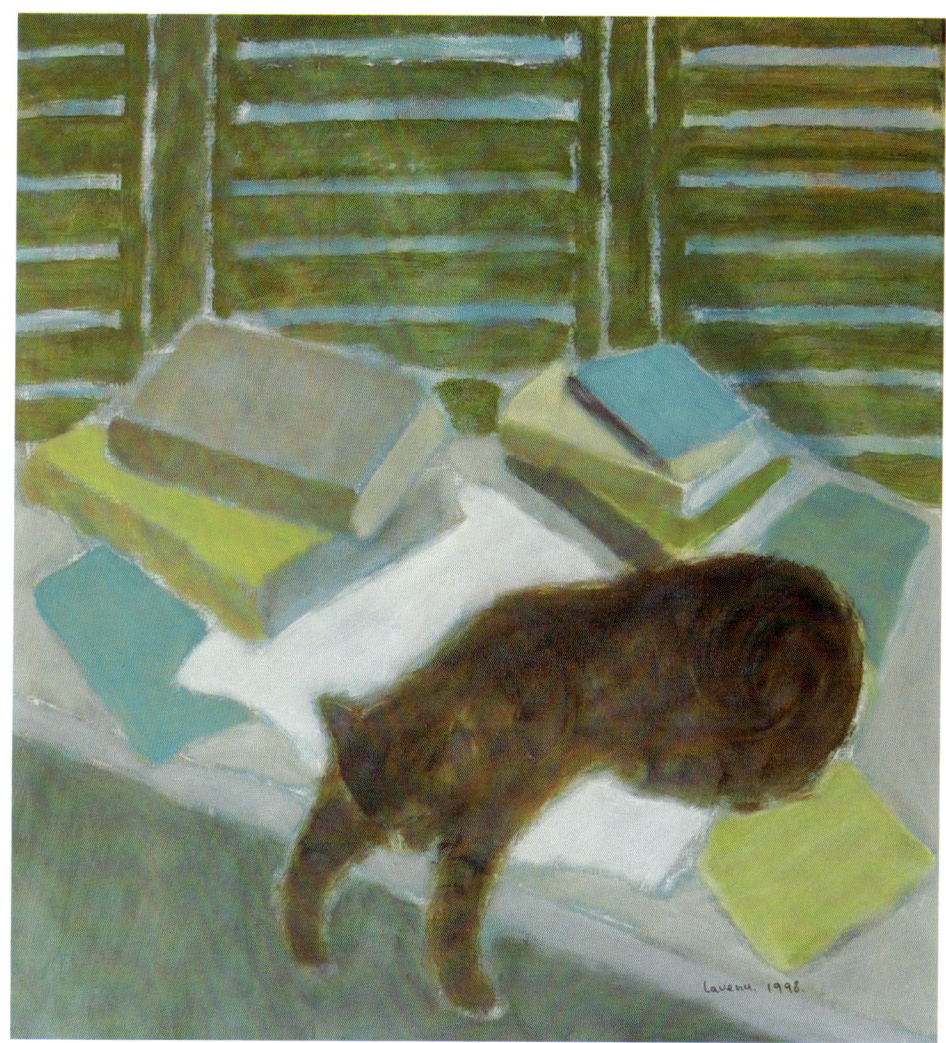

Chat et livres, oil on canvas, 100x90 cm, 1998.

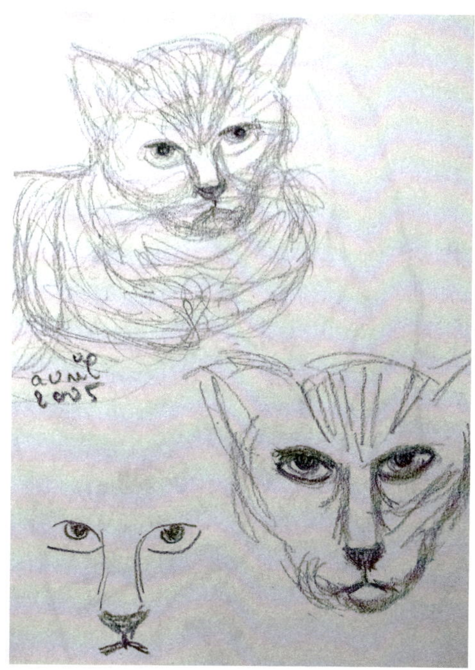

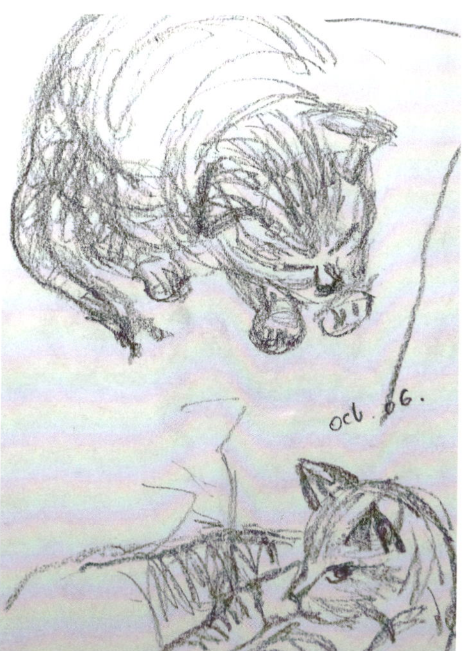

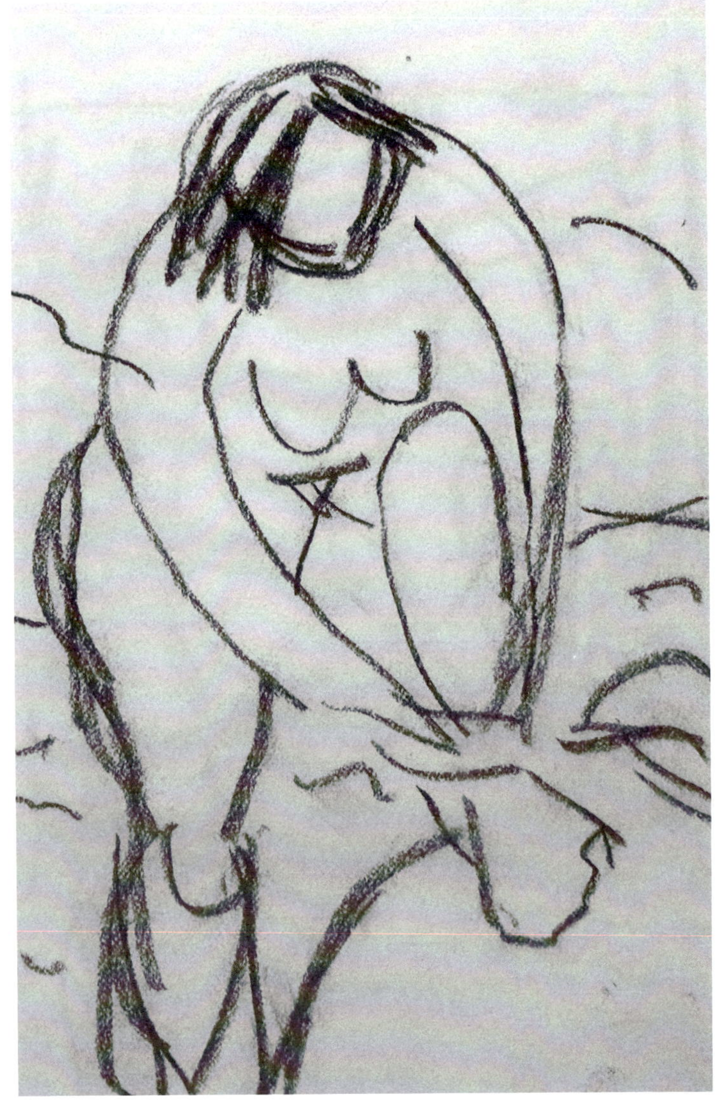

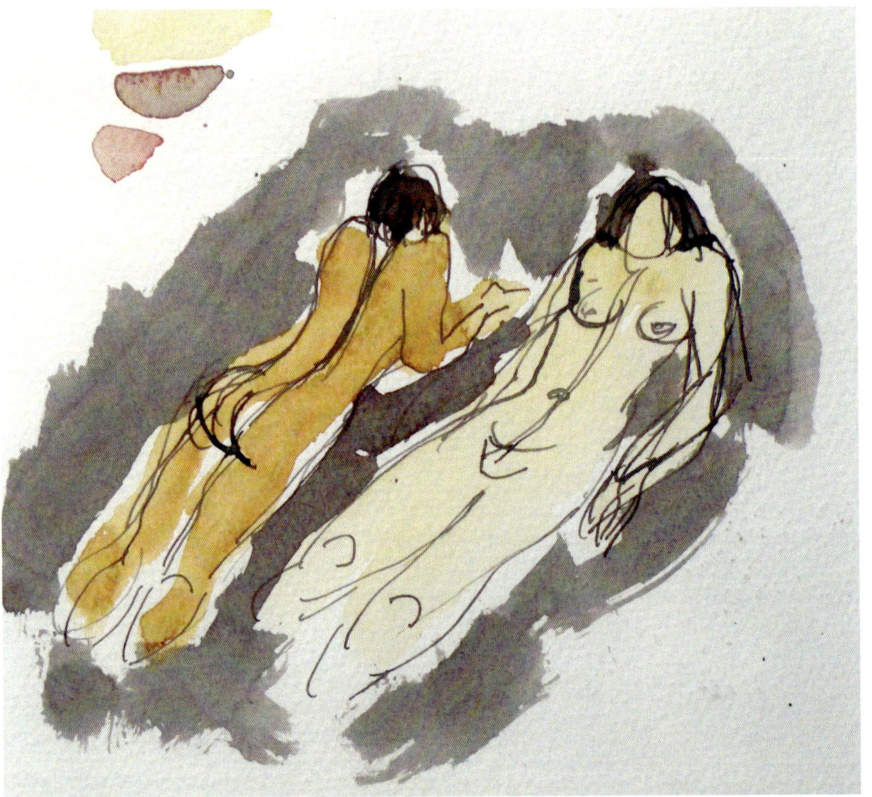

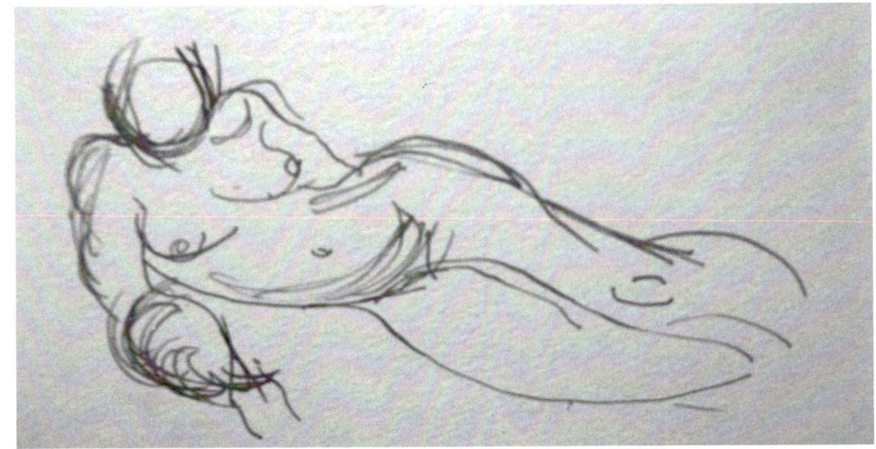

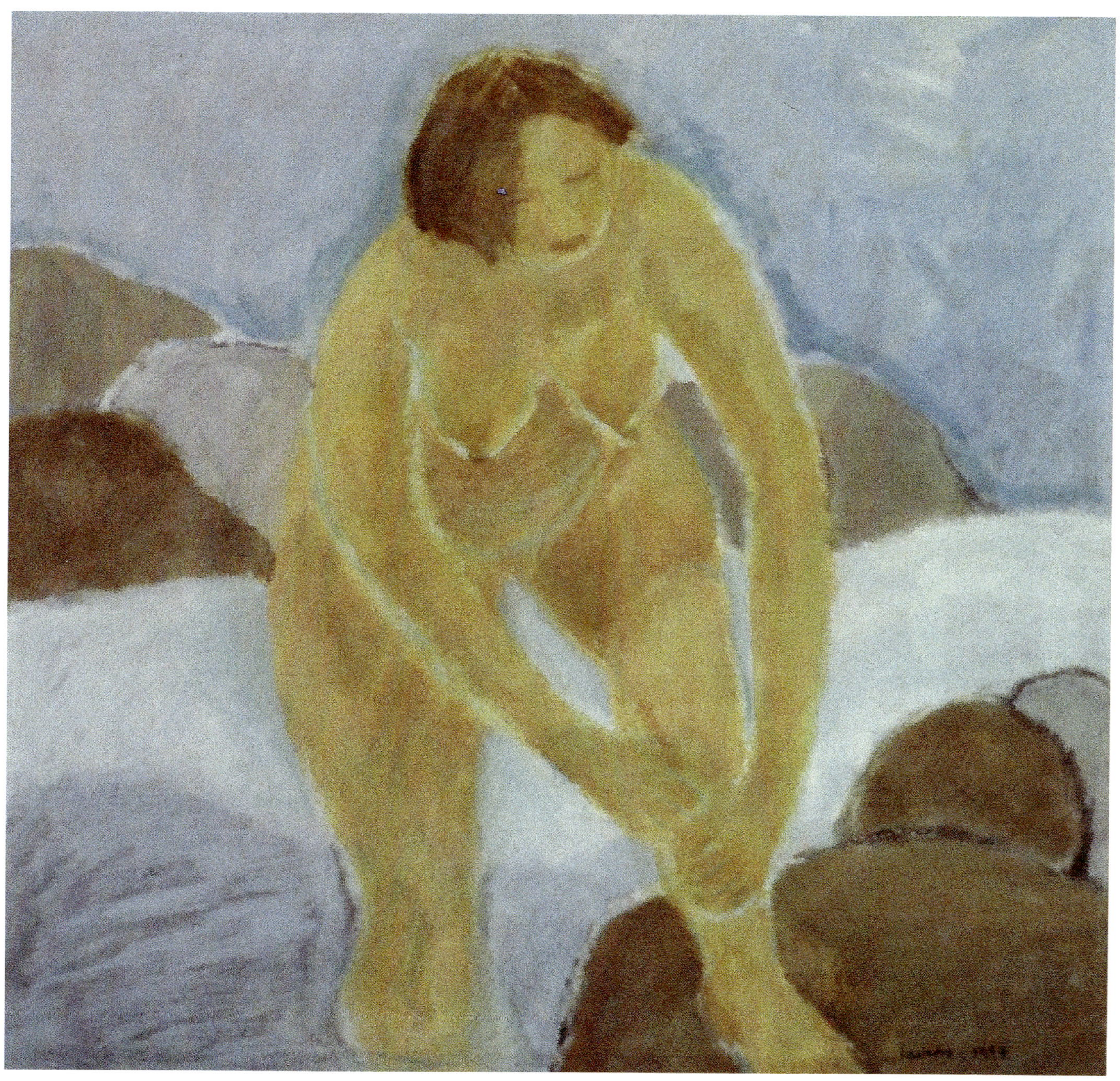

Nu dans les rochers, oil on canvas, 95x95 cm, 1997. Private collection.

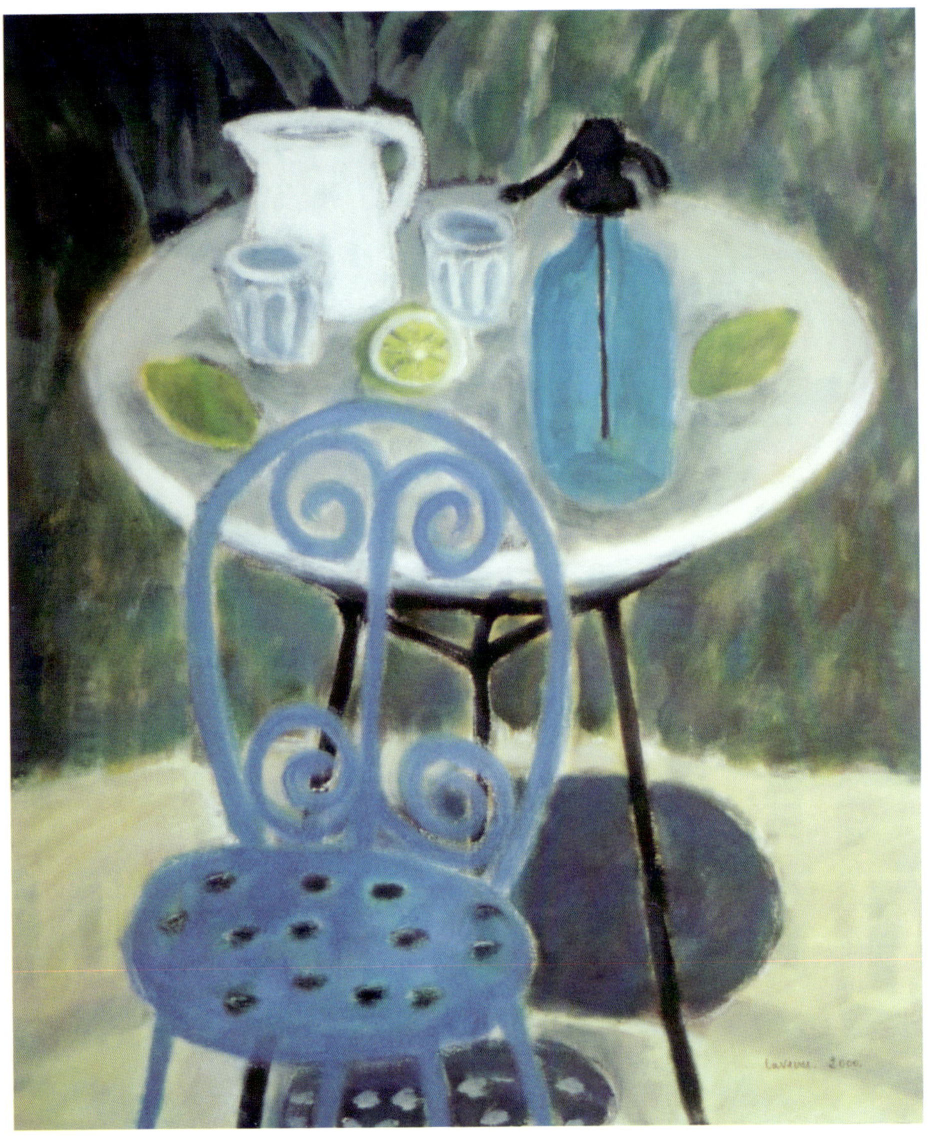

Nature morte et siphon, oil on canvas, 116x97 cm, 2000. Private collection.

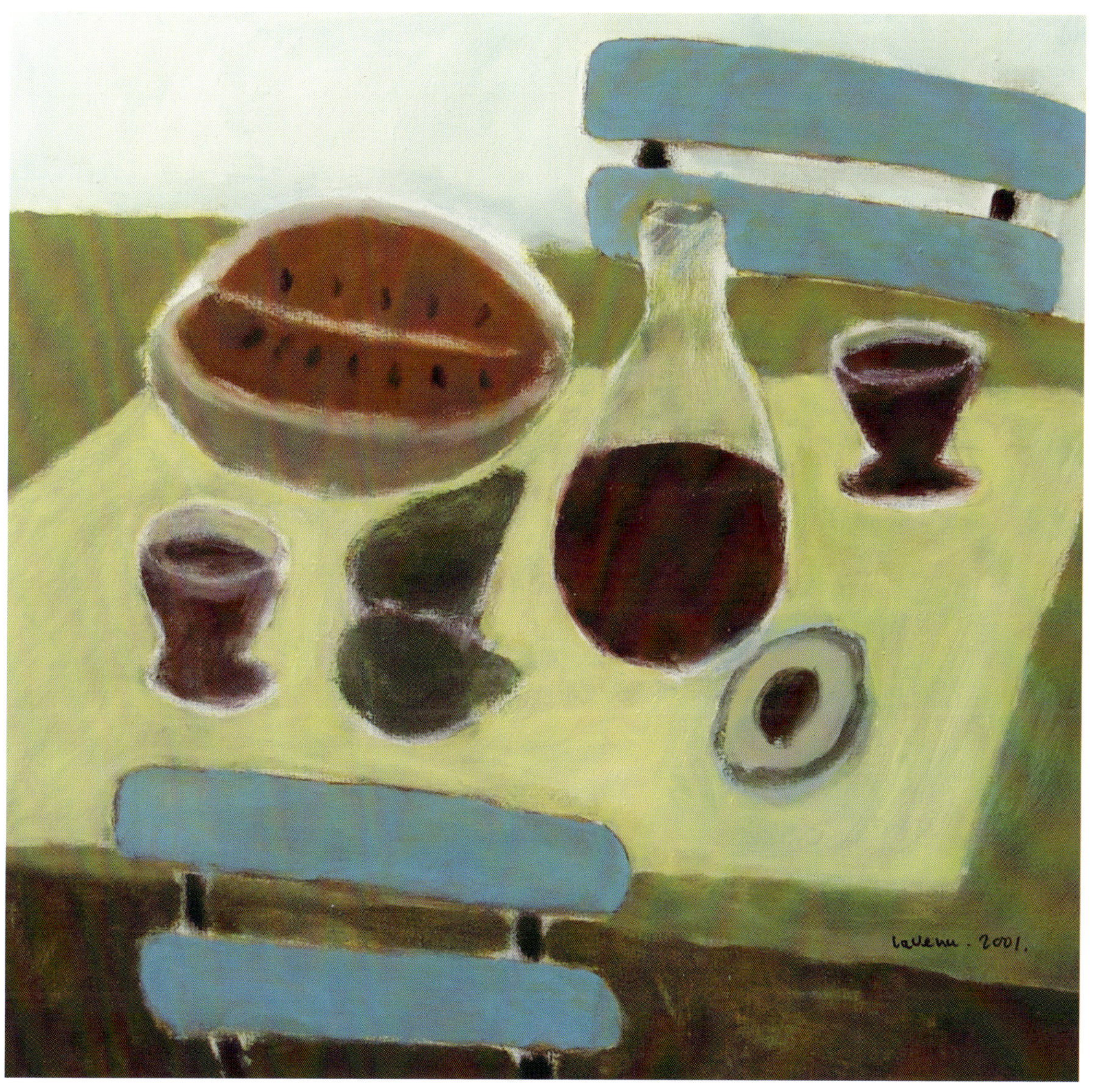

Avocats et pastèque, oil on canvas, 92x92 cm, 2001. Private collection.

Jacqueline's work allows me to feel like an obscured viewer to a seemingly simple scene, into which I can step and journey and discover, or stay safely tucked away to watch and wait.

Her art simultaneously offers me nostalgia and possibility.

I can return to a quiet afternoon in a place of my own gentle design or meet an unusual character offering me experiences unknown.

When I need the comfort of the sun and an open field, a simple meal, or my beloved pet's warmth, I turn to her pieces.

When I want to daydream of a clandestine adventure, or a surprising scene just around the bend, I turn to her pieces.

Jacqueline Lavenu's gift to me is memory and imagination.

Victoria Joes
Policy Advisor, City of San Diego

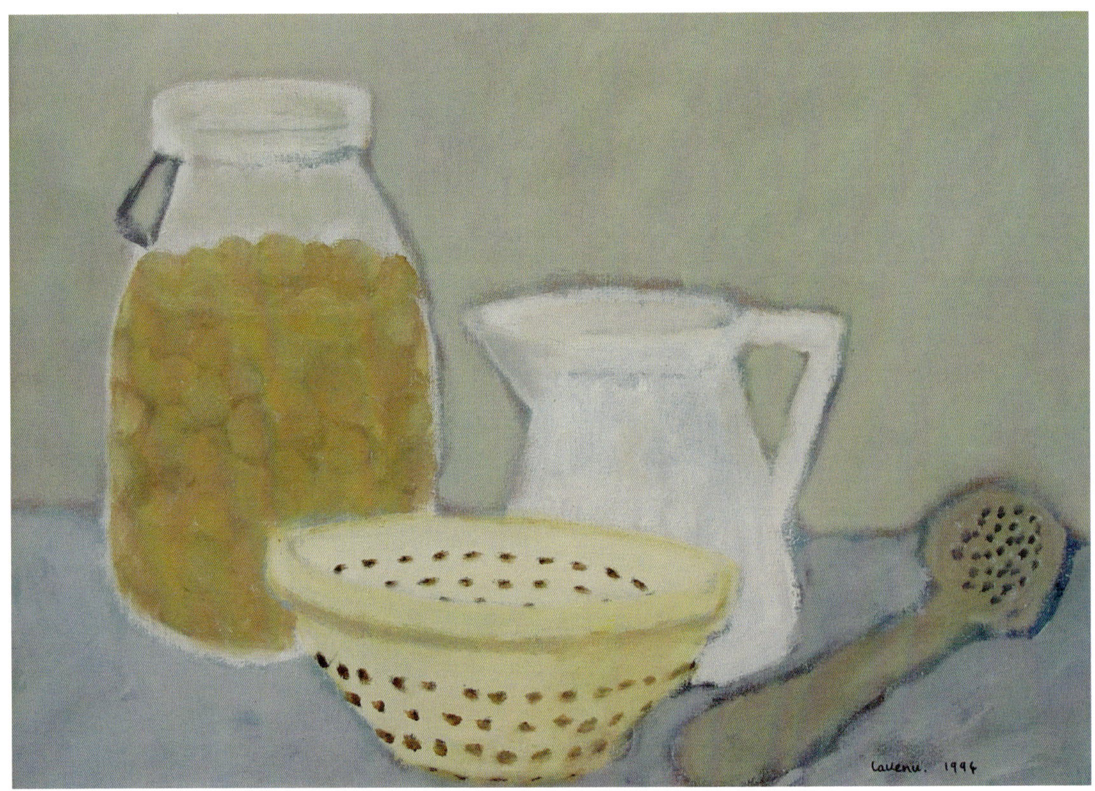

Nature morte aux mirabelles, oil on canvas, 73x100 cm, 1994. Private collection.

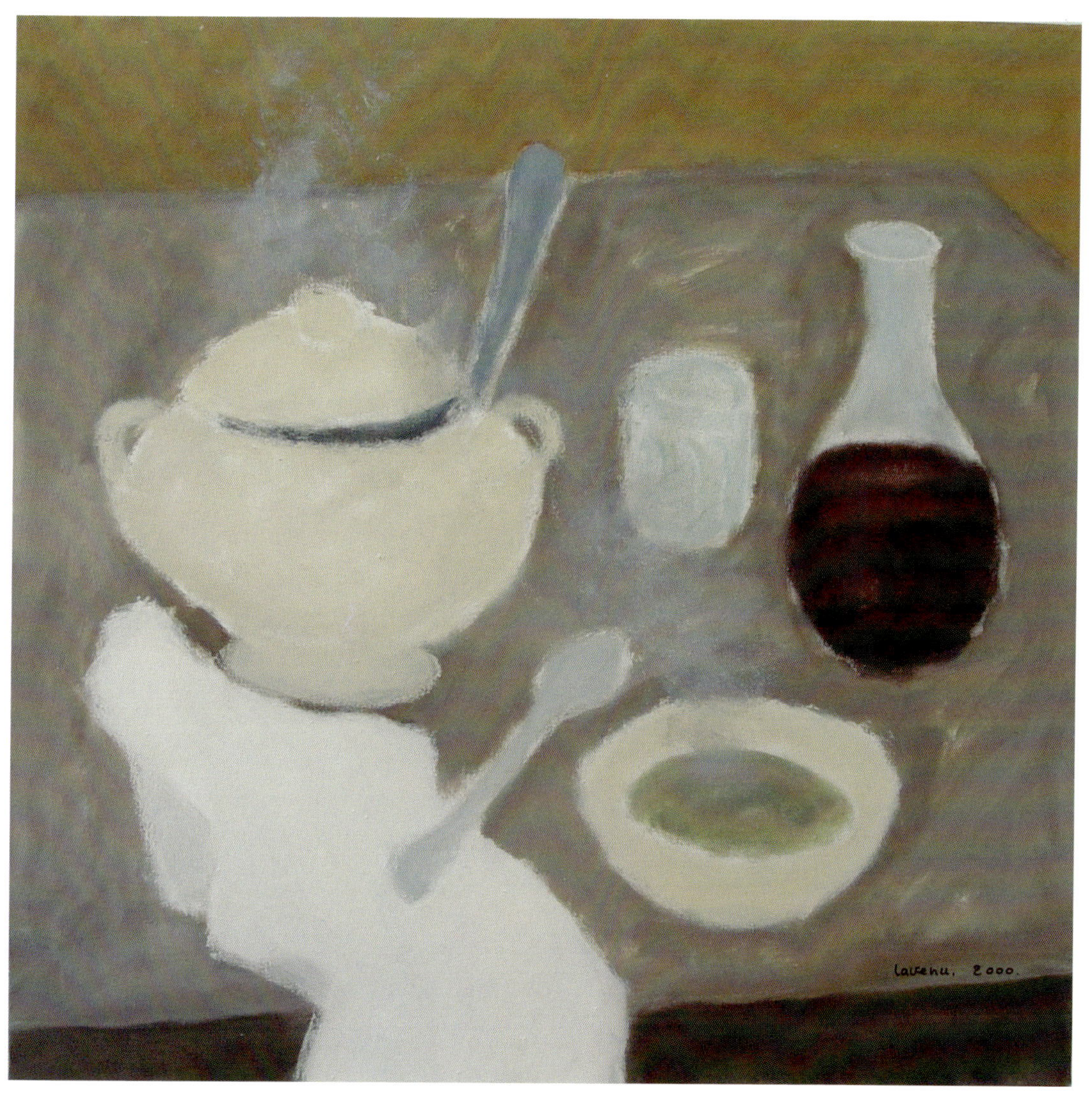

Nature morte et soupière, oil on canvas, 92x92 cm, 2000.

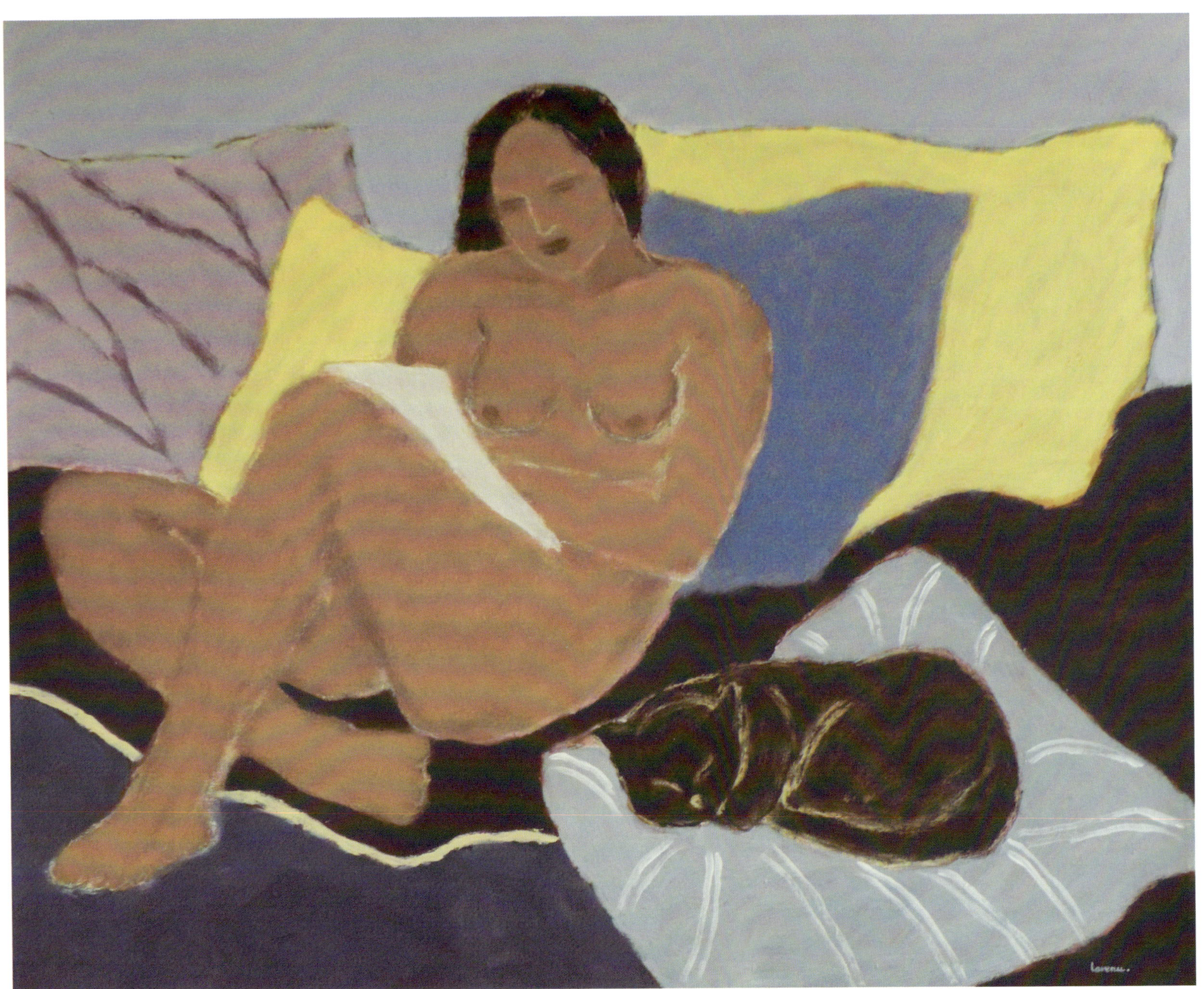

Reading with cat I, oil on canvas, 97x116 cm, 2002.

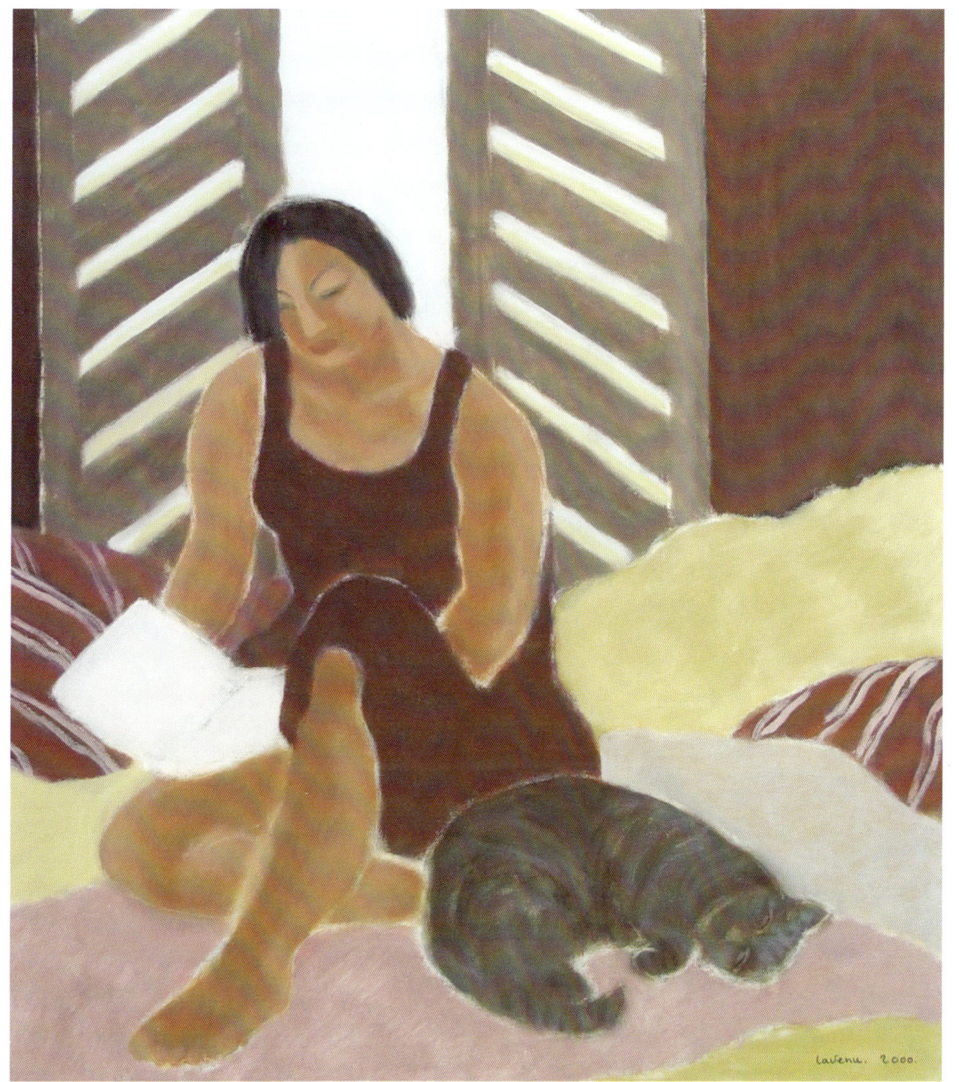

Reading with cat II, oil on canvas, 138x122 cm, 2005.

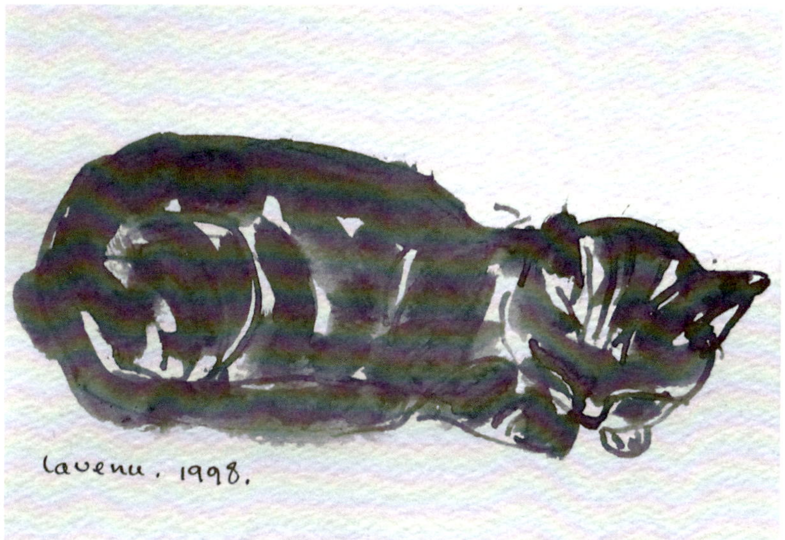

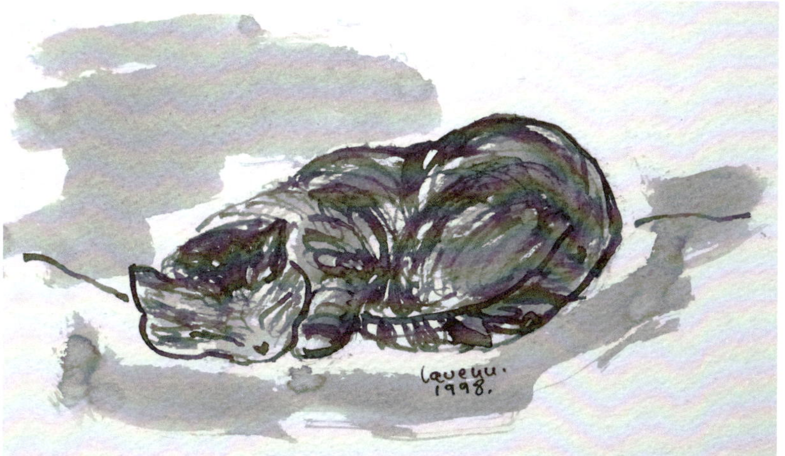

"Mrs. Freeman's mother and Mrs. Freeman are imaginary names. However, they are real people. I saw Mrs. Freeman's mother sitting on her porch. Mrs. Freeman was comfortably installed in a furniture store. Both made a strong impression that I captured with a sketch."

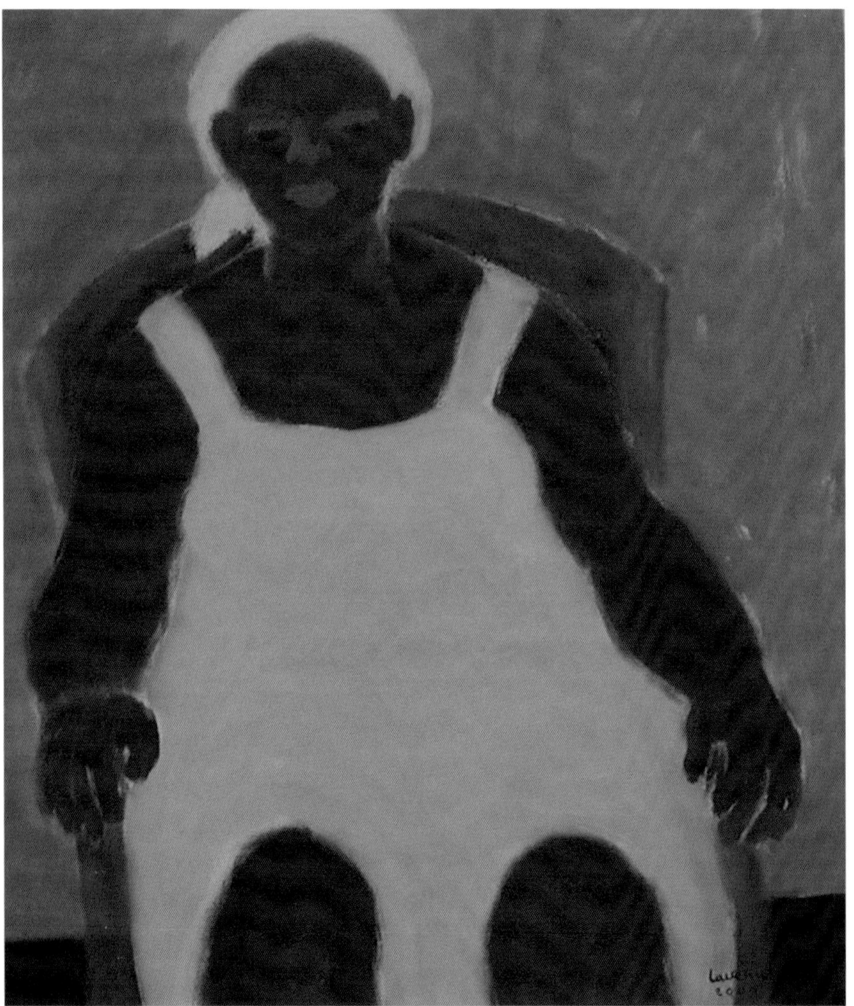

Mrs. Freeman's mother, oil on canvas, 92x76 cm, 2000. Private collection.

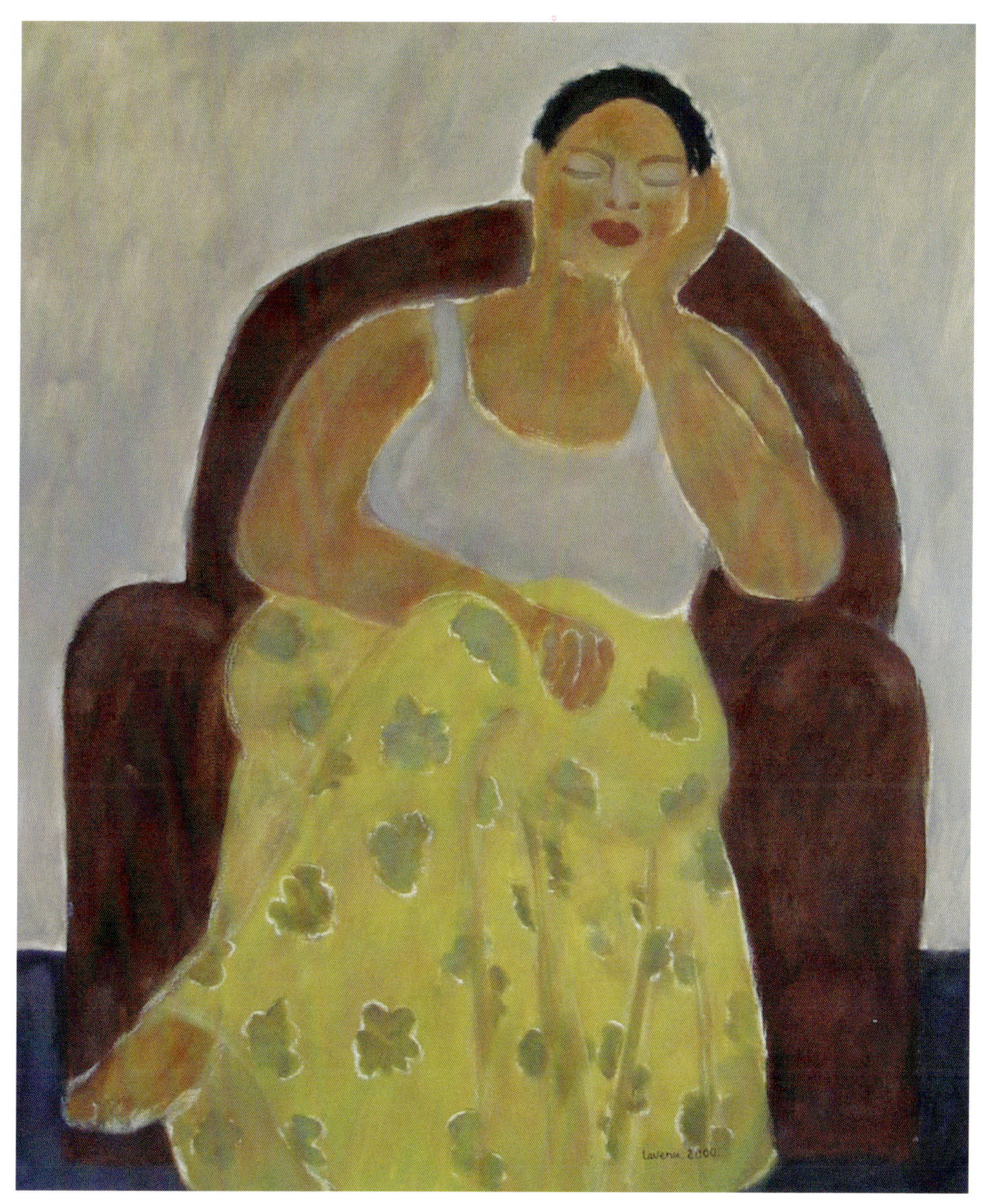

Mrs. Freeman, oil on canvas, 122x102 cm, 2000.

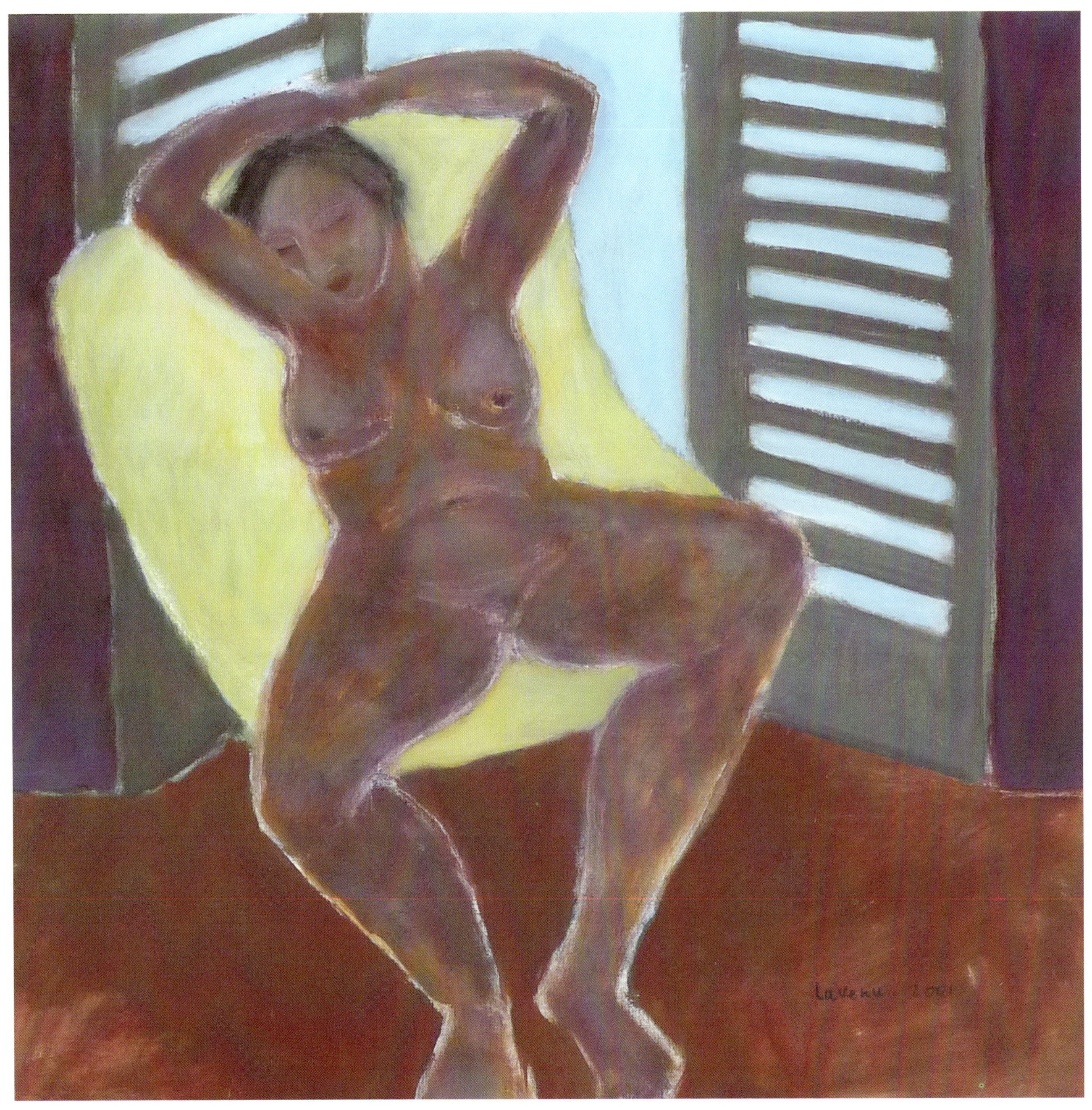

Nu à contre-jour, oil on canvas, 92x92 cm, 2001. Private collection.

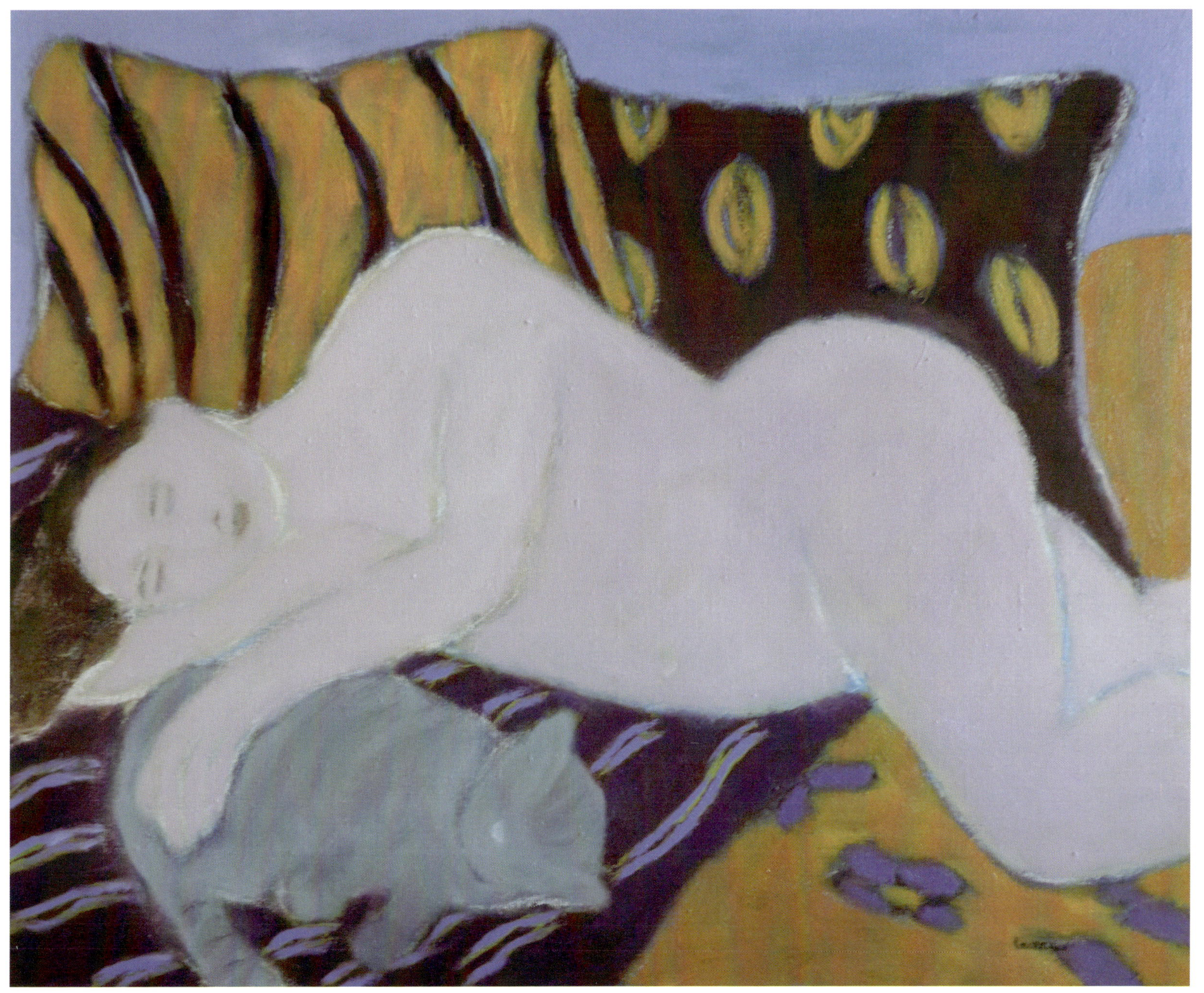

Nude and cat, oil on canvas, 76x92 cm, 2008-2011.

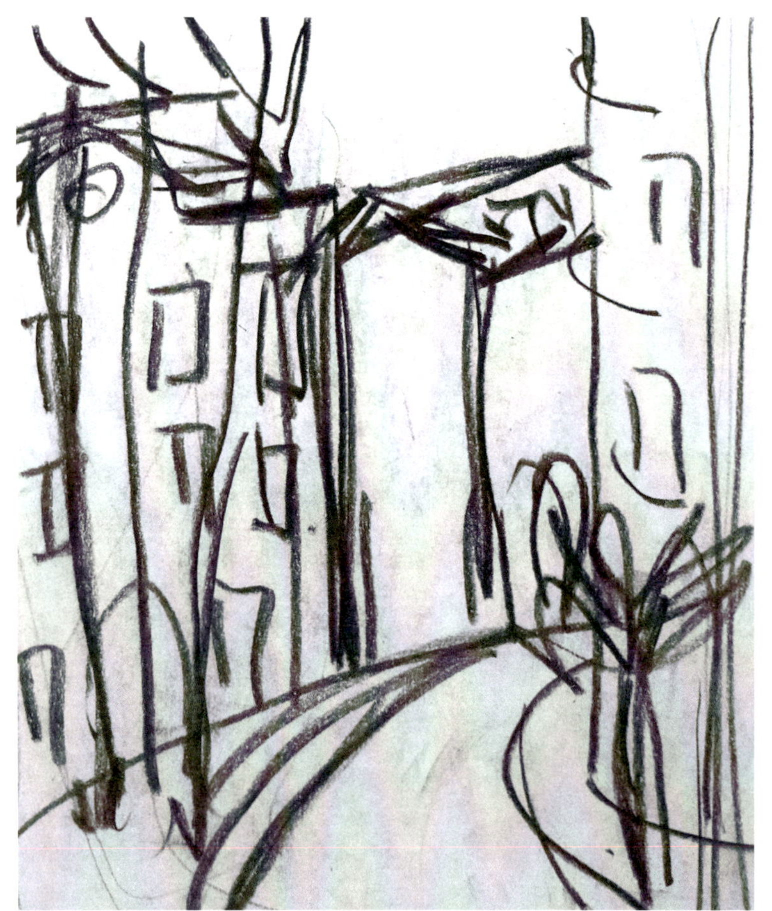

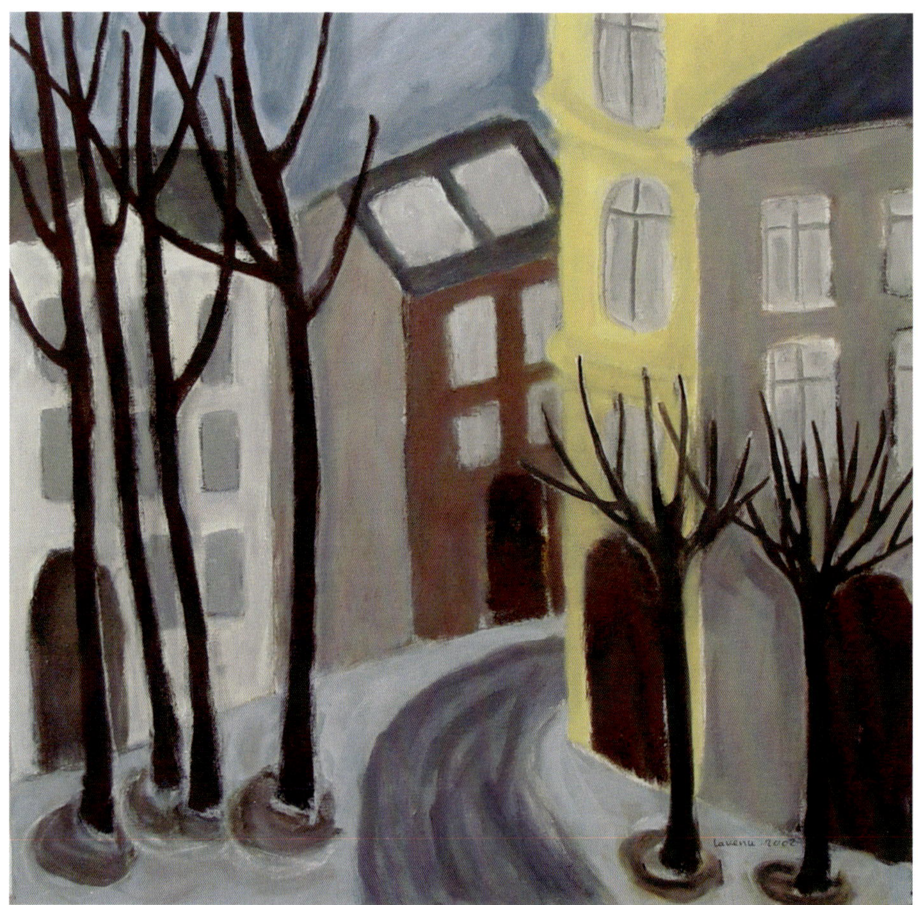

Viktoria-Luise-Platz Berlin, oil on canvas, 92x92 cm, 2000. Private collection.

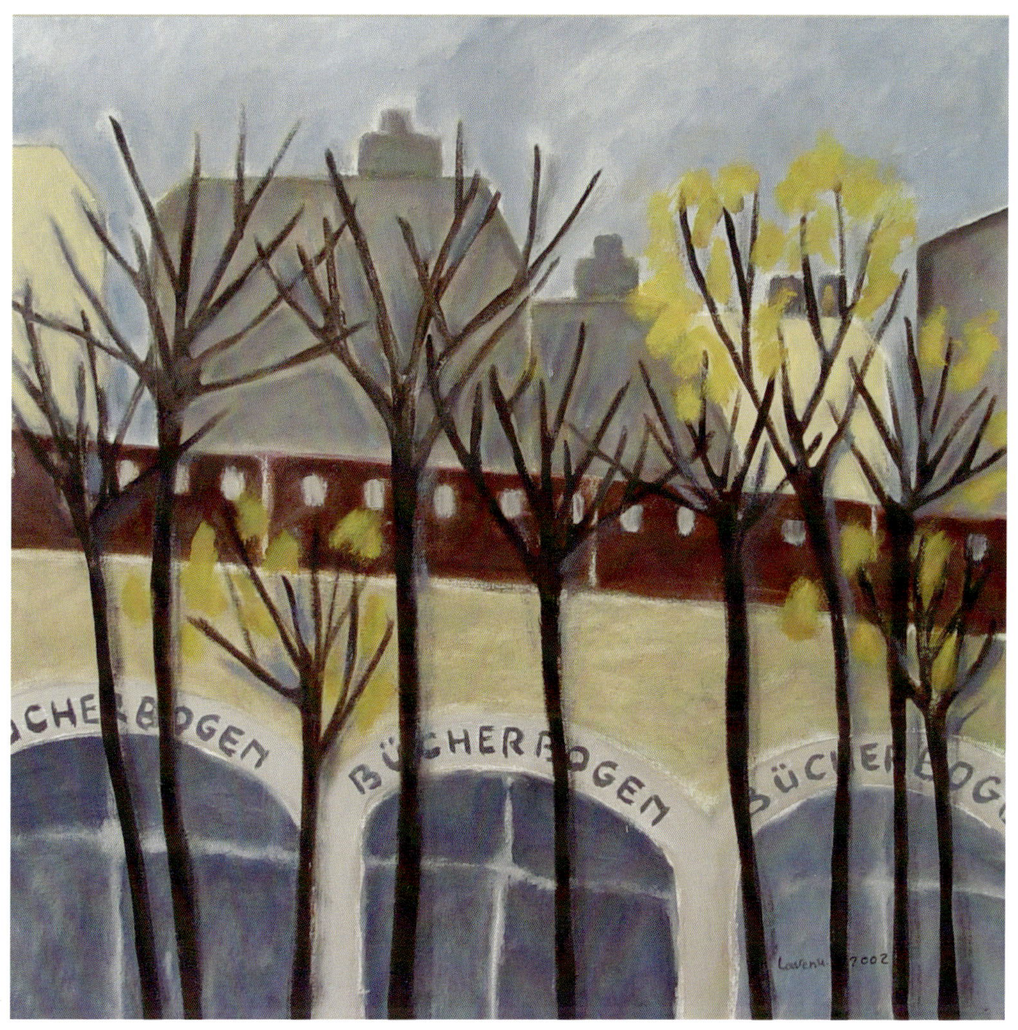

Savignyplatz Berlin, oil on canvas, 92x92 cm, 2002. Private collection.

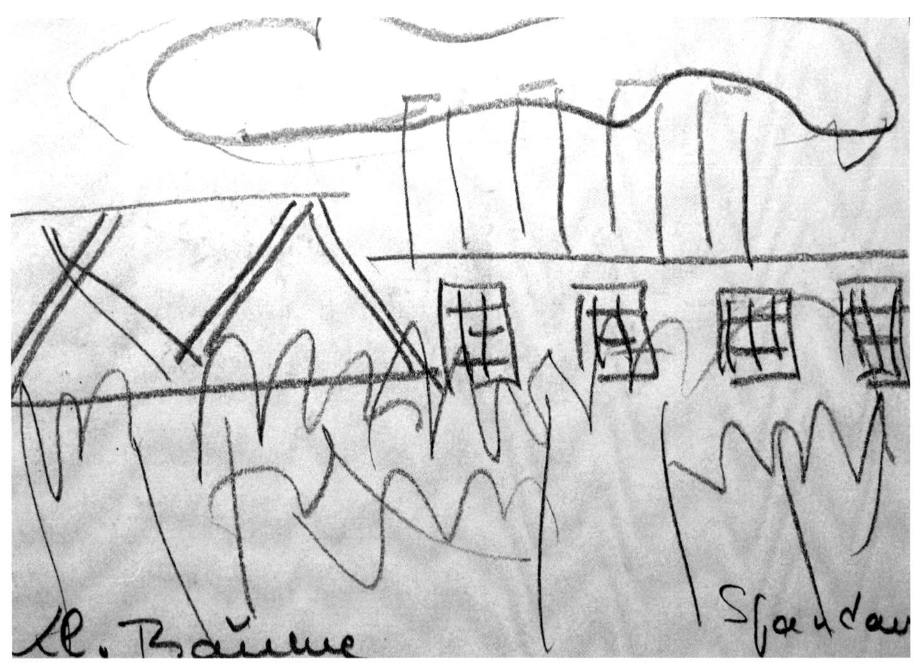
Kl. Bäume
Spandau

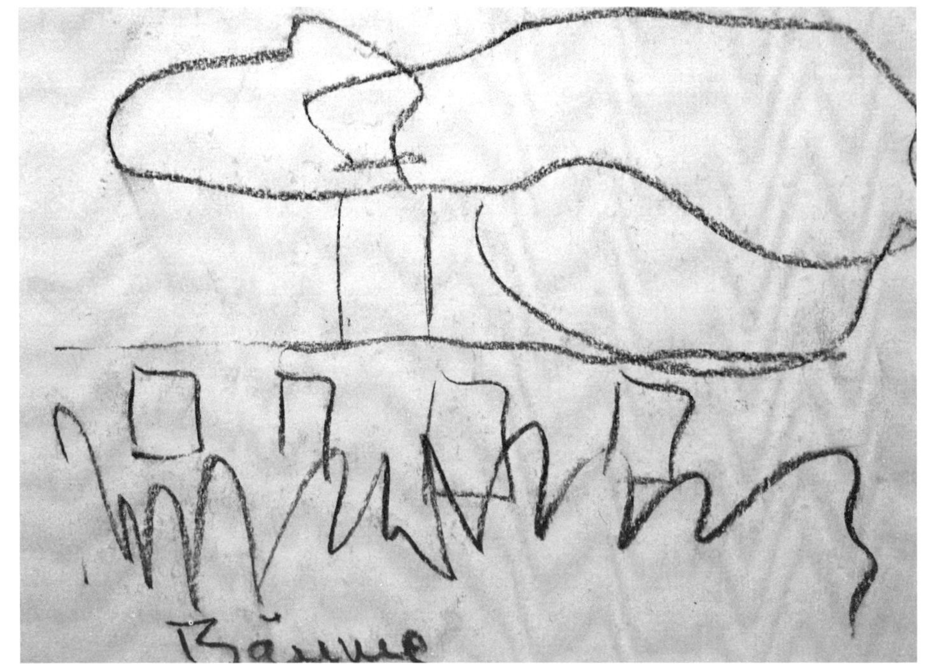
Bäume

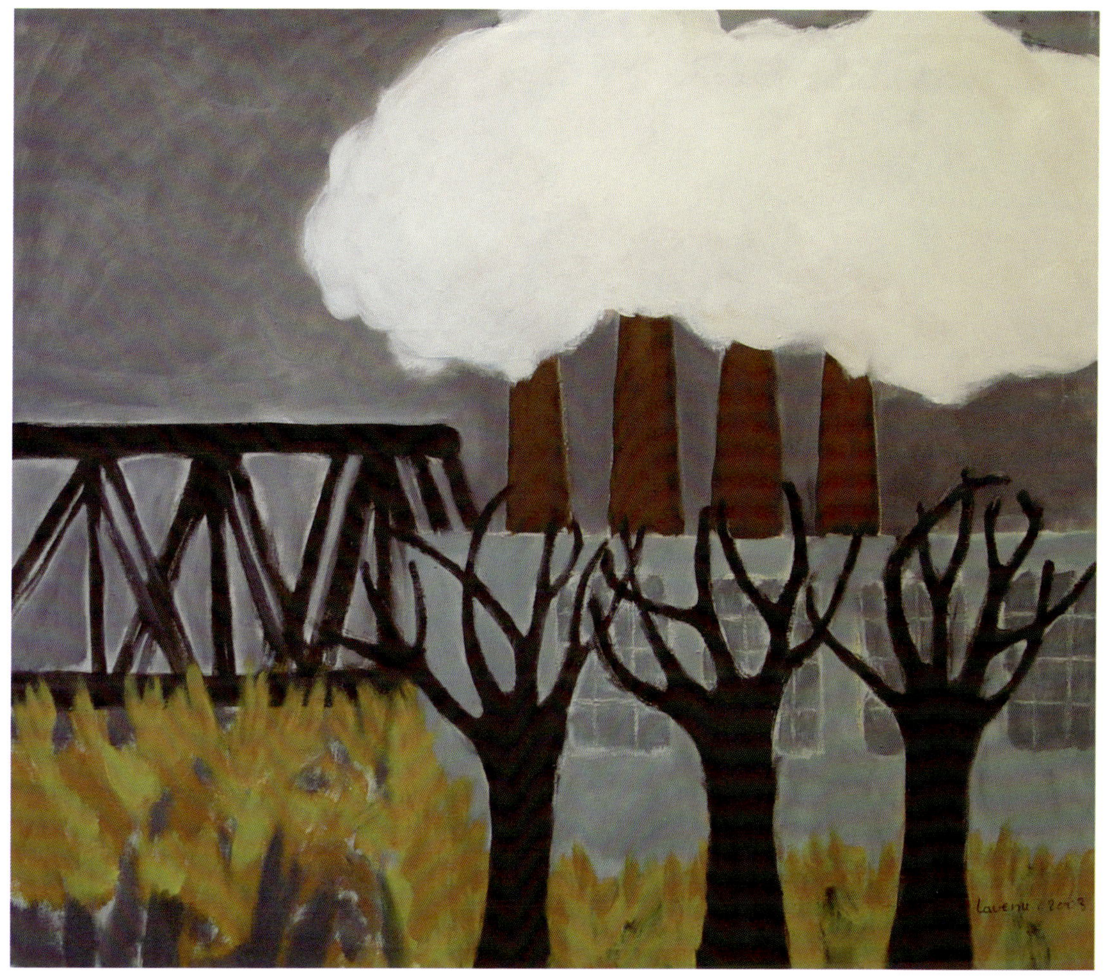

Factory in Berlin-Spandau, oil on canvas, 122x138 cm, 2003.

“Once a year Berliners used to clear out their attics and cellars leaving everything on the sidewalk for pickup. This beer garden chair I made mine and is featured in many of my paintings.”

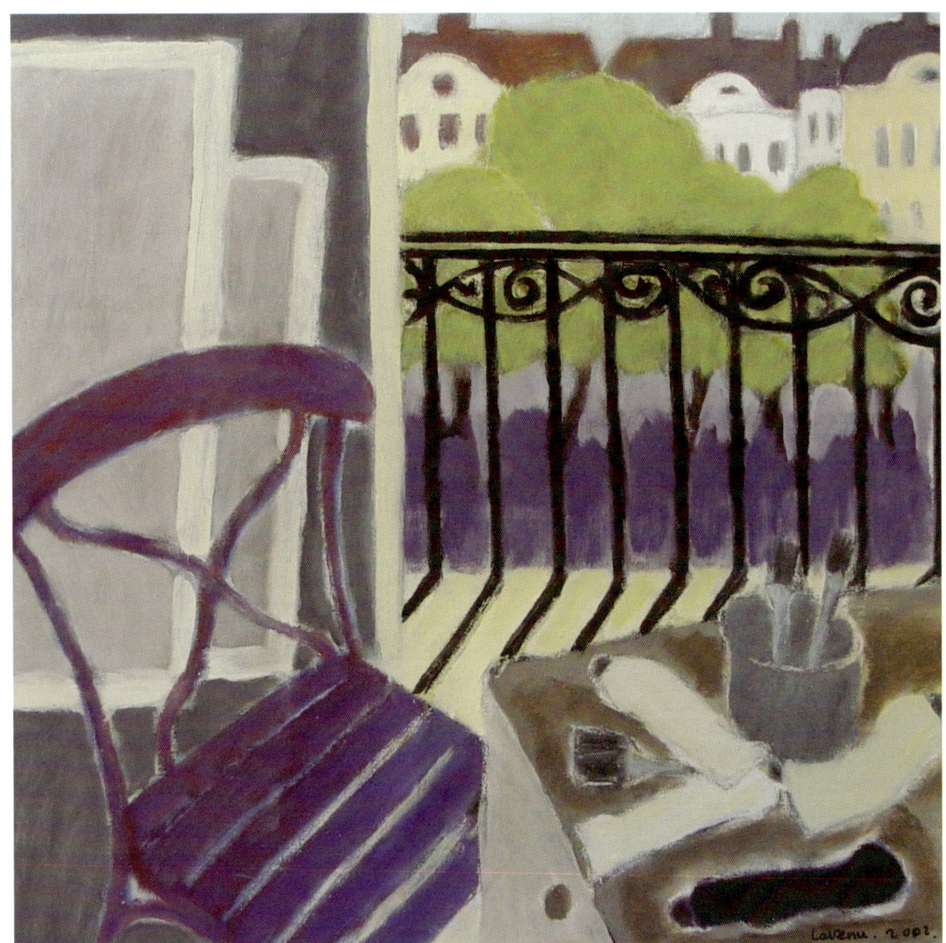

Atelier Berlin, oil on canvas, 92x92 cm, 2002. Private collection.

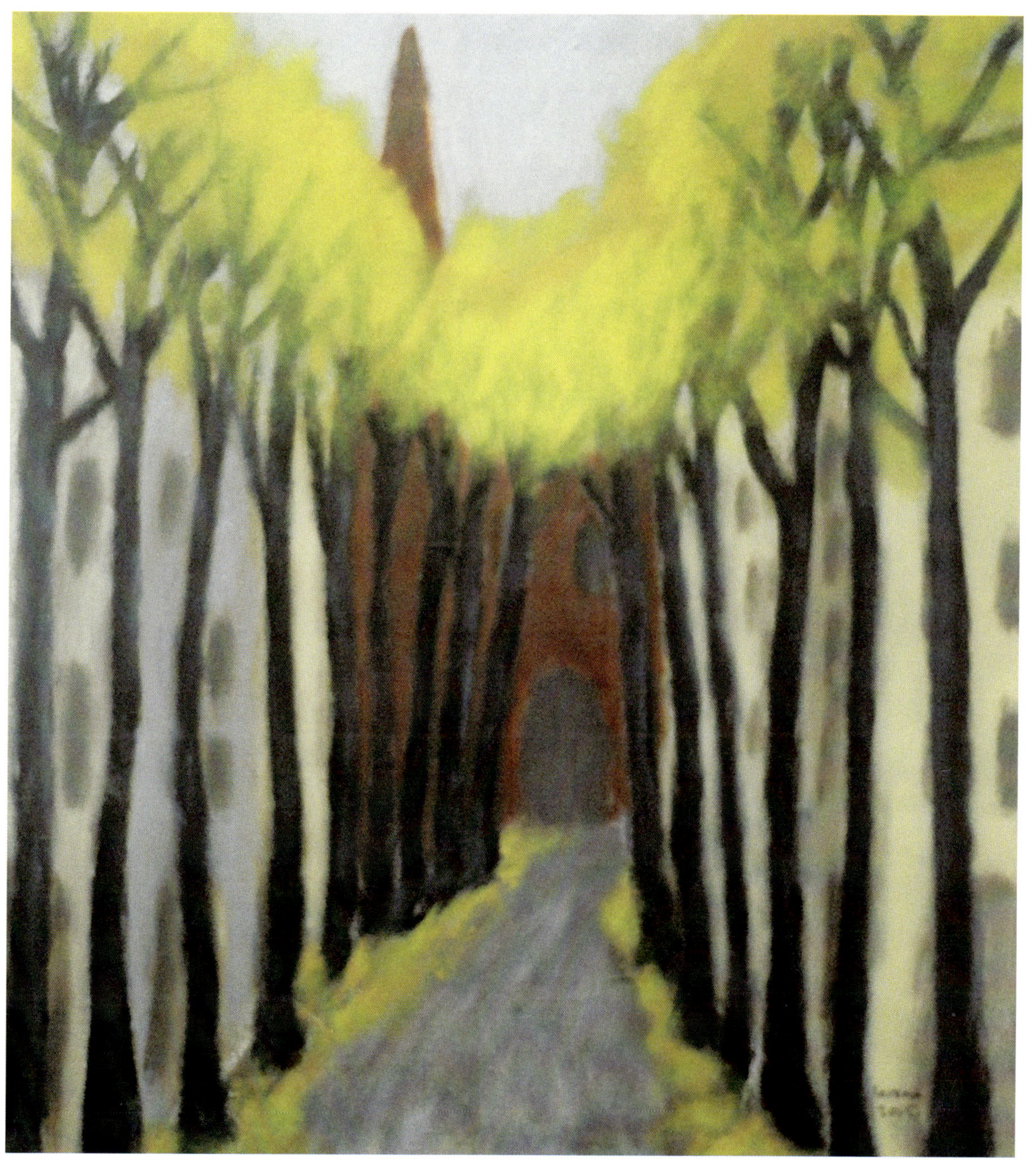

Pariserstrasse Berlin, oil on canvas, 102x92 cm, 2005. Private collection.

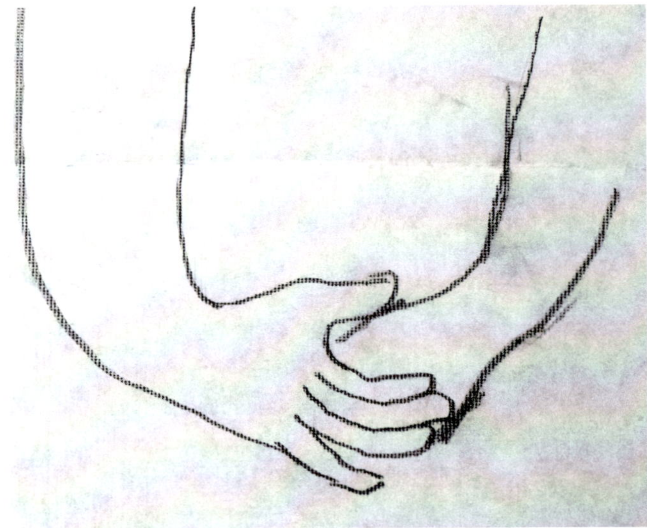

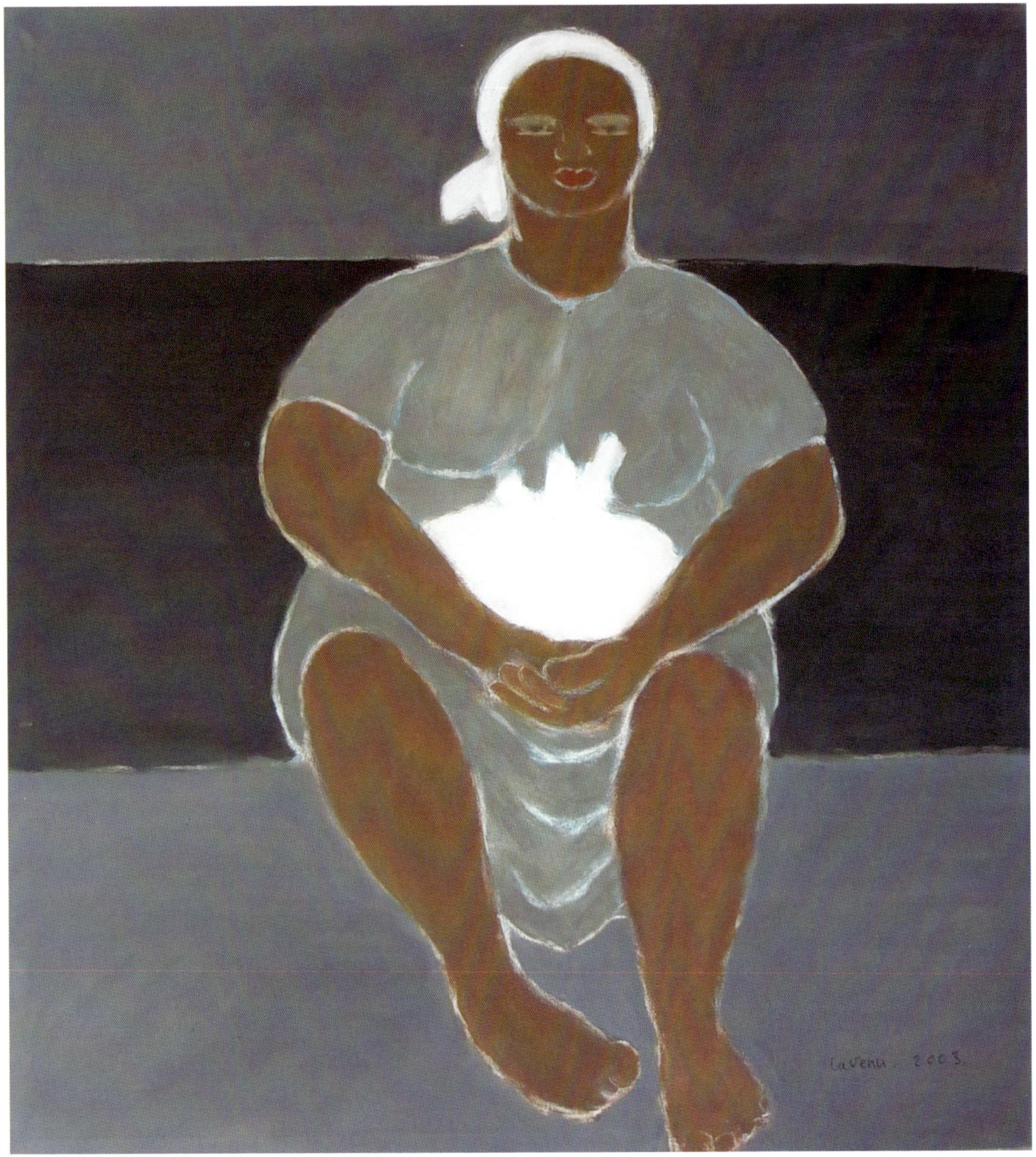

Waiting on bus, oil on canvas, 138x122 cm, 2003. Private collection.

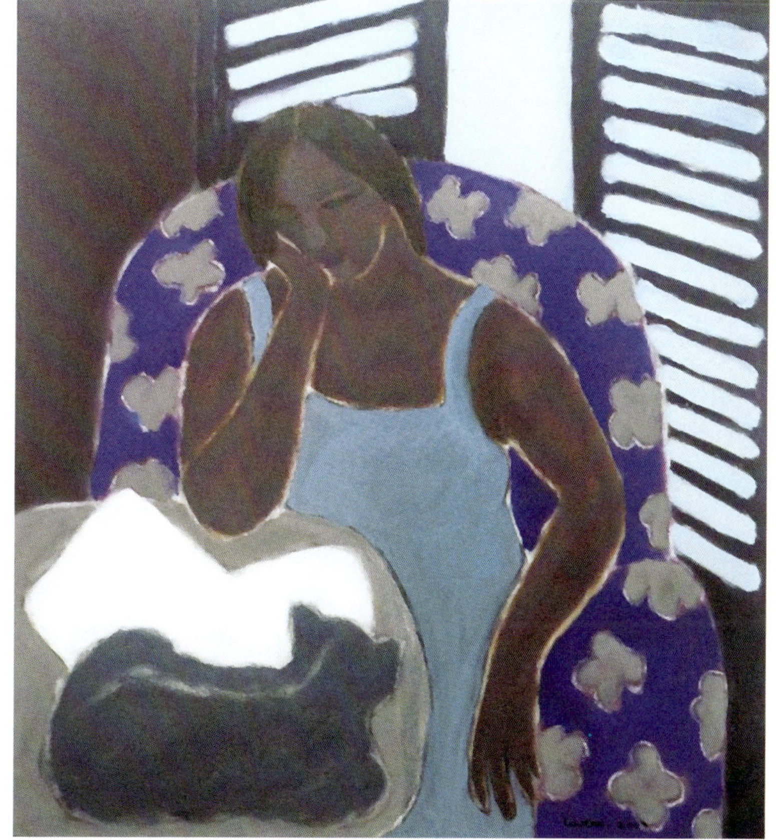

Reading with cat III, oil on canvas, 102x92 cm, 2003. Private collection.

Lavenu's paintings are like a good book – there is a story waiting to be told and the more you read the painting the more you are held captive by the visual prose.

The first time I looked at her work I was stopped short by a memory, real or imagined, that I once walked on that street, stood under that tree, or sat in that chair.

Oddly, with the sense of the familiar also comes a time where you just have to stop and wonder what is it that makes the work feel strange.

That odd sense comes from both the warmth and coolness of the subject and also from Lavenu's unusual and extraordinary use of color that makes daylight seem almost liquid, the air something dense enough to hold in your hands, and the cat a creature from another world."

Elizabeth Cumming
Art Consultant

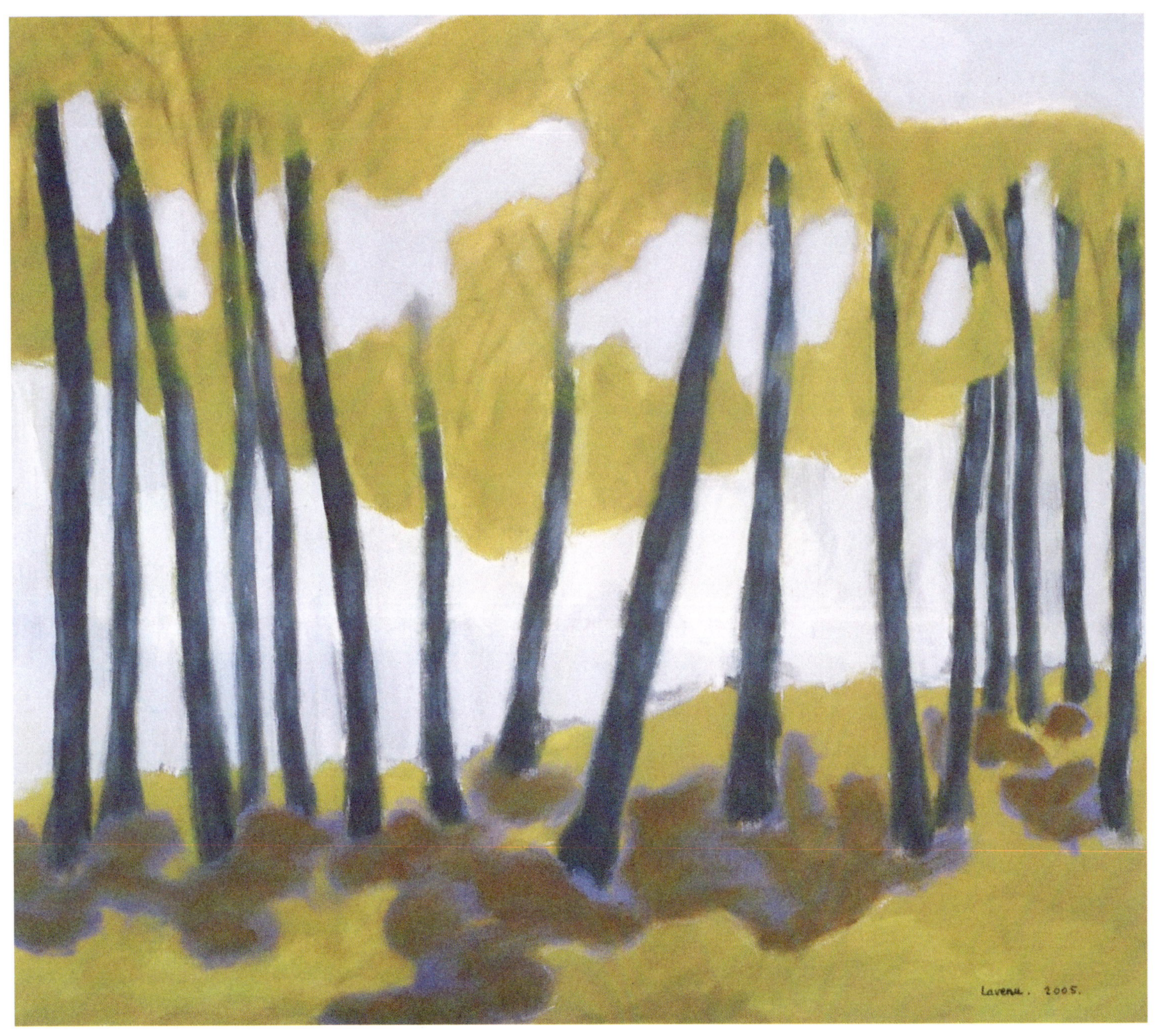

Vogelsang Berlin-Dahlem, oil on canvas, 122x138 cm, 2005.

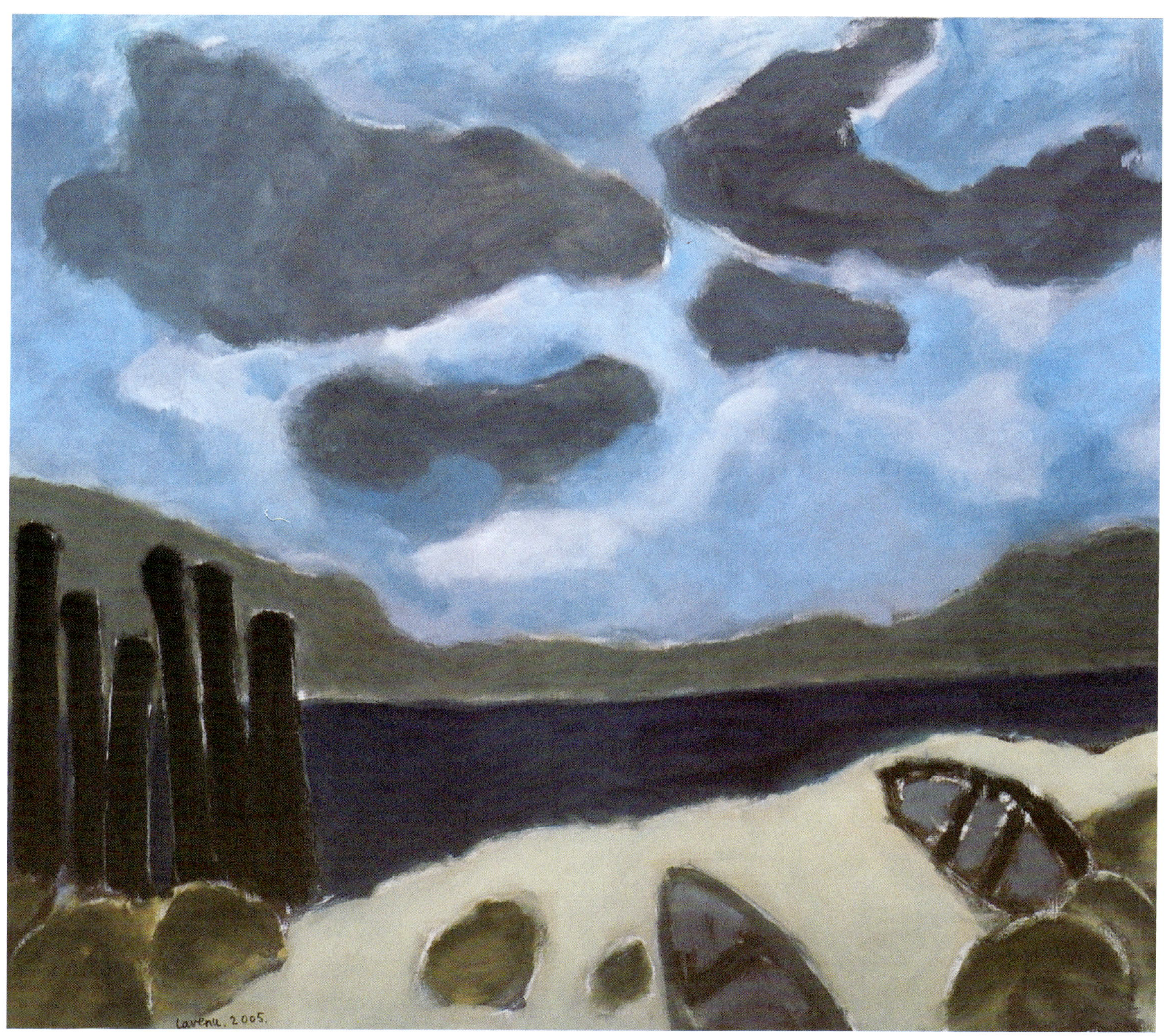

Irlande, oil on canvas, 122x138 cm, 2005.

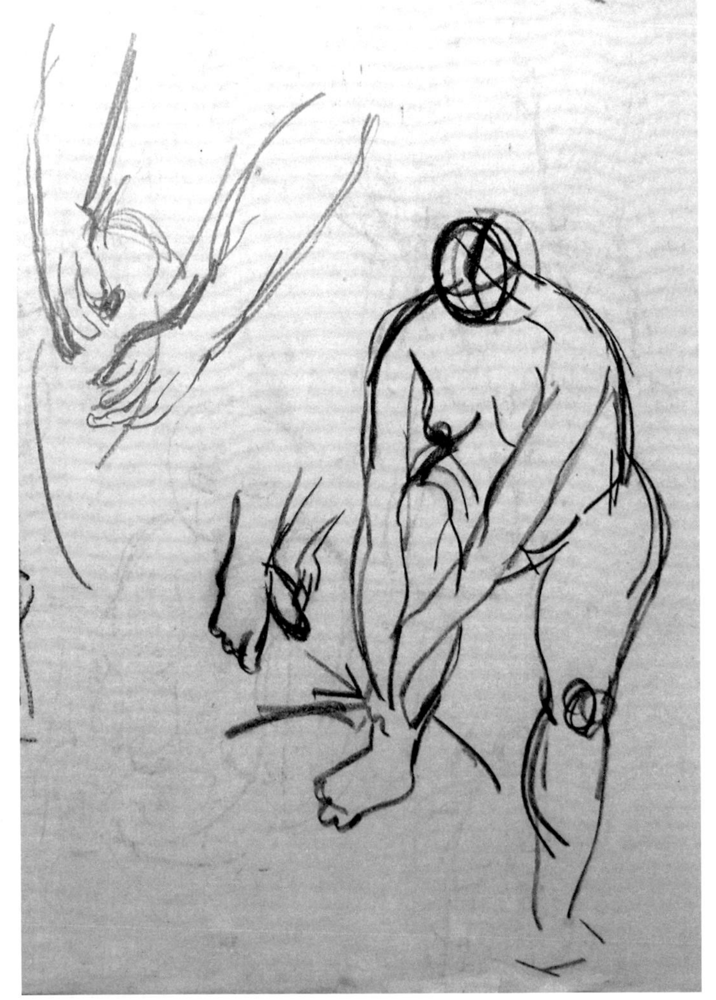

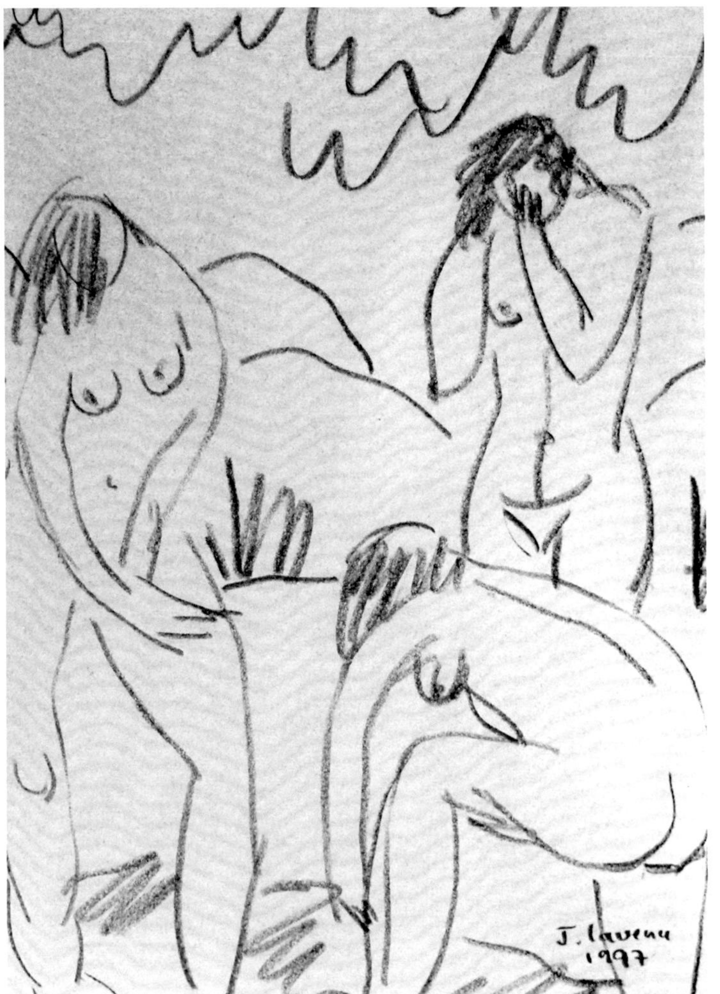
J. Lavenu
1997

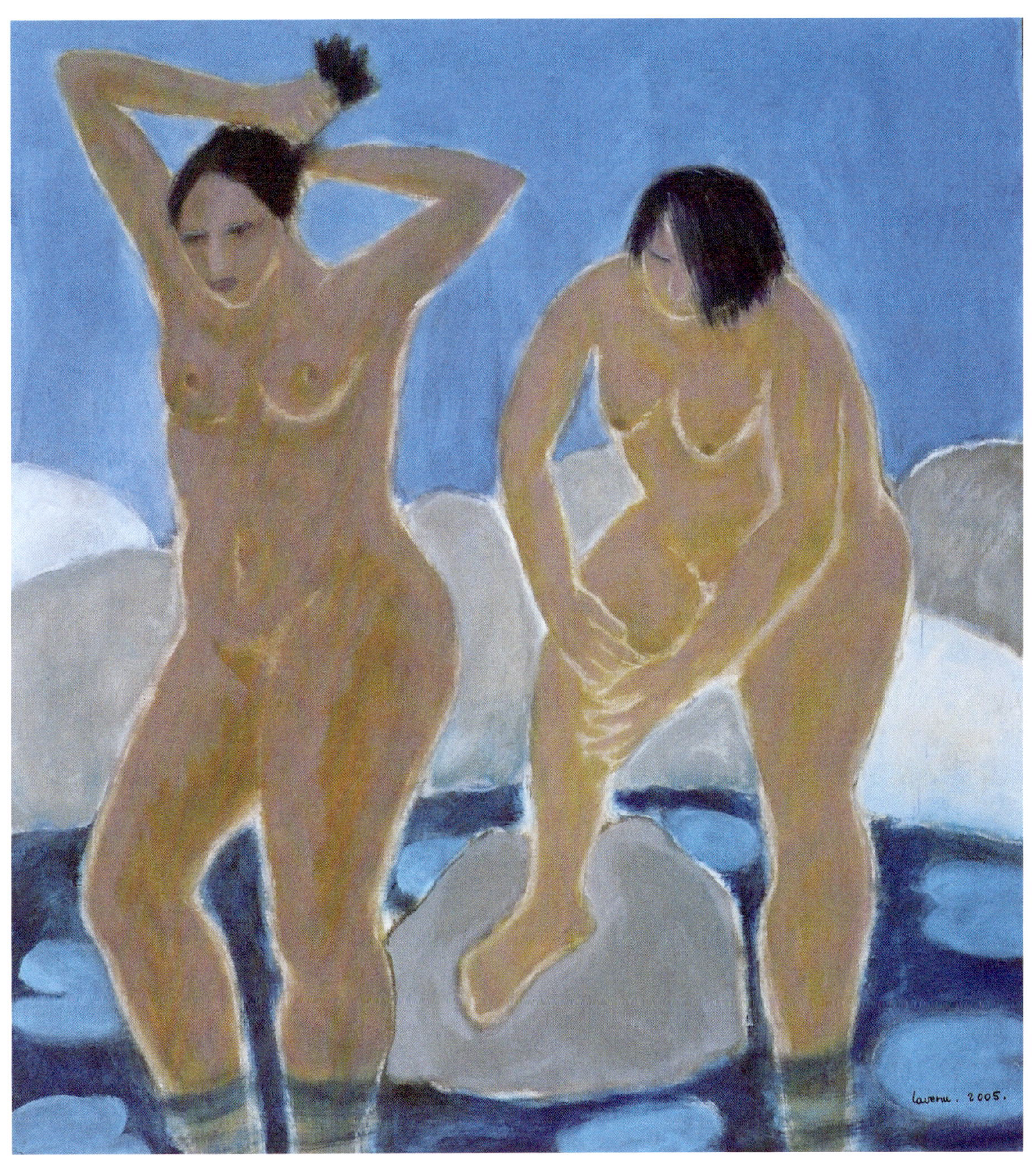

Deux grandes baigneuses, oil on canvas, 138x122 cm, 2005.

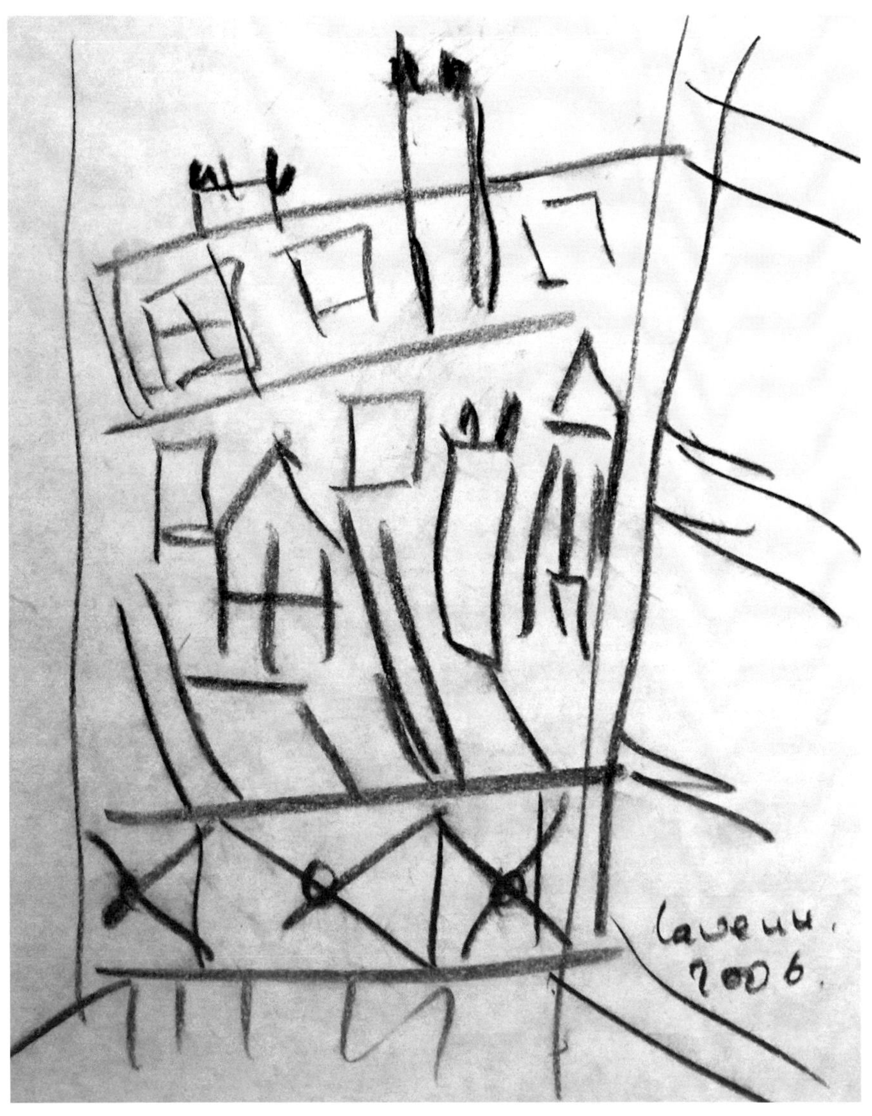

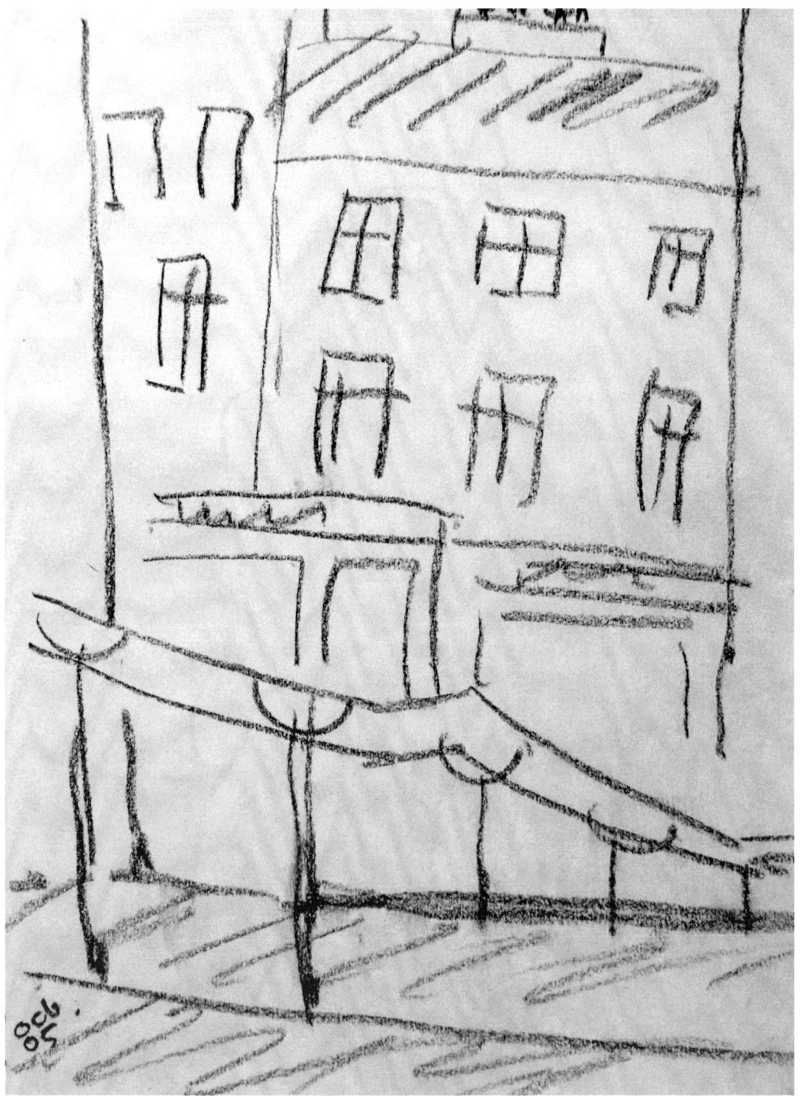

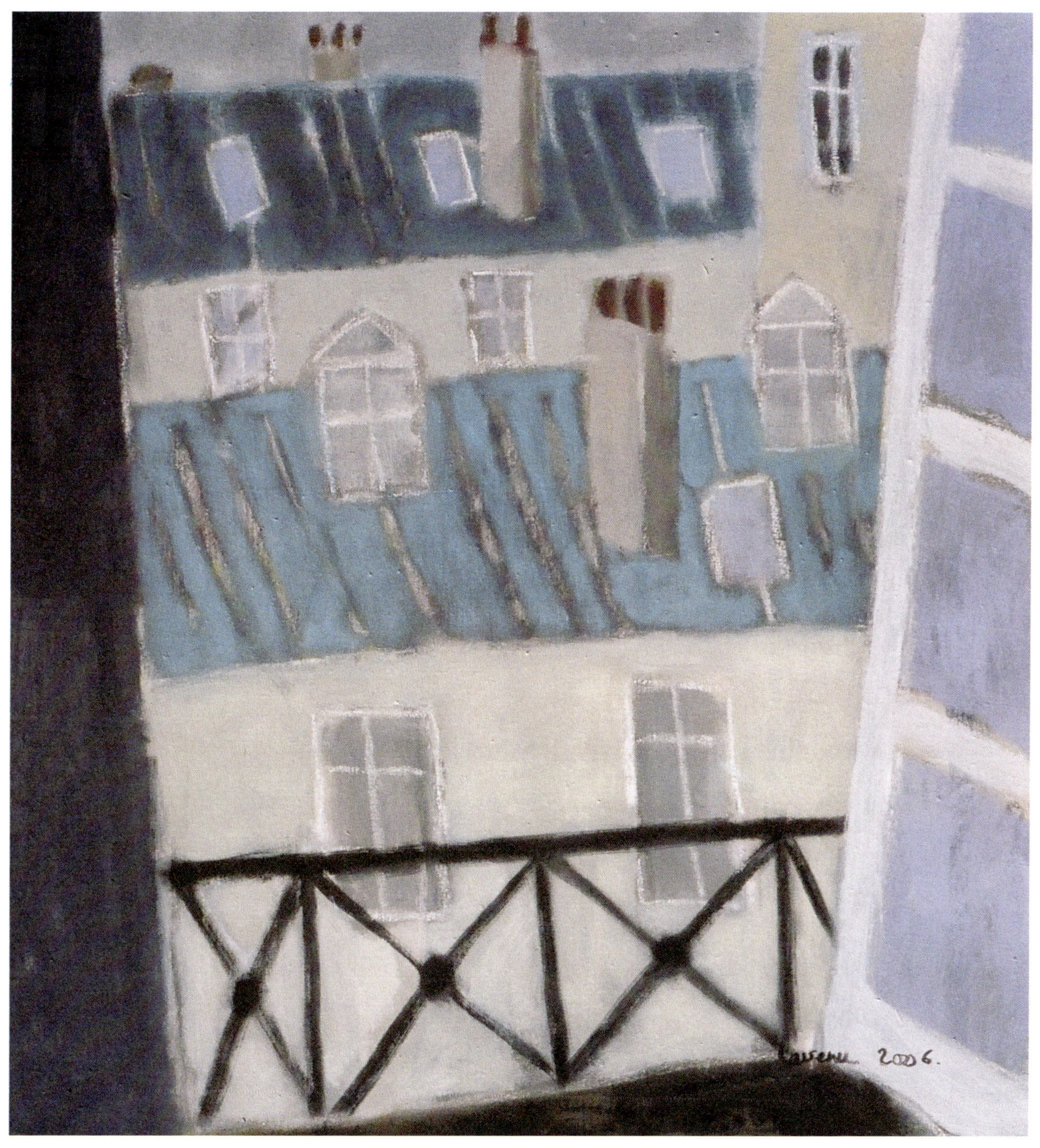

Window in Paris, oil on canvas, 102x92 cm, 2006. Private collection.

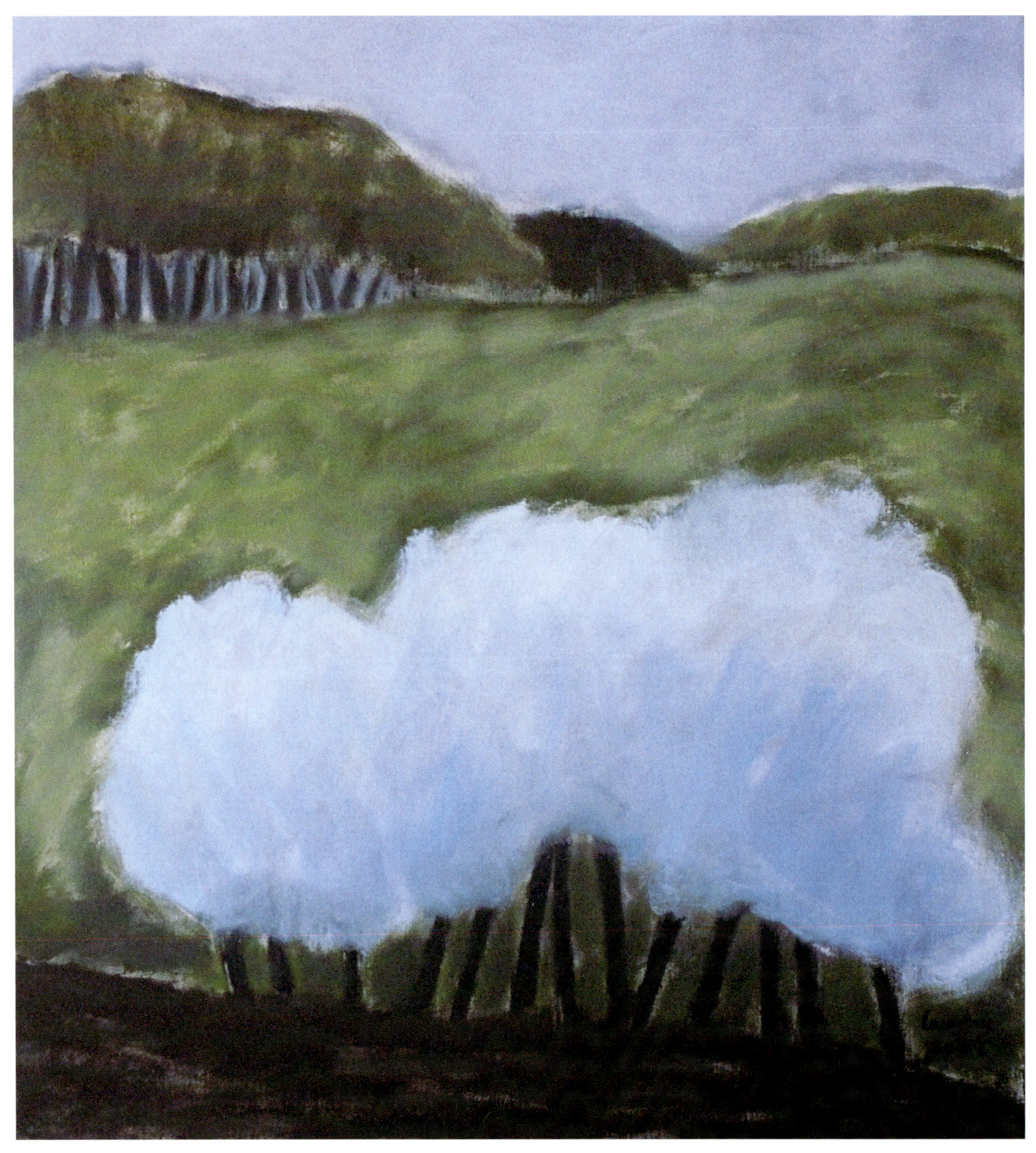

Beedenkirchen, Odenwald, oil on canvas, 102x92 cm, 2006.

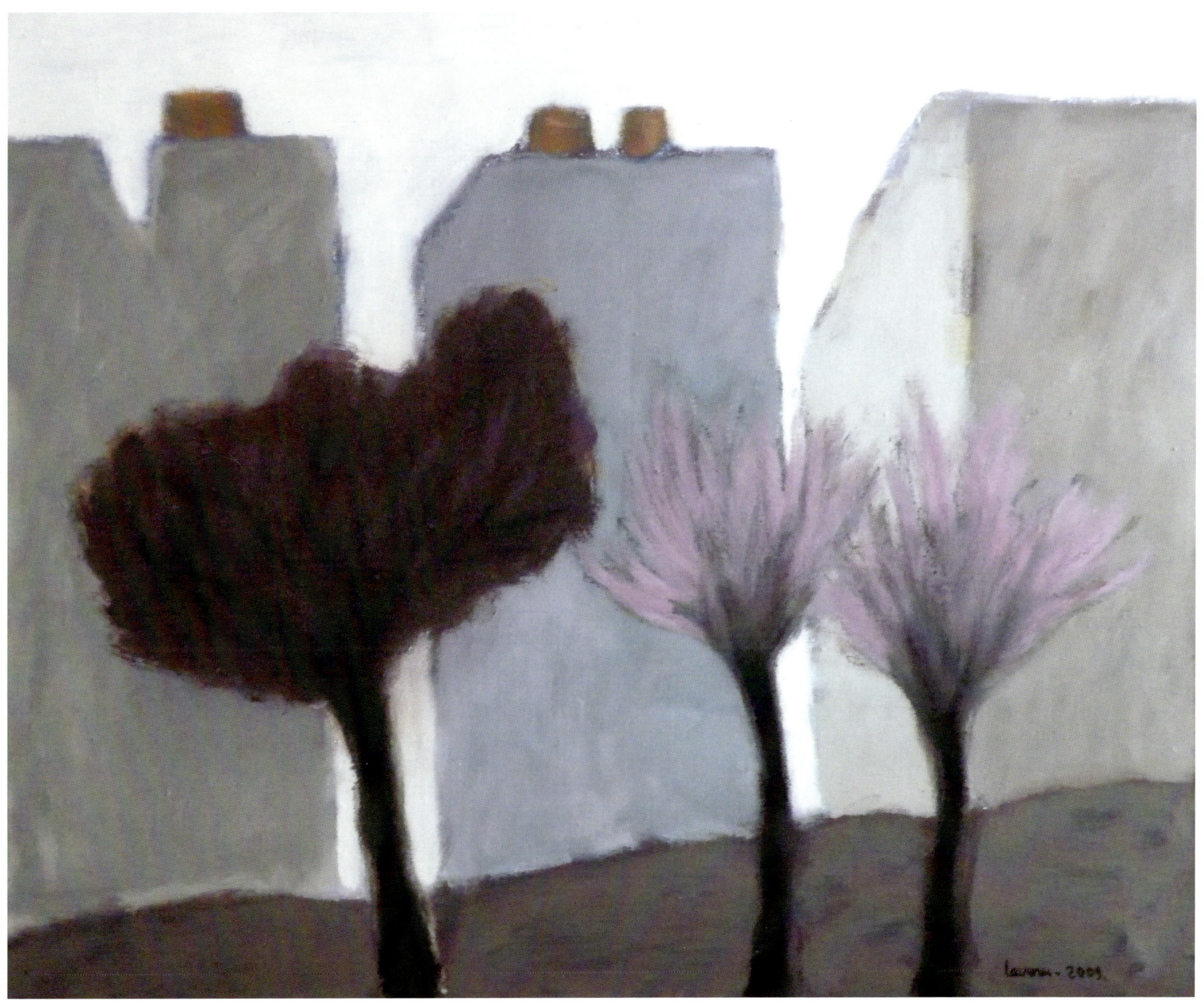

Am Holsteiner Ufer Berlin (II), oil on canvas, 76x92 cm, 2009.

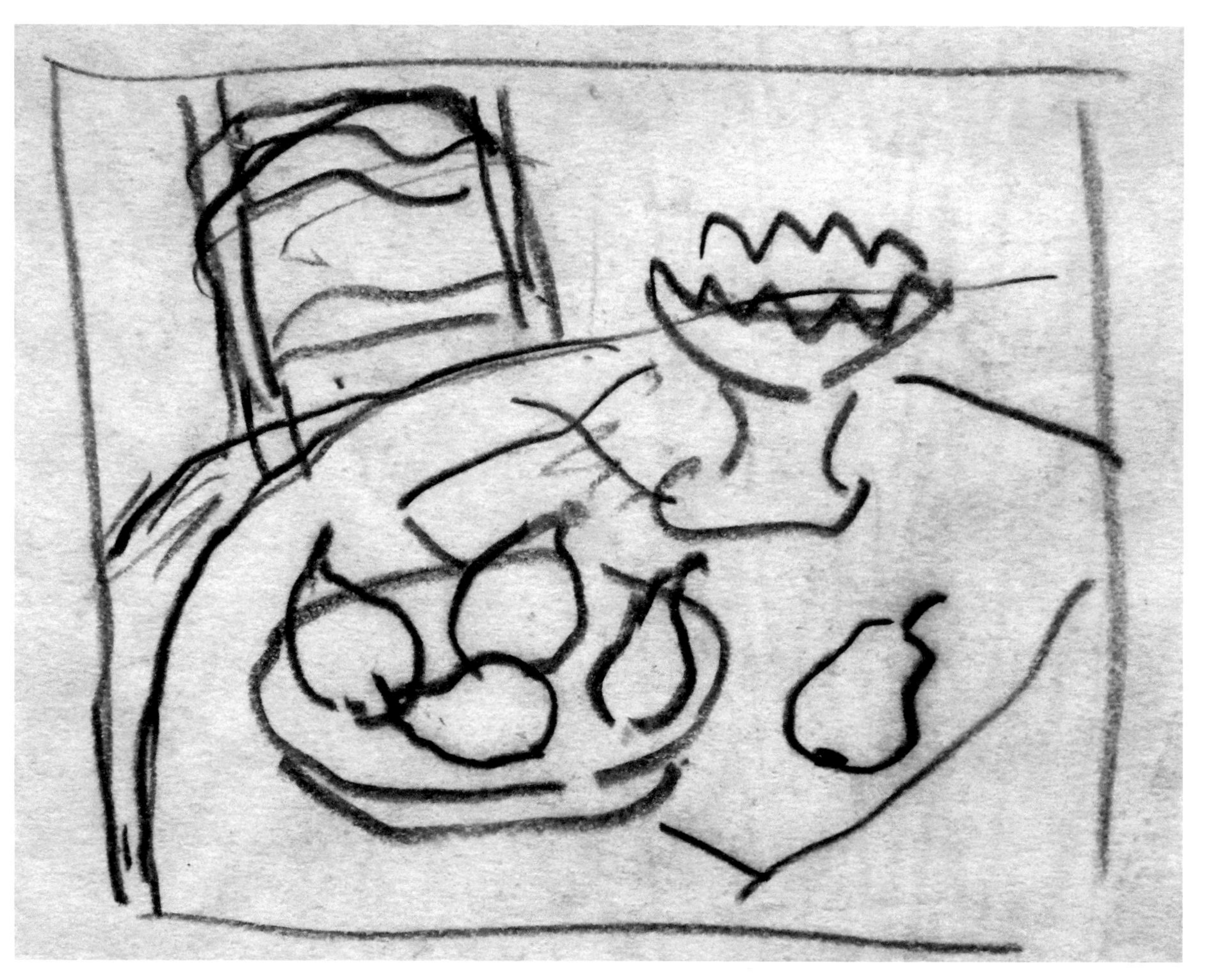

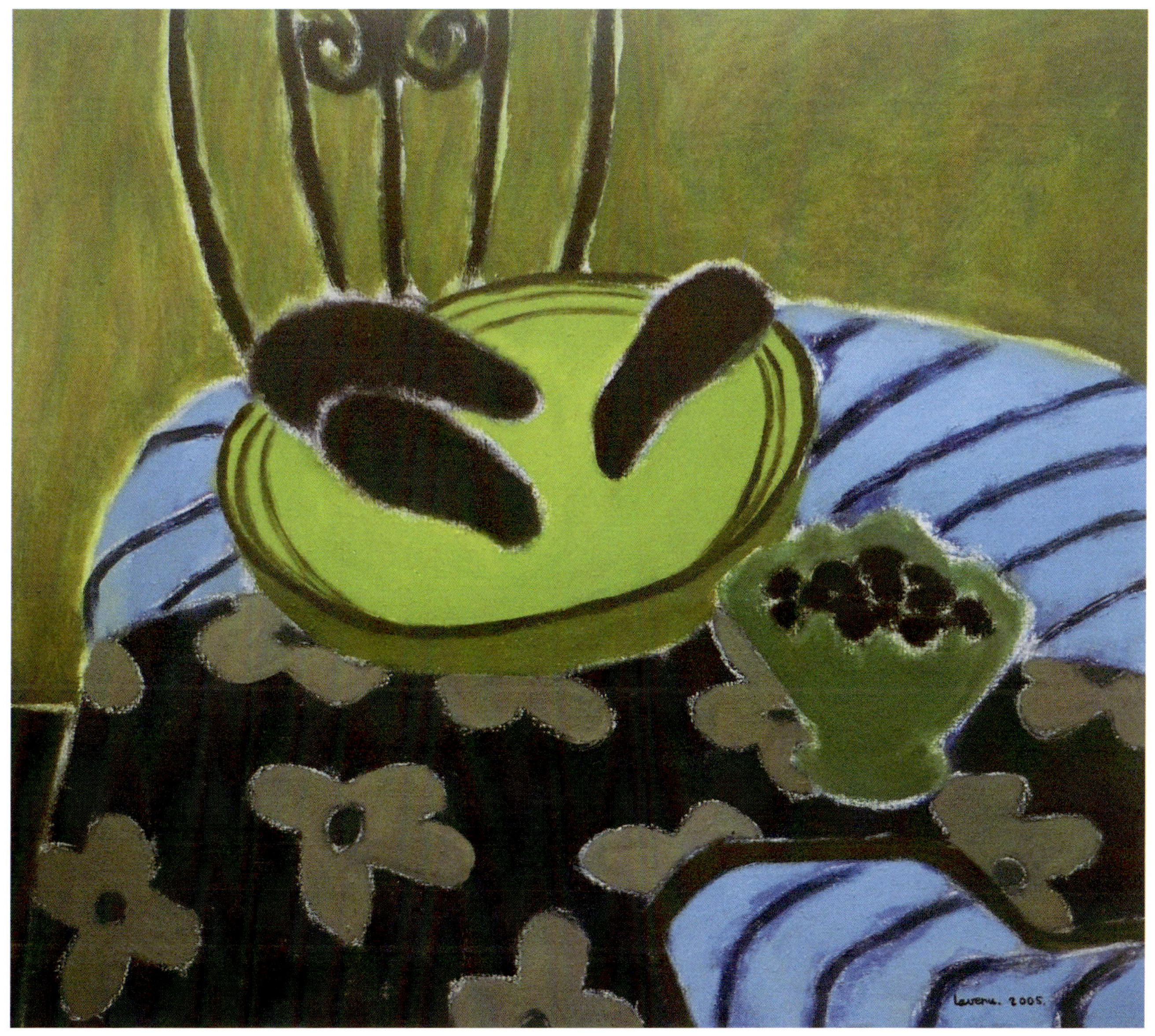

Nature morte aux aubergines, oil on canvas, 92x102 cm, 2005. Private collection.

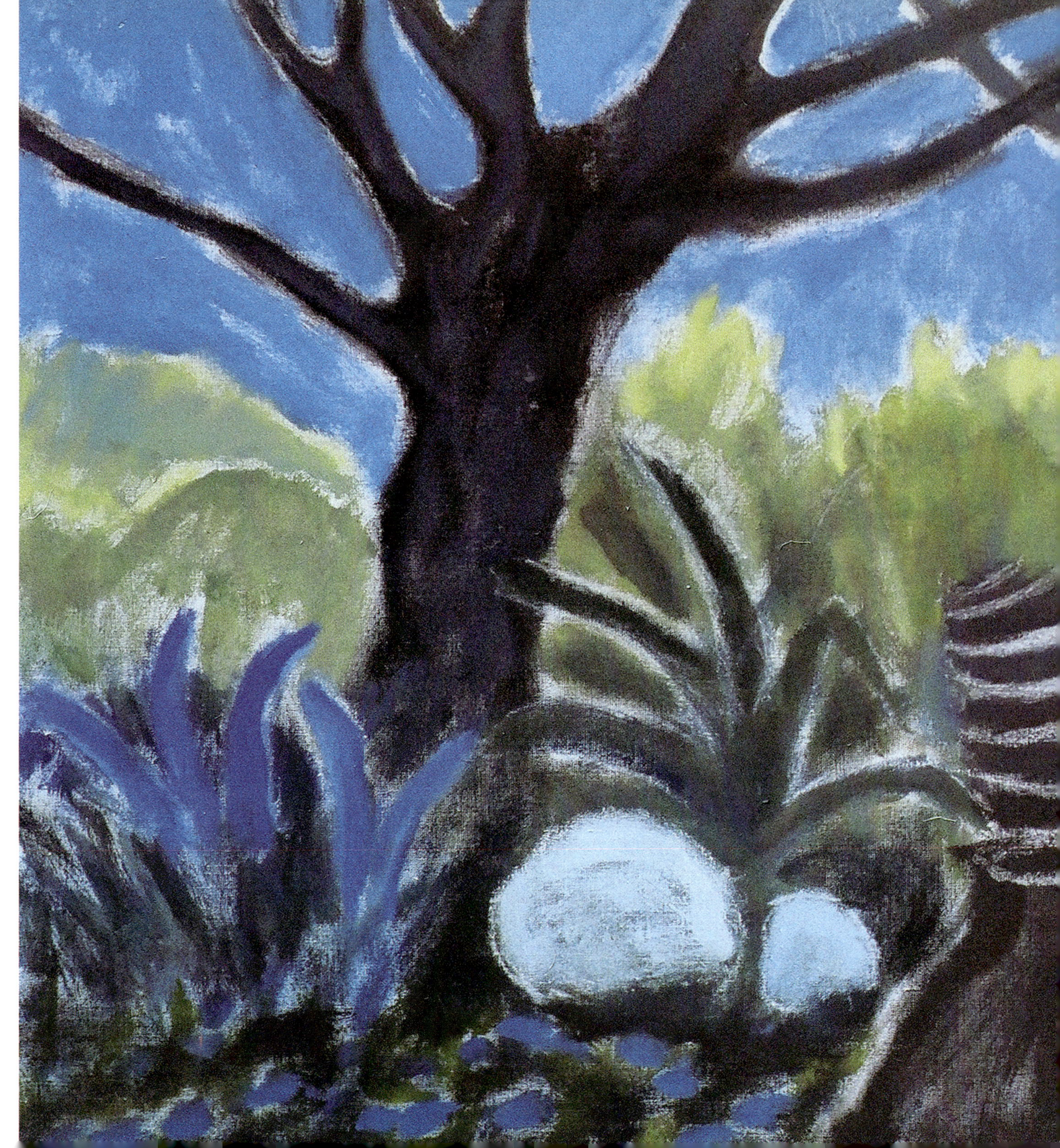

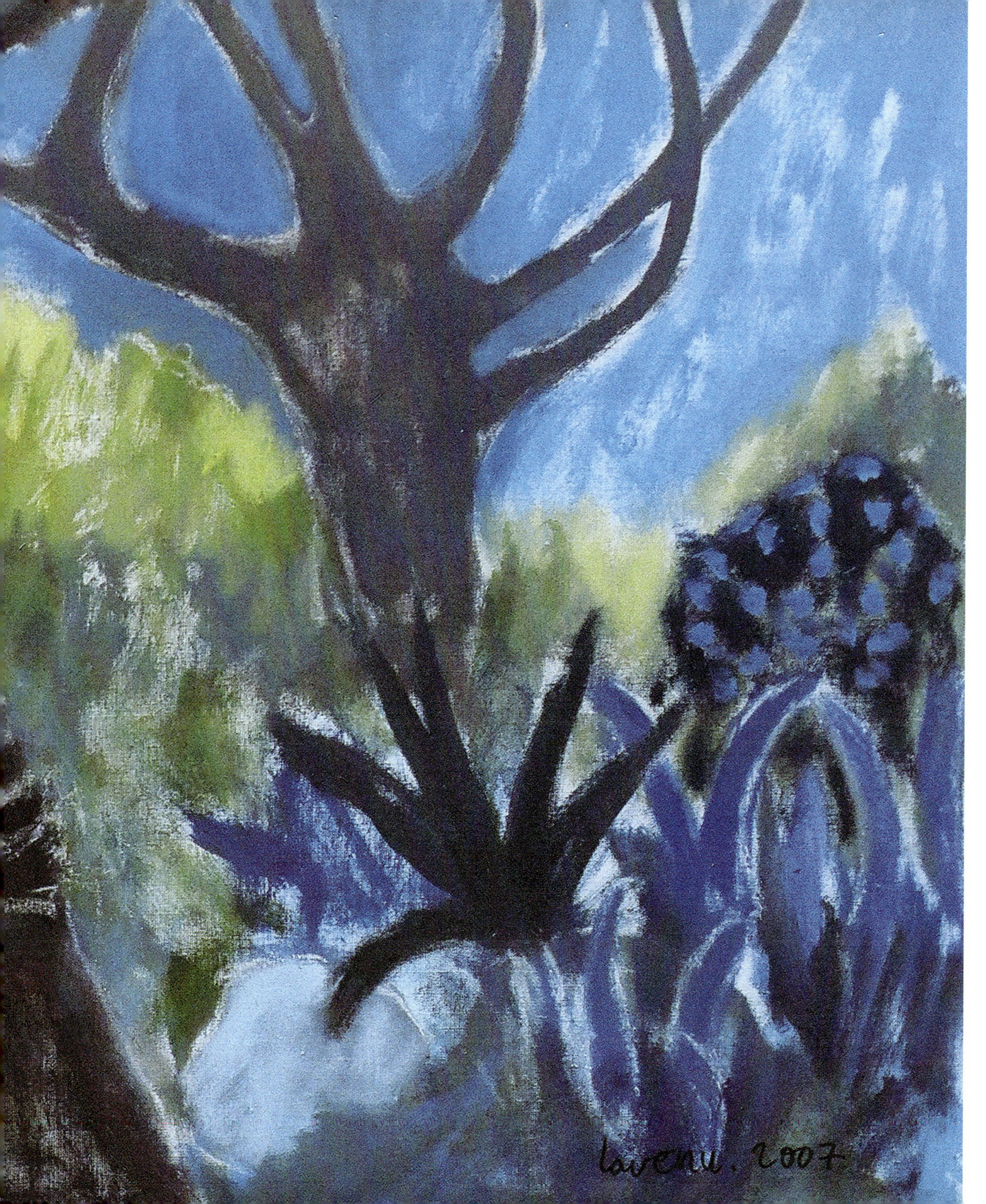

Mon jardin à San Diego, oil on canvas, 97x163 cm, 2007. Private collection.

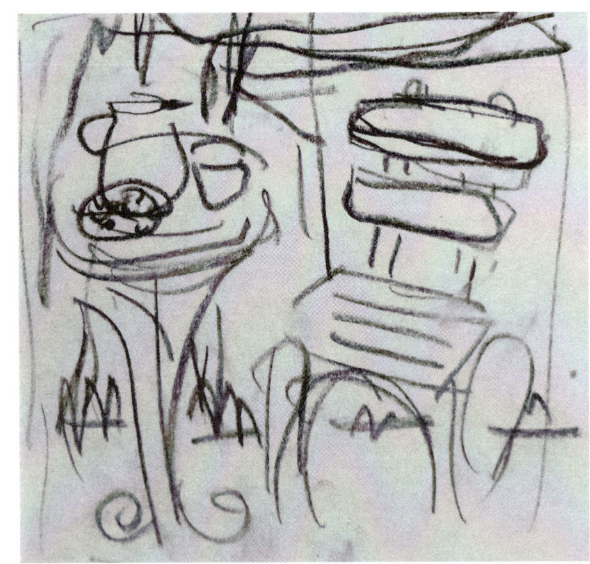

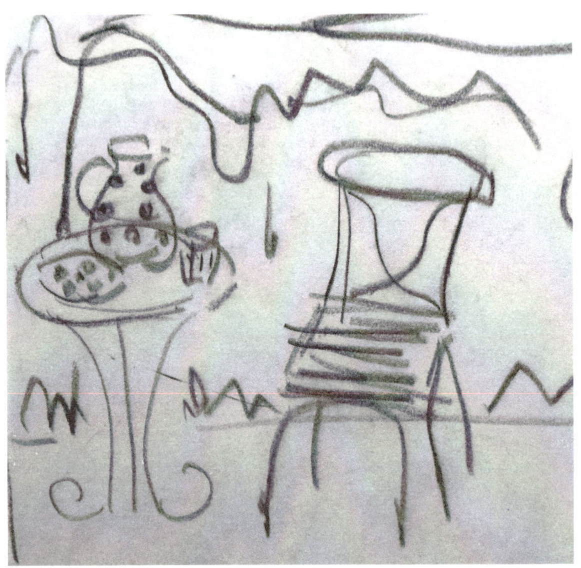

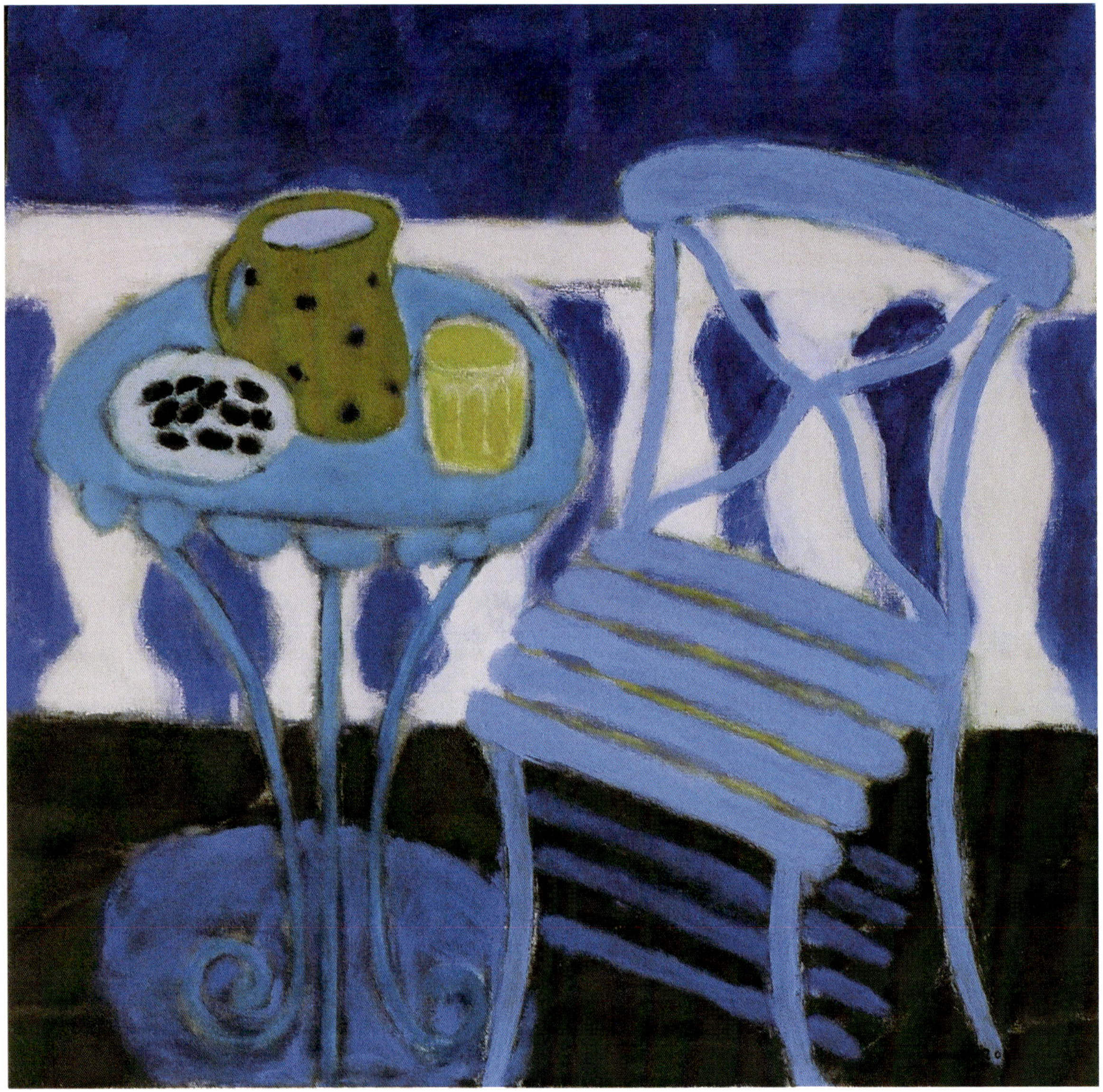

Chaise bleue, oil on canvas, 102x102 cm, 2008.

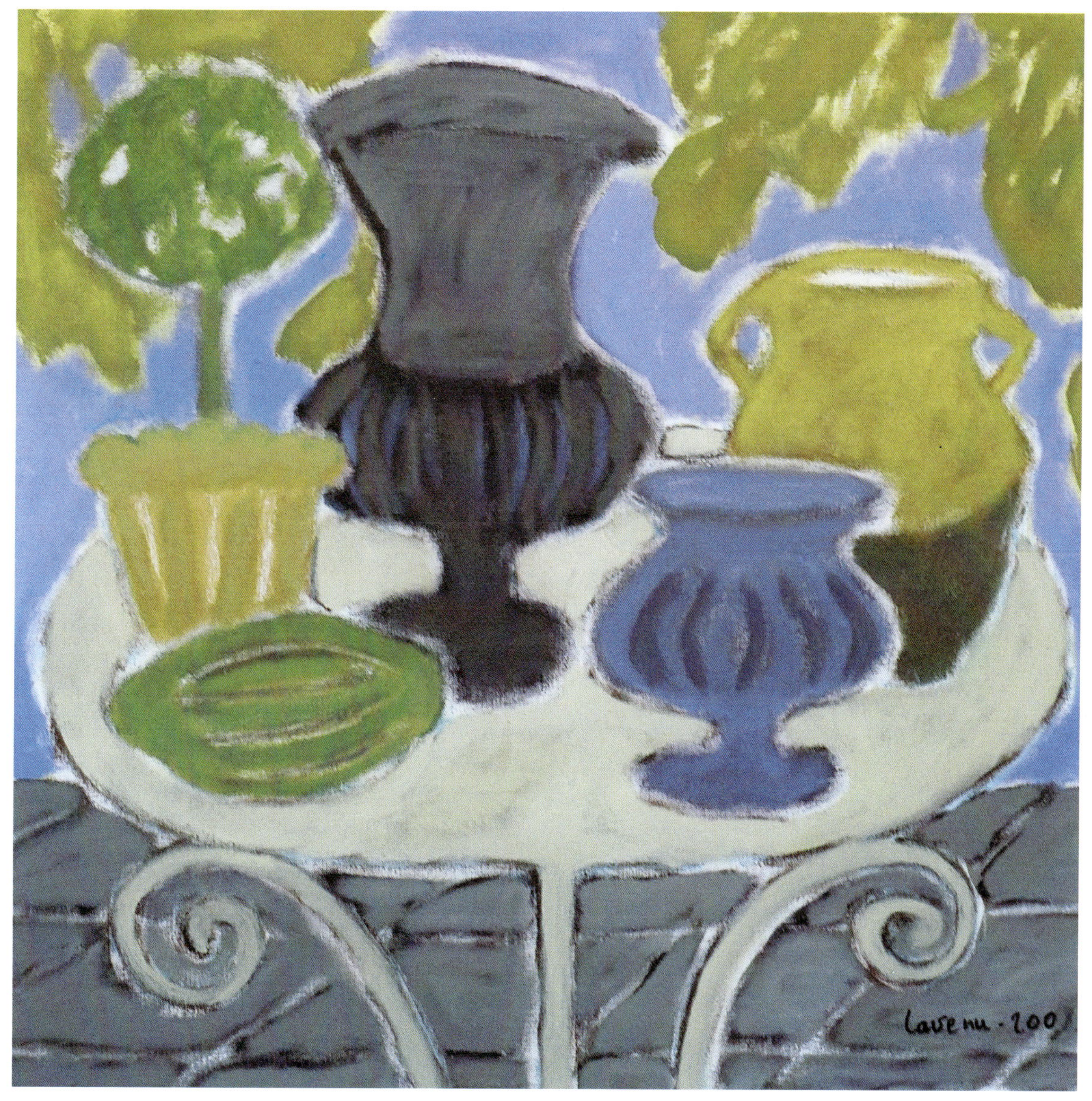

Garden table, oil on canvas, 92x92 cm, 2008. Private collection.

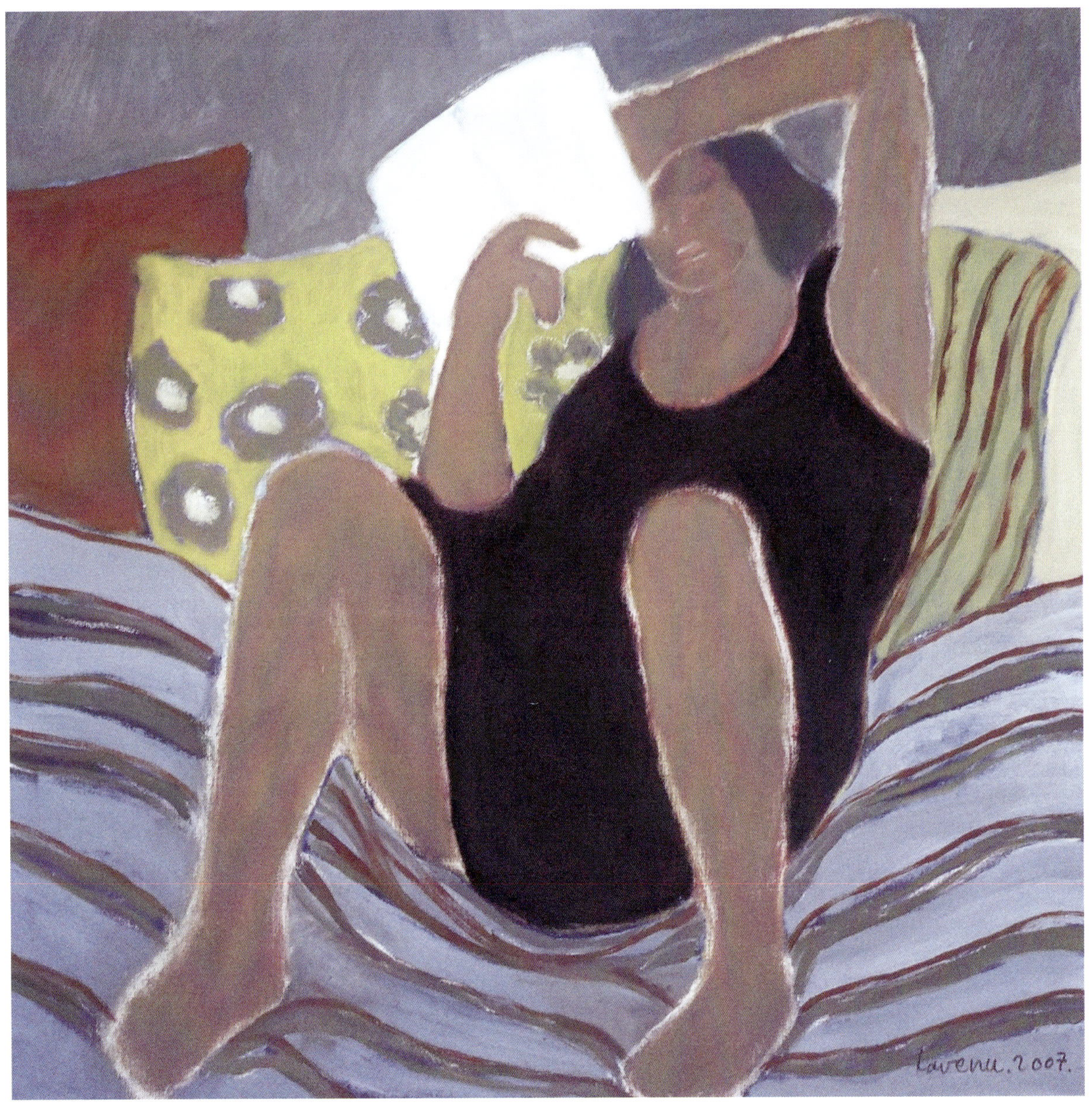

Reading, oil on canvas, 102x102 cm, 2007. Private collection.

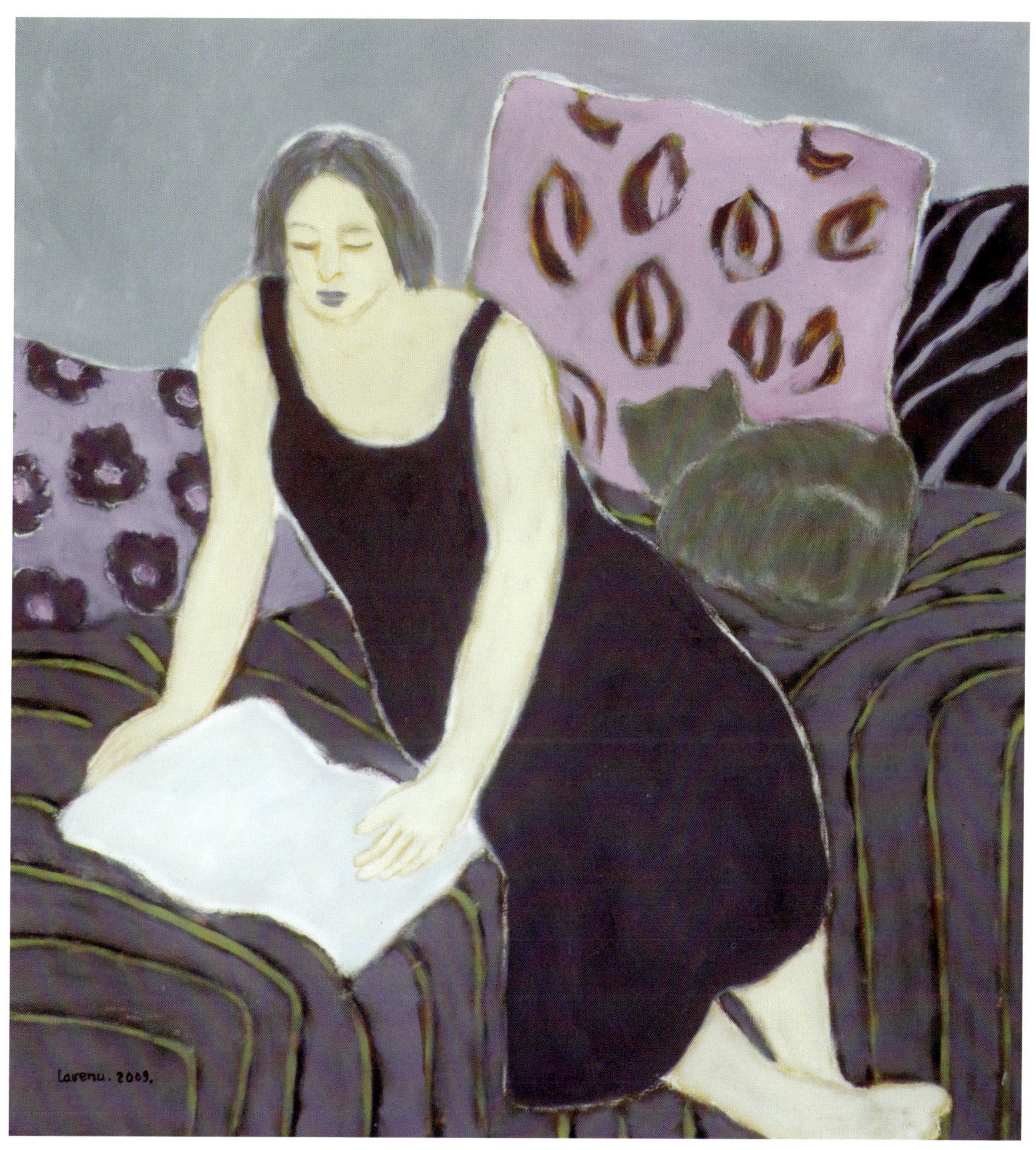

Reading with cat VI, oil on canvas, 138x122 cm, 2009.

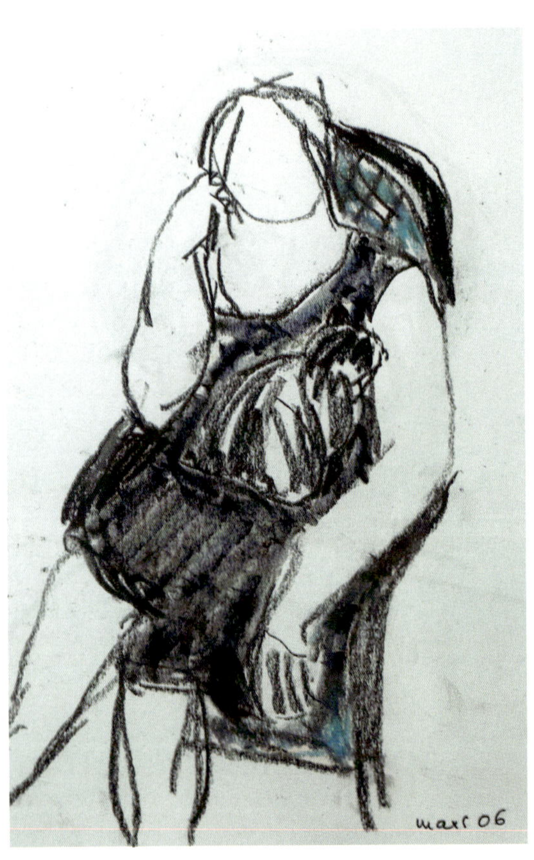

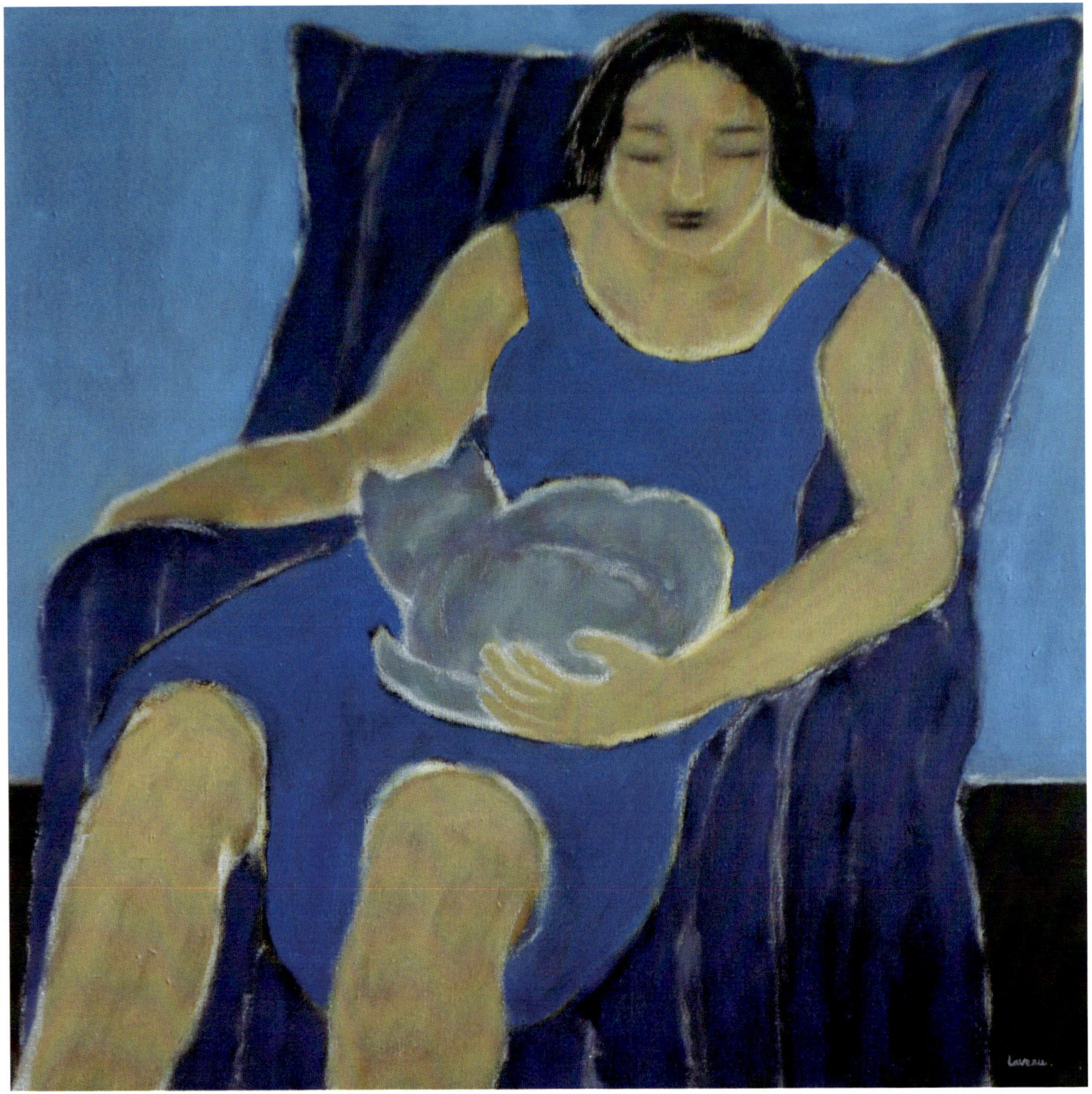

Woman with cat, oil on canvas, 92x92 cm, 2008.

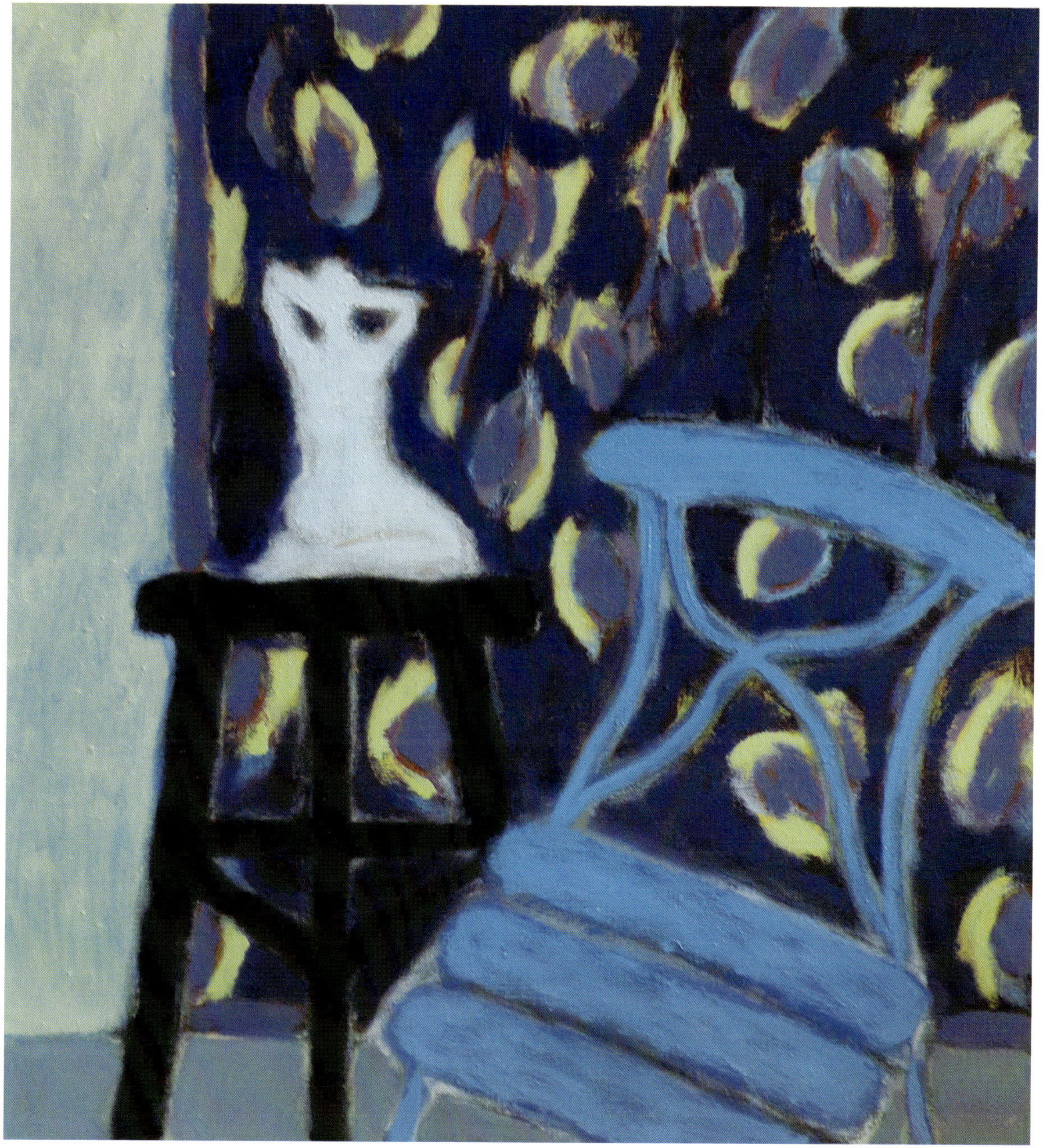

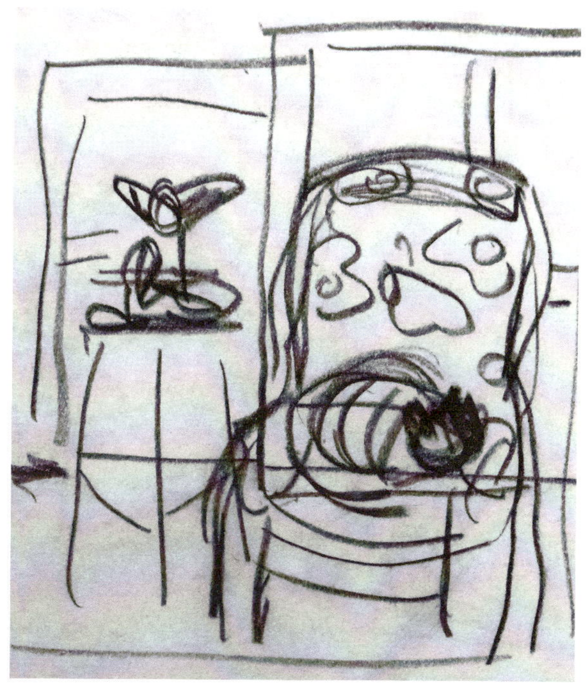

Atelier et chaise bleue, oil on canvas, 102x92 cm, 2007-2009.

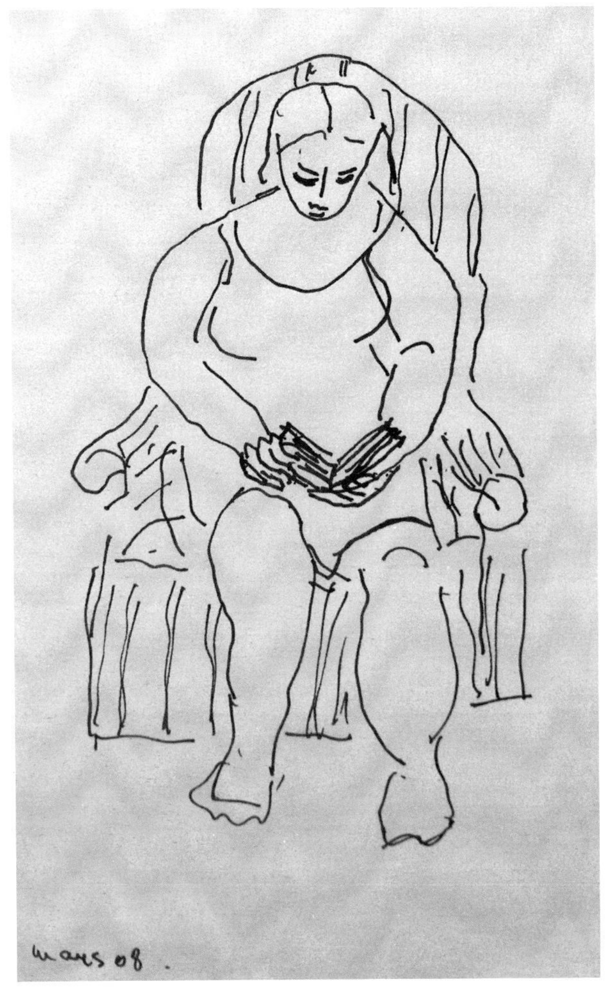
mars 08

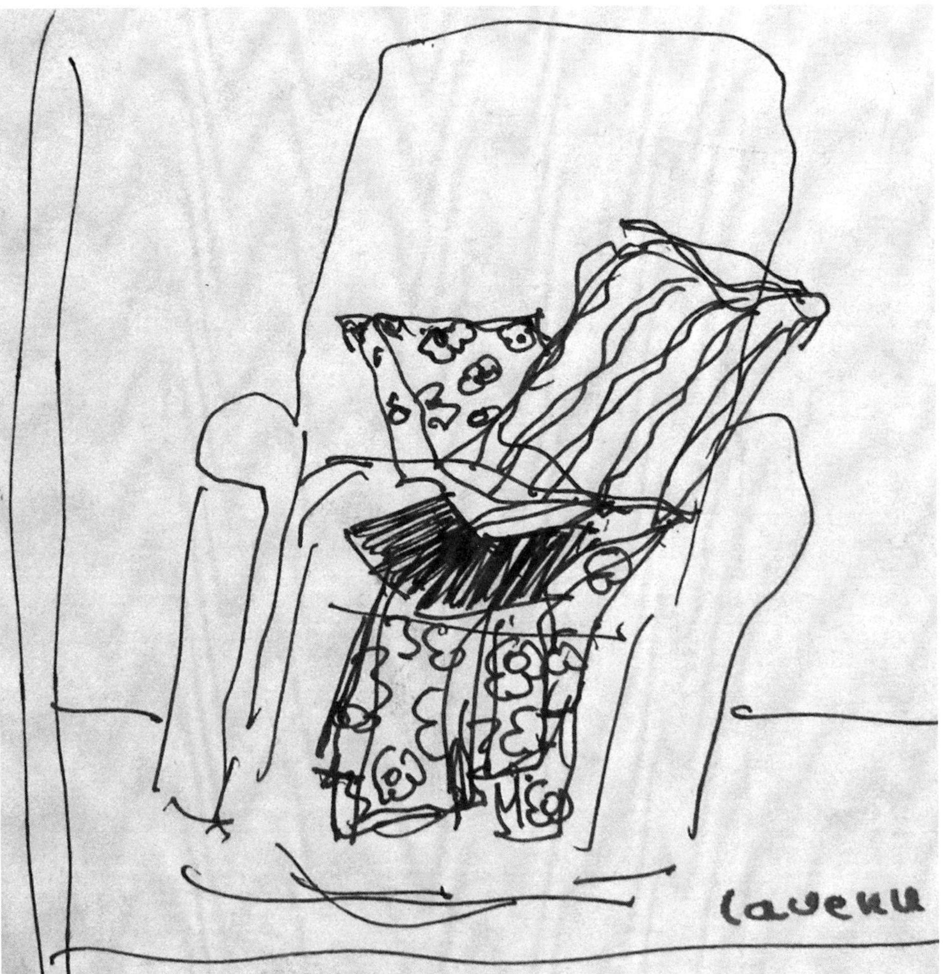

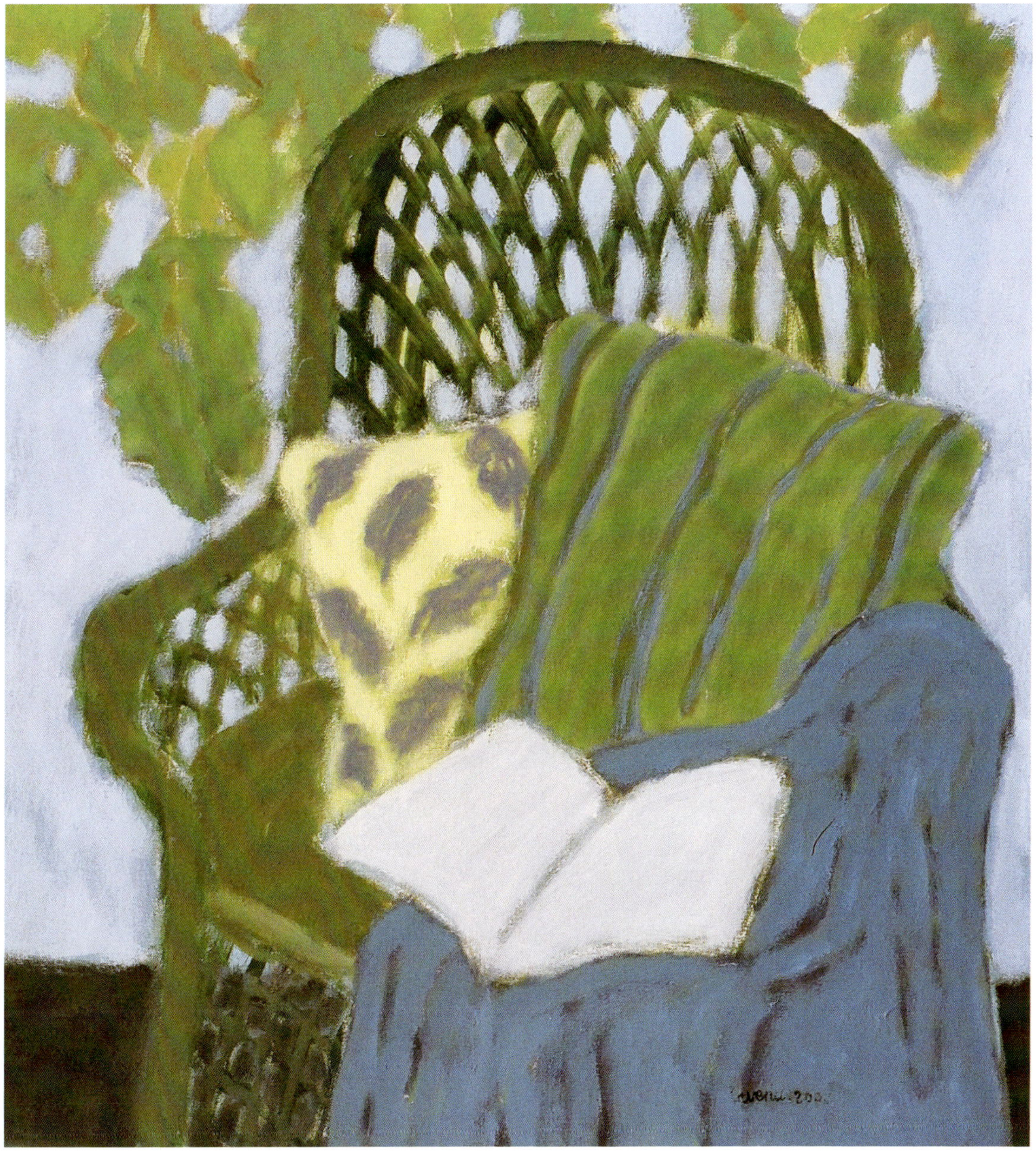

Reading in garden, oil on canvas, 102x92 cm, 2009. Private collection.

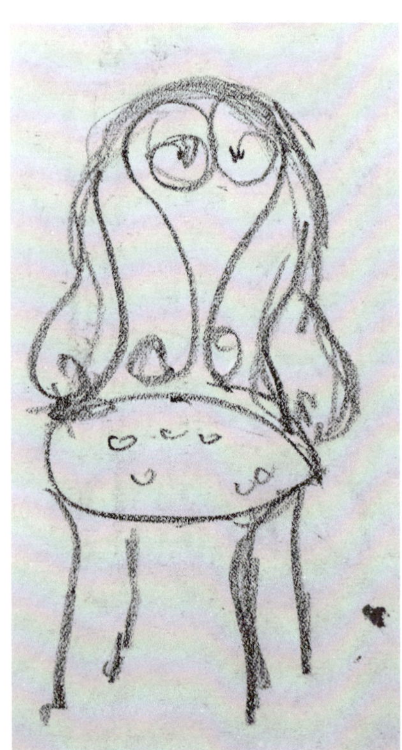

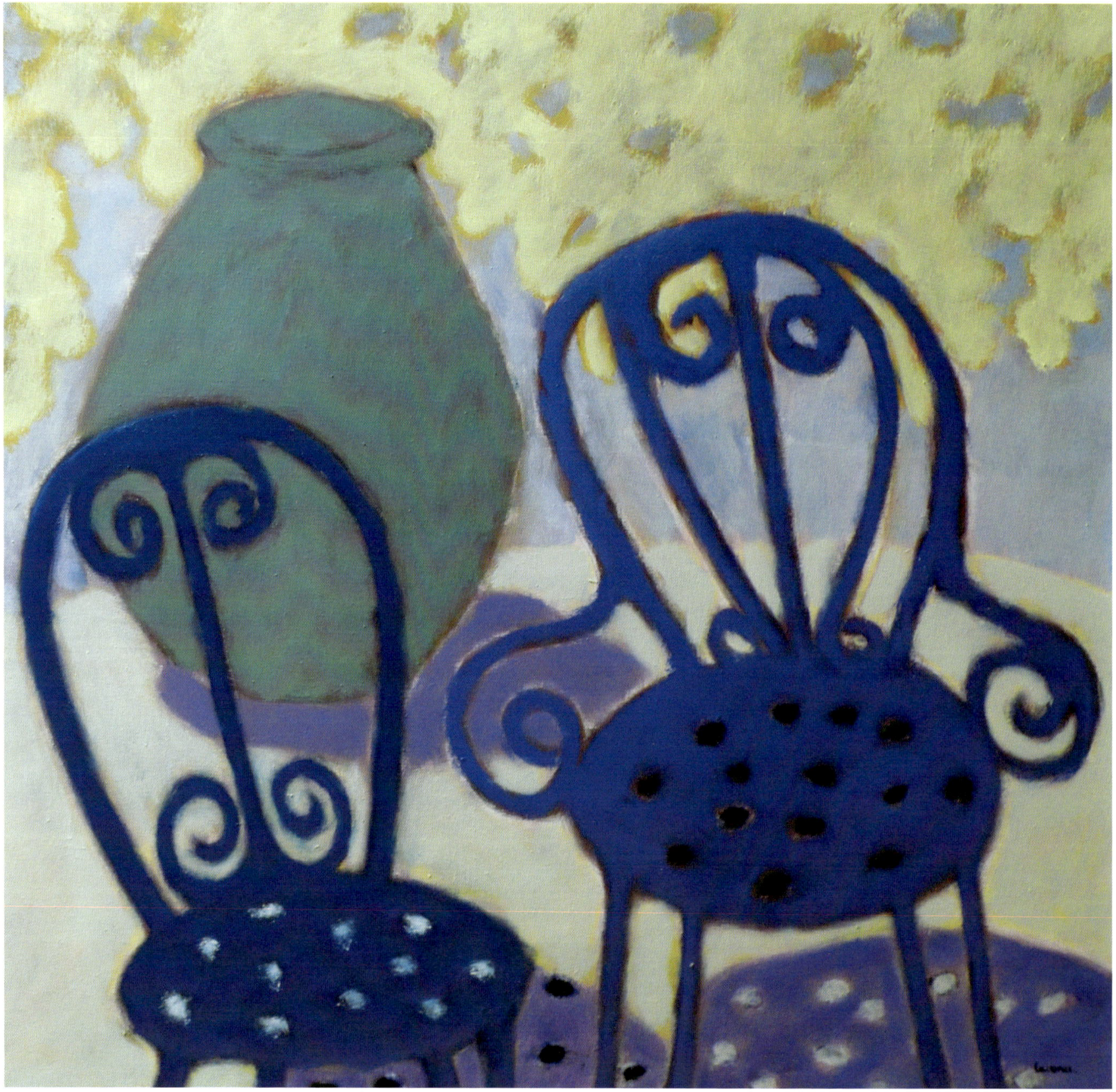

Chaises de jardin, oil on canvas, 102x102 cm, 2001.

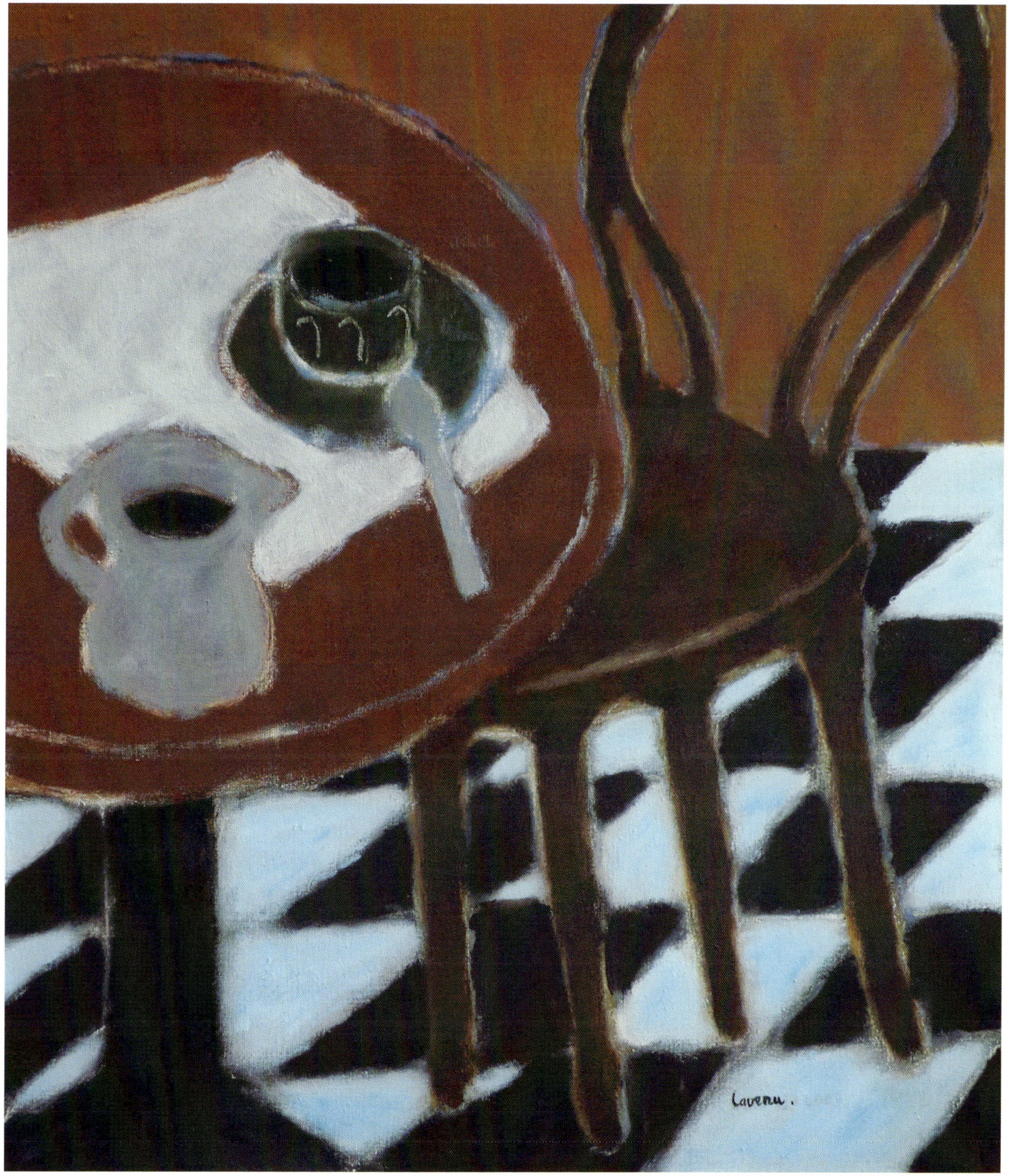

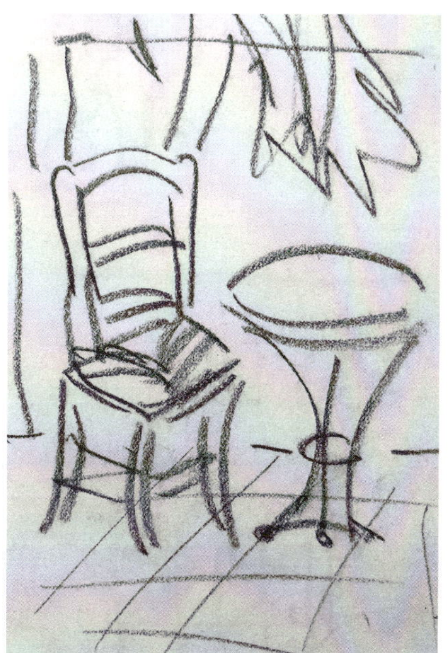

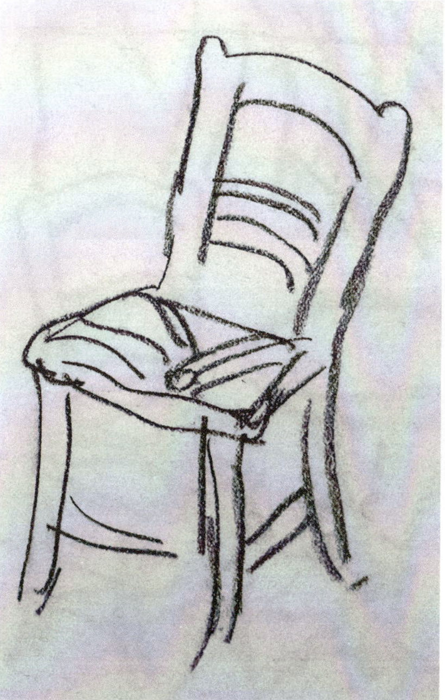

Café, oil on canvas, 92x76 cm, 2009.

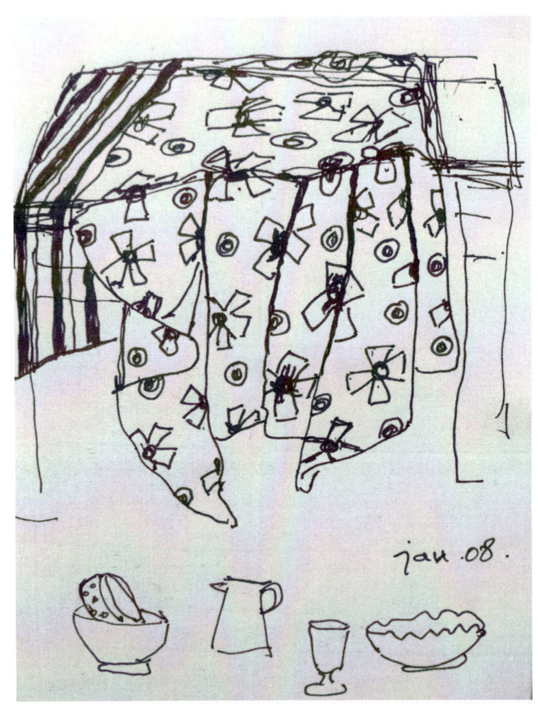

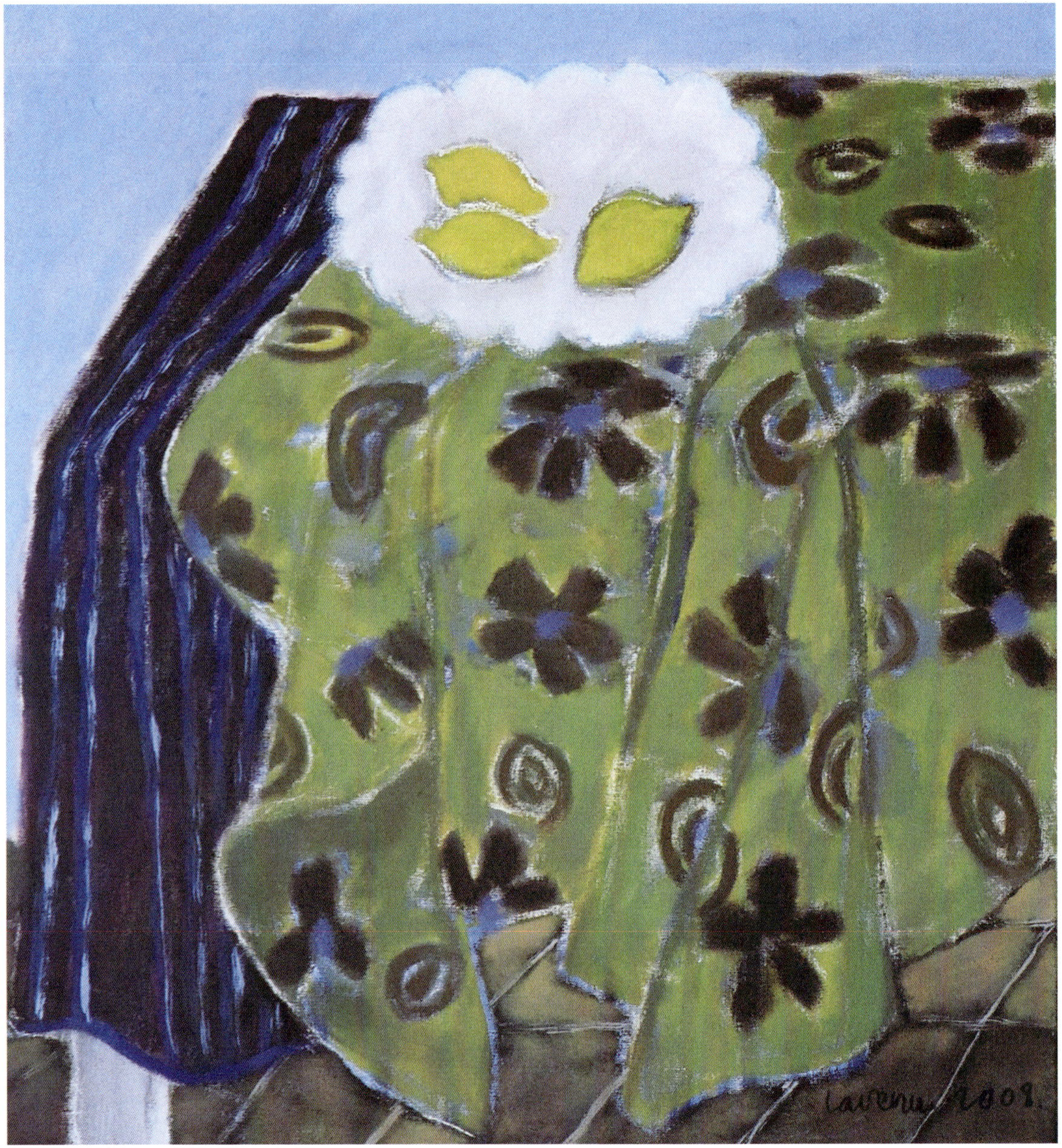

Green tablecloth, oil on canvas, 102x92 cm, 2008.

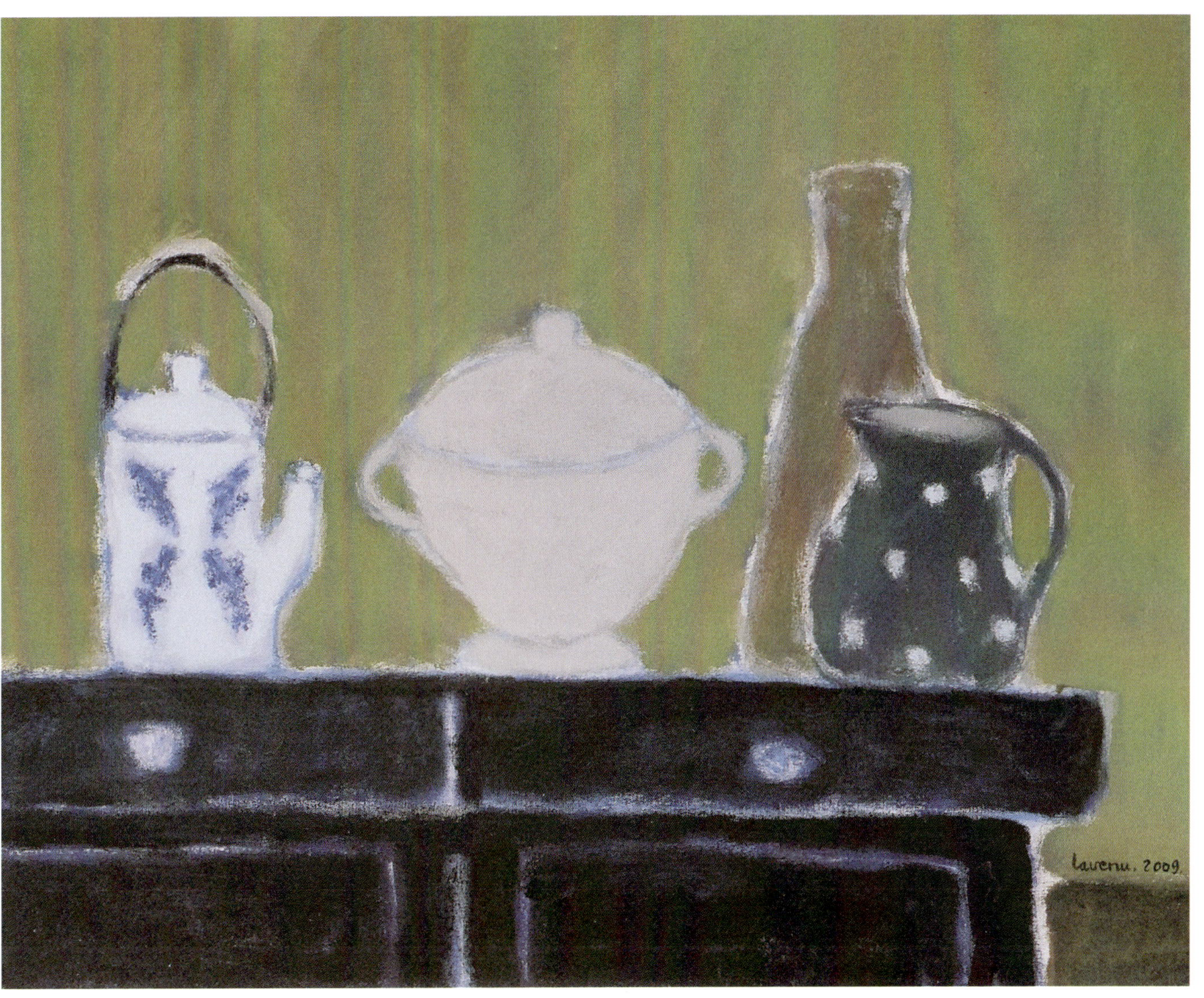

Nature morte sur buffet bleu, oil on canvas, 76x92 cm, 2009.

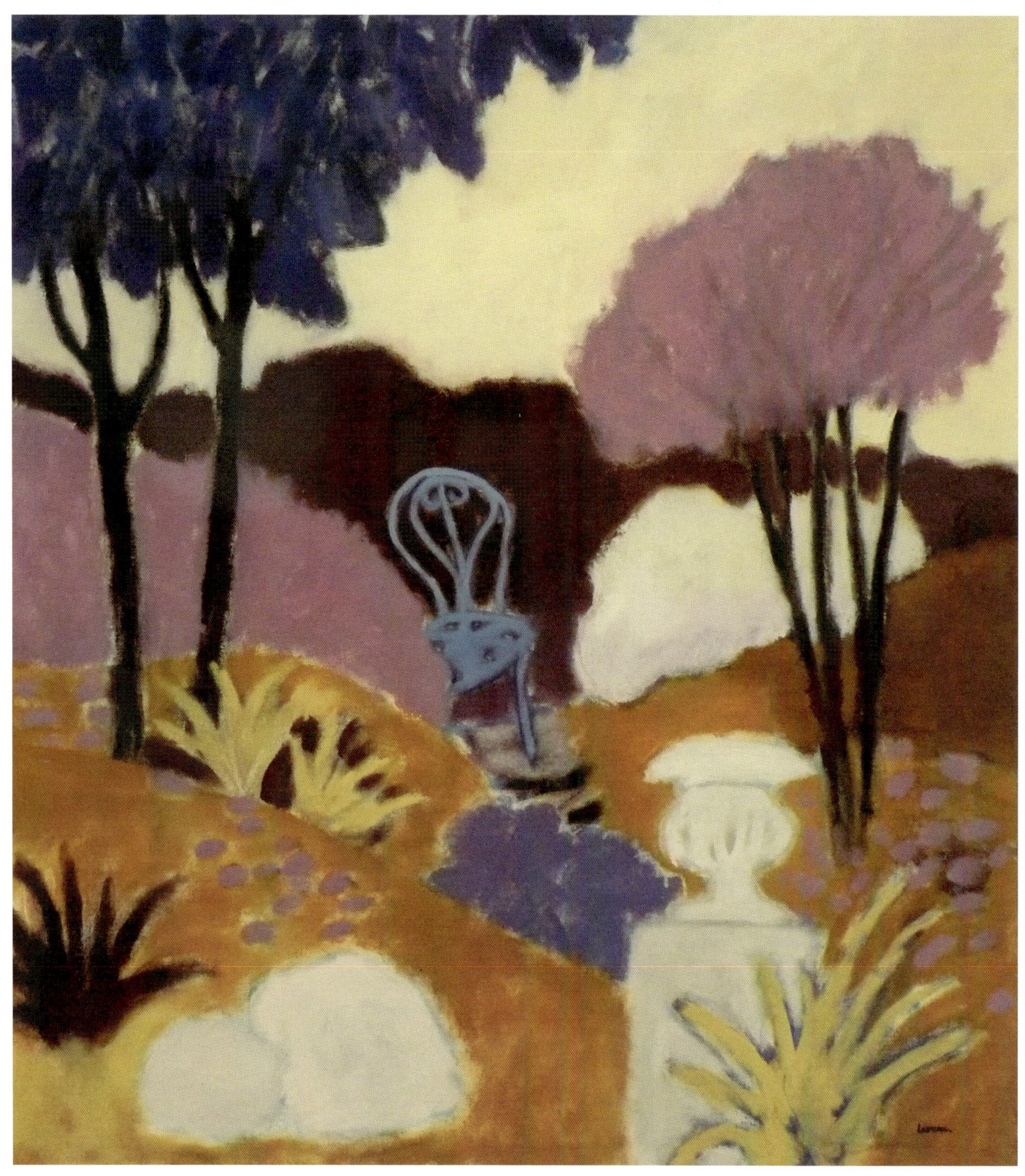

Mon jardin à San Diego IV, oil on canvas, 152x138 cm, 2010. Private collection.

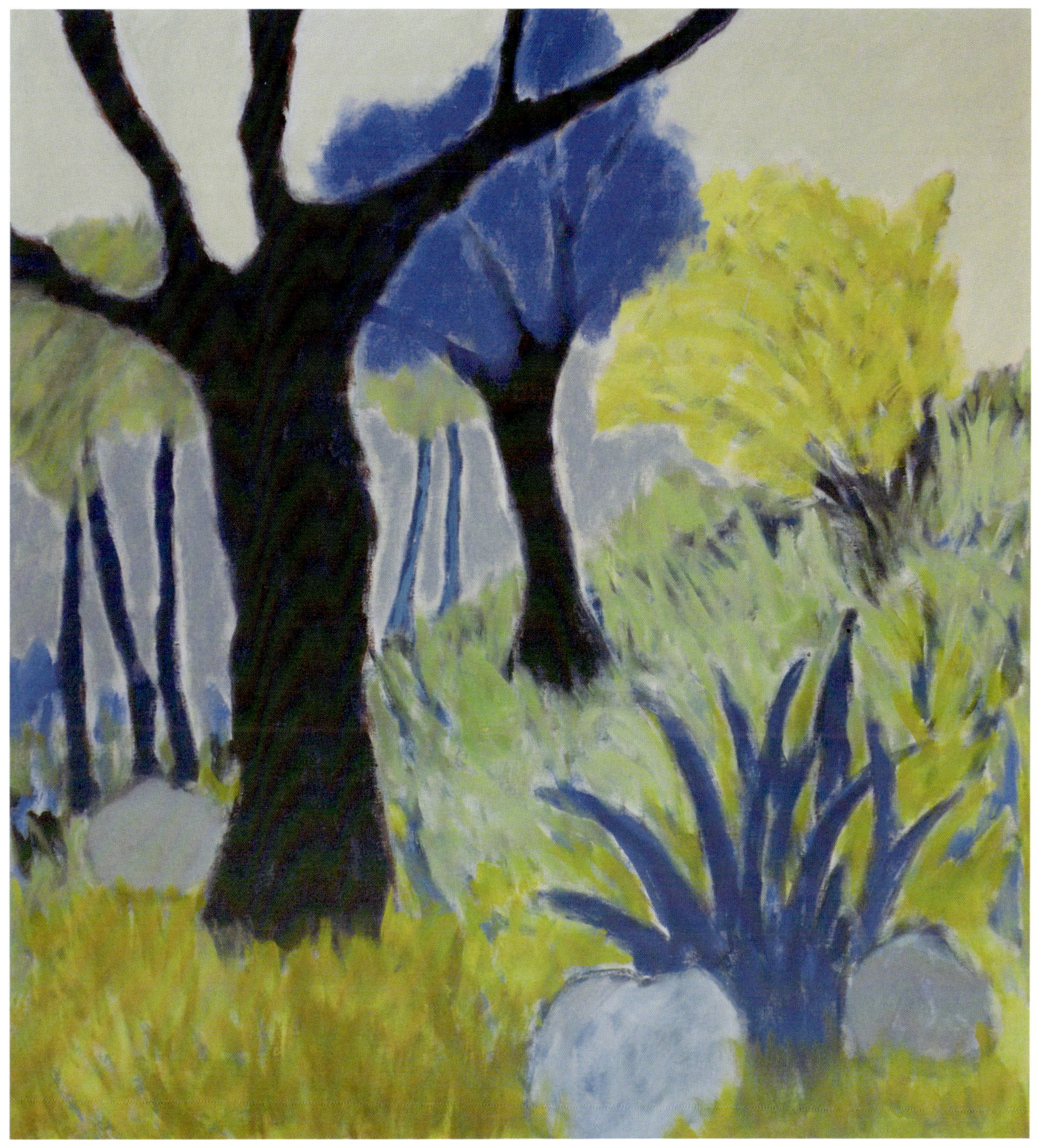

Mon jardin à San Diego I, oil on canvas, 152x138 cm, 2010. Private collection.

Because I like it

Ok, I've written those fatal words, because I've thought it, felt it, seen it and I like it. No more attempts at objective analysis; let's move on to pure unsubstantiated subjectivity to get at the essence of Jacqueline Lavenu's work.

Ms. Lavenu's intriguing compositions, often many times over painted, offer the opportunity to look, and then look again, into the heart of her paintings until we truly see the painter's mind and supple hand at work. Each piece has its own story to tell; sometimes contemplative other times mysterious, where inert objects are transfused with feeling.

Her subtle colors, their juxtaposition between forms and the space they create, and the use of defining linear white voids, offer a wonderful way to appreciate the nuances of the artist's vision.

Ms. Lavenu's use of light, both European and Californian, provides a basis for comparing two distinctly different cultures and climates. The flat gradations often exhibited in her Franco-German pieces contrast sharply with the luminous landscapes of her adopted Californian countryside.

The memory of space and time is vividly portrayed in Ms. Lavenu's oeuvre. With only rough sketches and her emotional memory, Ms. Lavenu paints depictions of places, events and personages both past and present with bold confidence.

The ability of Ms. Lavenu to transport the viewer to a time and place is almost beyond description. Her scenes of Paris roof tops eloquently evoke not only the city's urban geometry but also provide a base for the projection of the viewer's emotions. One can easily imagine the thoughts of a young, lonely, homesick au-pair sequestered in her attic chambre de bonne gazing over the cold, lead gray roofs beyond.

In other works, voluptuous females, alone and in the company of others, make classic reference to bygone poses. Often serenely set, these figurative portraits are studies in an inner contemplation which magically transfers to the viewer.

It is the depiction of timelessness, whether it is past, present or future, that provides the foundation of Ms. Lavenu's work. One can observe its progression from her earliest work to her most current as a representation of continuity of effort in a recognizable, unified direction.

Her landscapes, still lifes, and portraits, while individual pieces, are one of a whole in an ever evolving and growing body of remarkable work.

That's why I like it.

James T. Frost
Architect, Artist and Collector

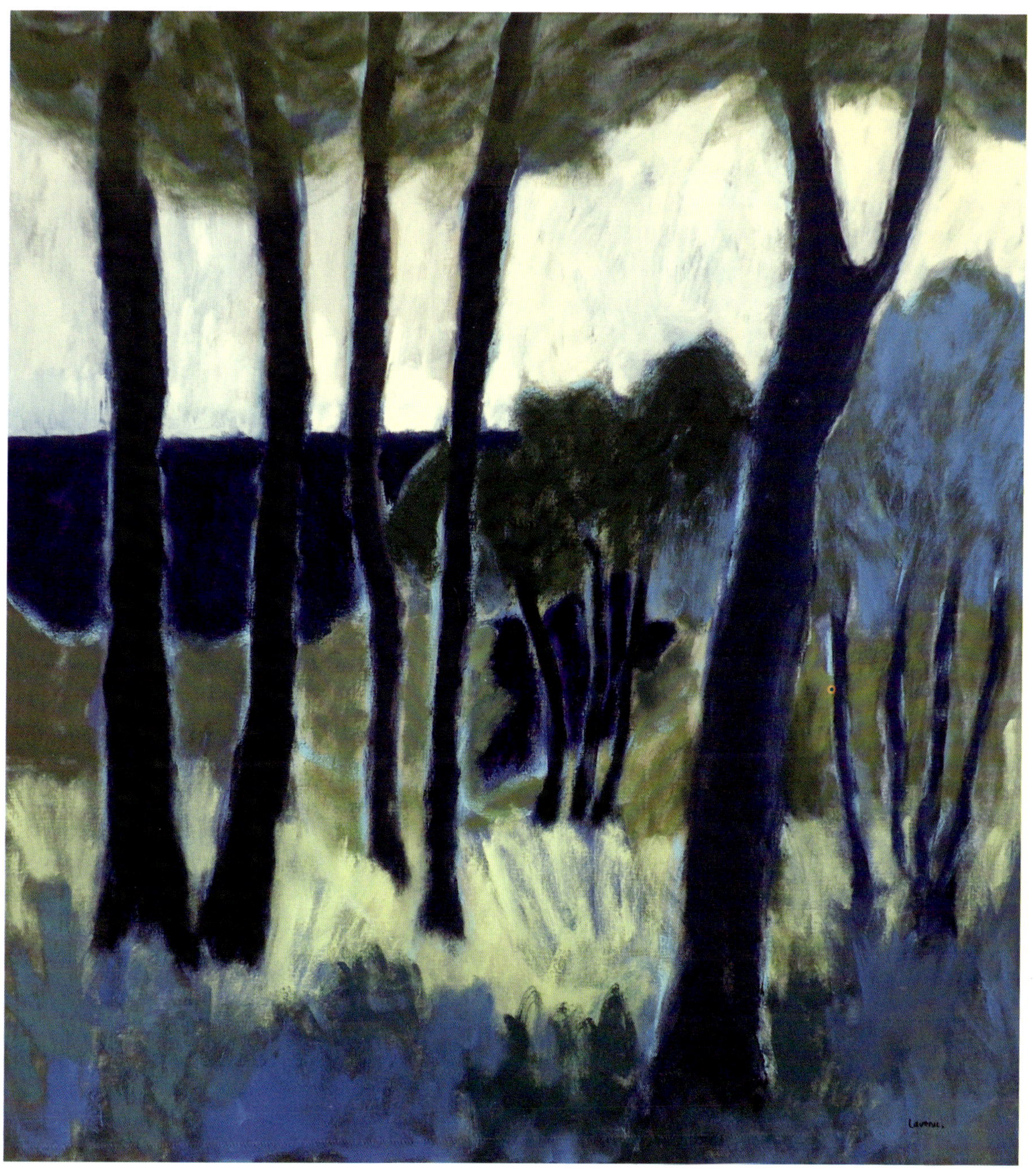

Legion of Honor Park, San Francisco, oil on canvas, 138x122 cm, 2010. Private collection.

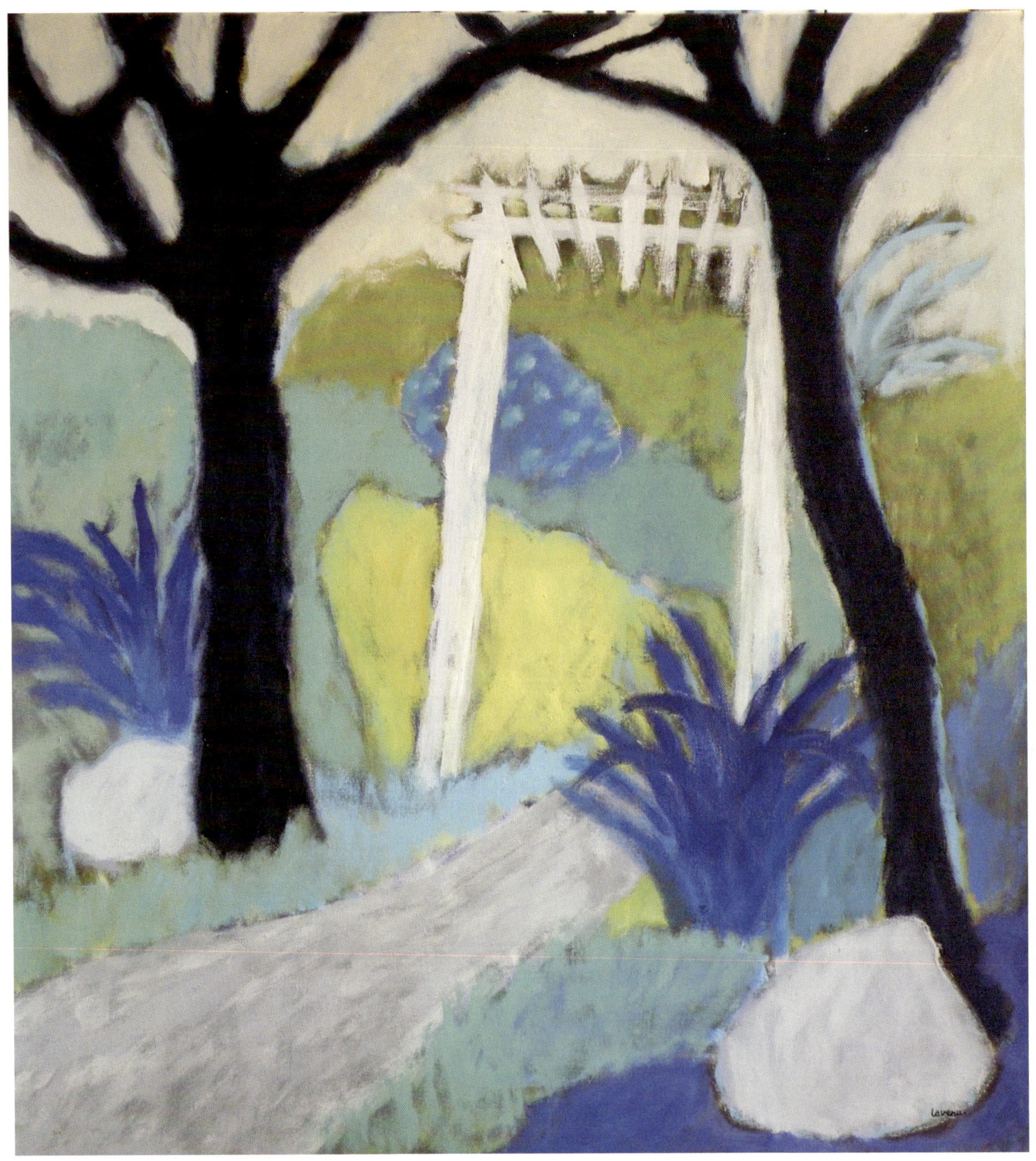

Mon jardin à San Diego II, oil on canvas, 138x122 cm, 2011.

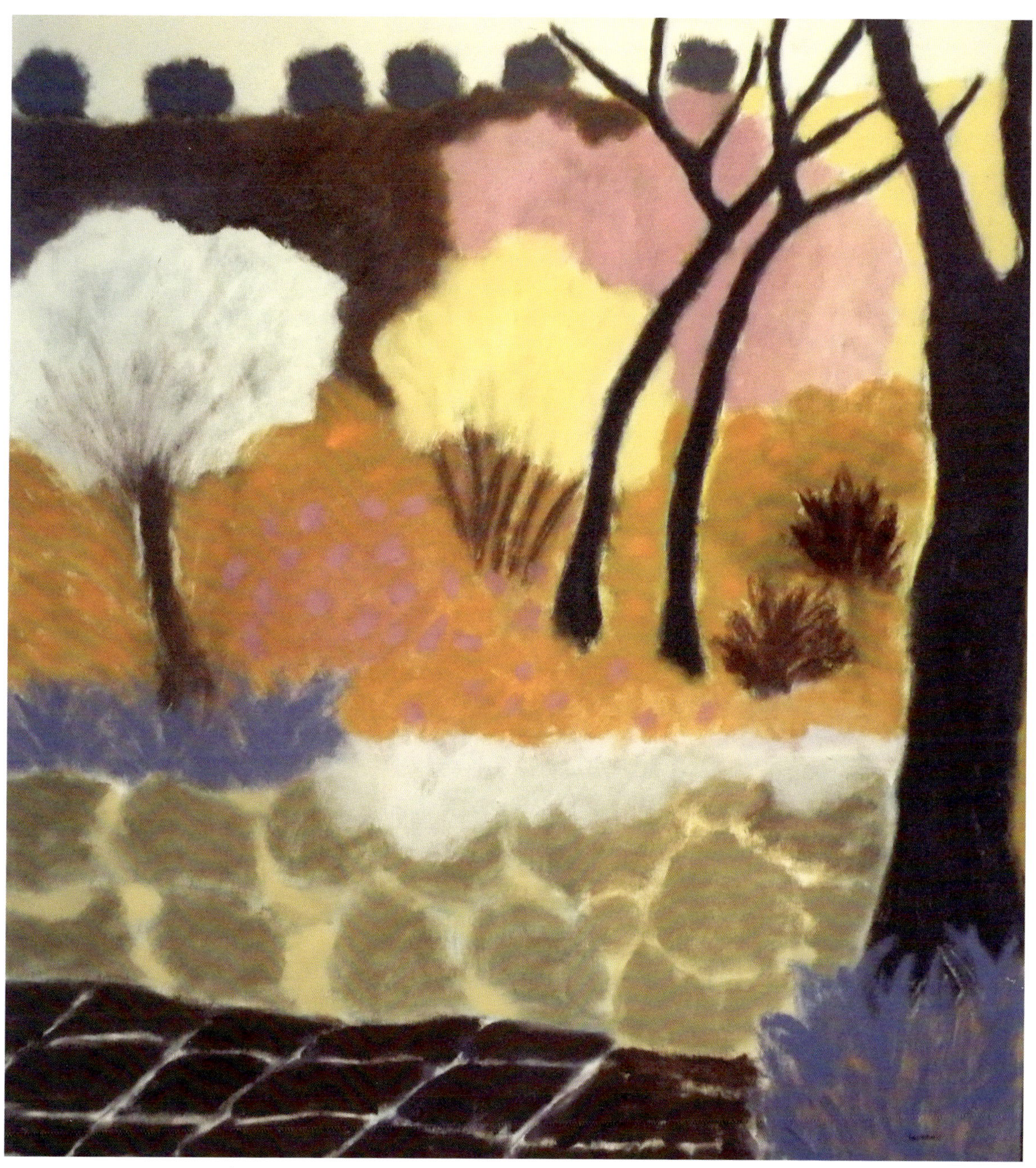

Mon jardin à San Diego V, oil on canvas, 152x138 cm, 2010.

"I discovered the forests around Lützelbach (Odenwald) perchance in 1993. I was totally enchanted as if transported into the Nibelungen legends of a Wagner Opera. This magic returns every year I visit and is a continual source of inspiration."

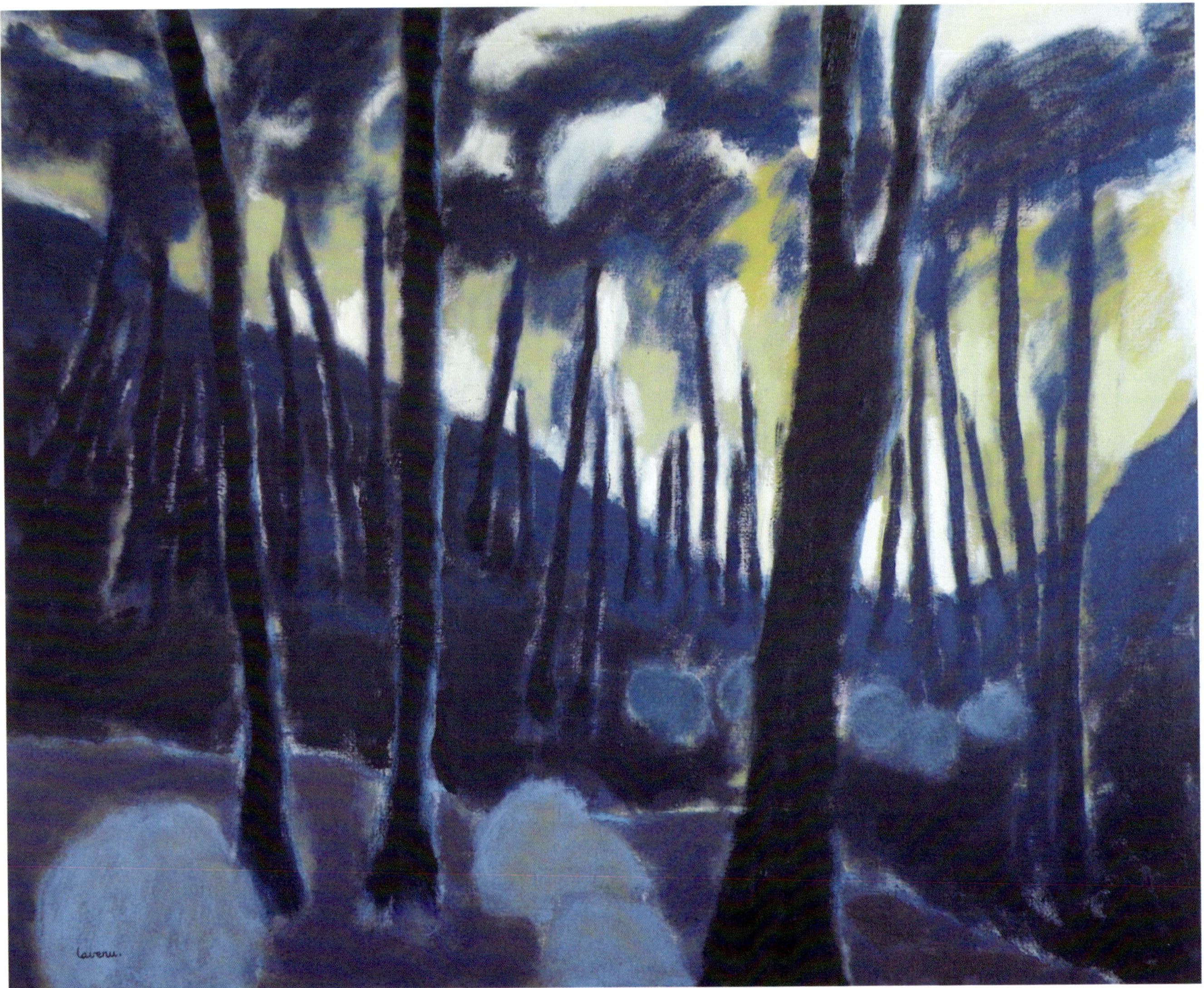

Lützelbach forest III, oil on canvas, 102x122 cm, 2011. Private collection.

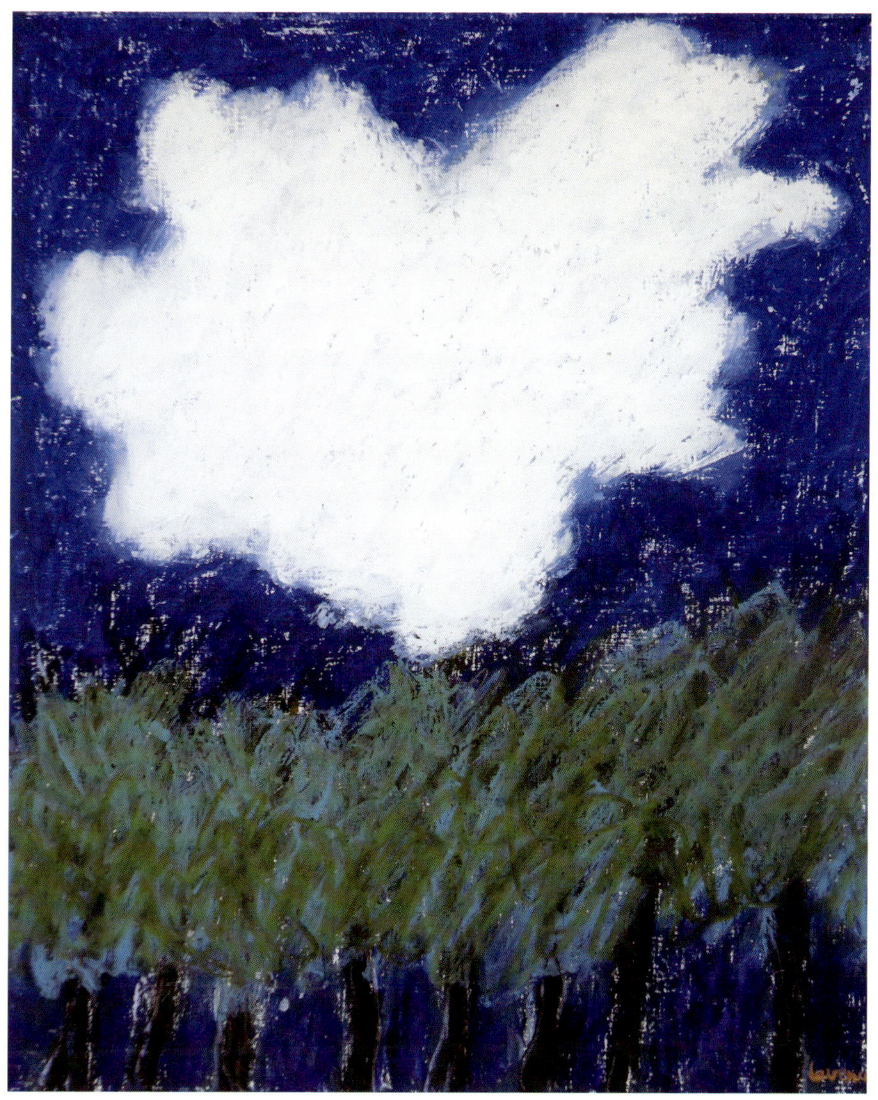

Twilight in Odenwald, oil pastel 49x39 cm, 2011.

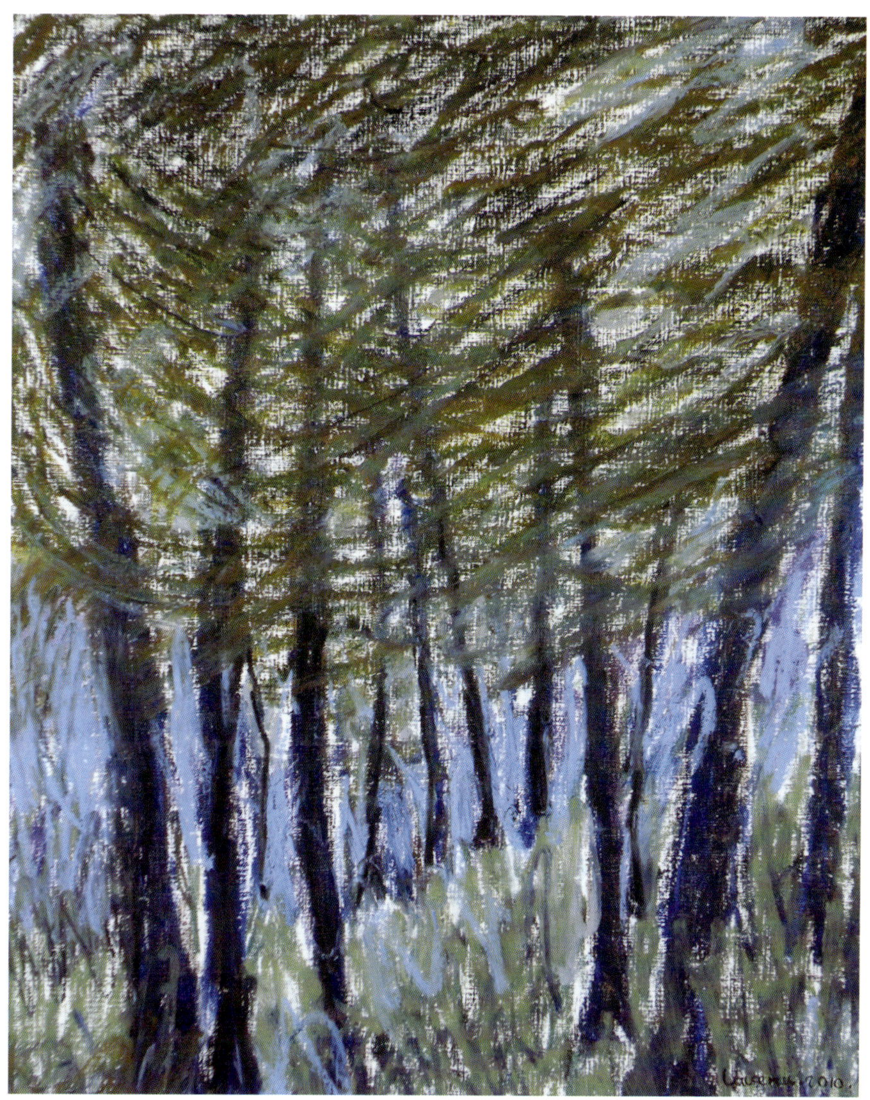

Lützelbach forest III, oil pastel 49x39 cm, 2010. Private collection.

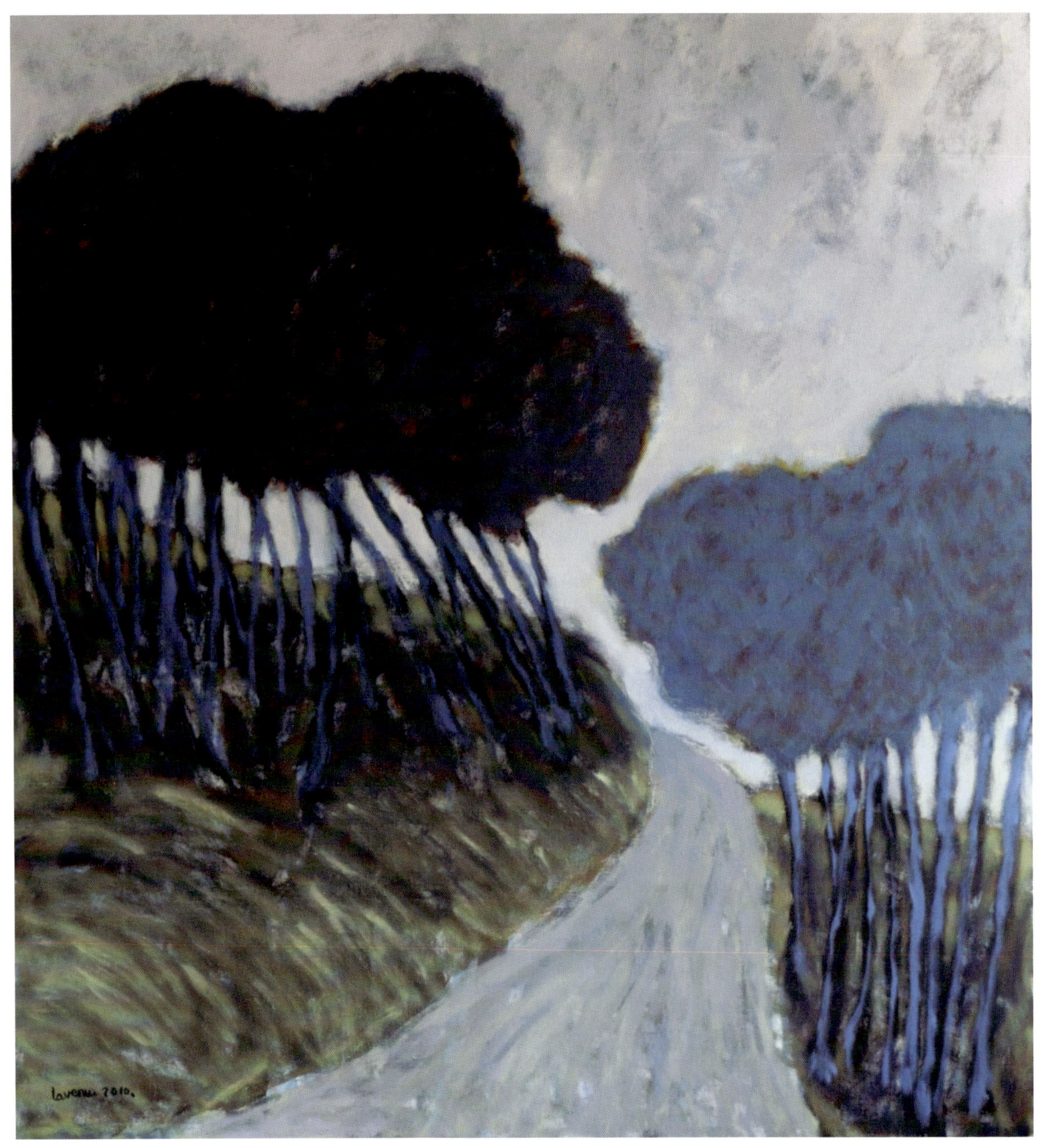

Lützelbach forest I, oil on canvas, 152x138 cm, 2010. Private collection.

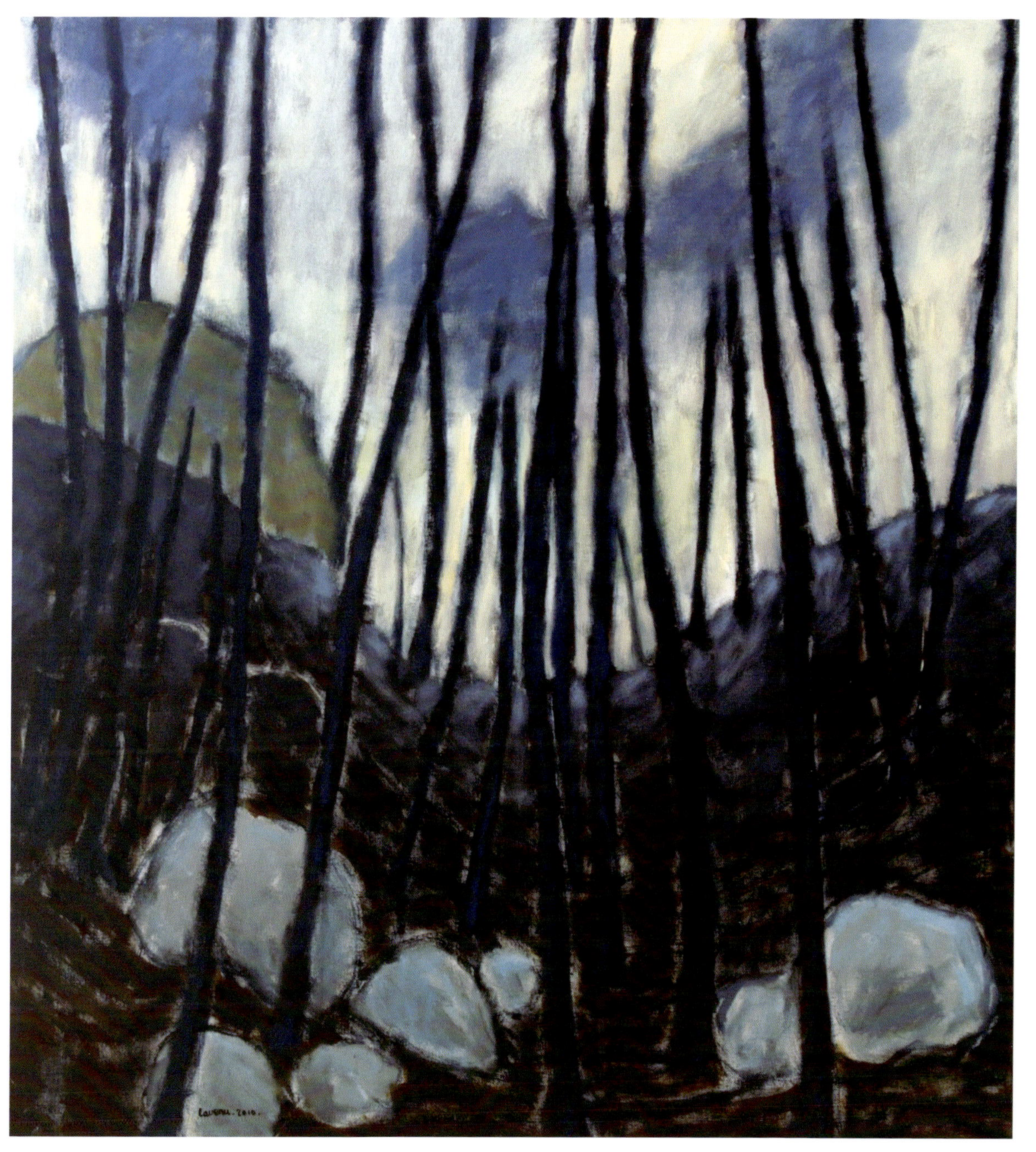

Lützelbach forest II, oil on canvas, 152x138 cm, 2010.

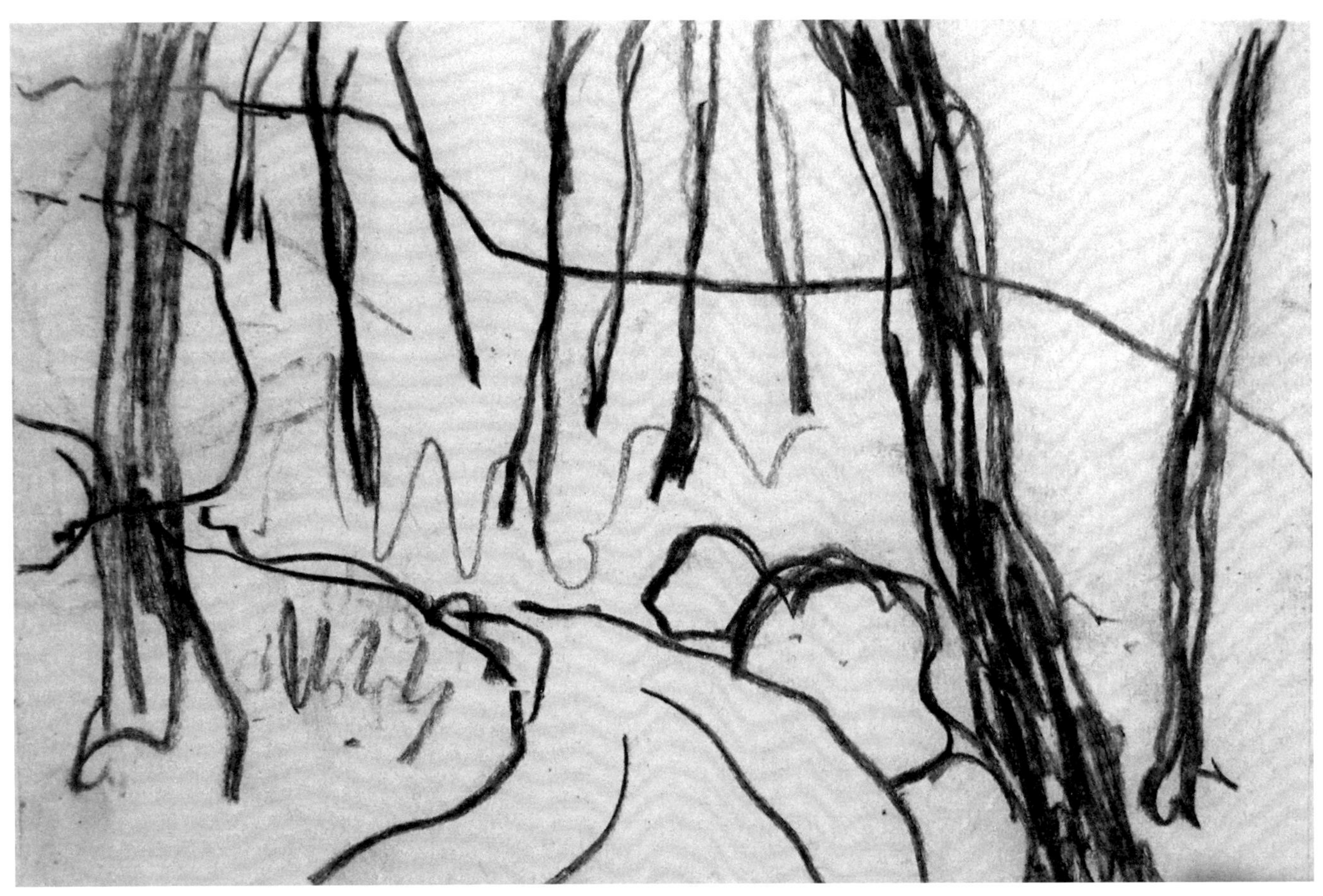

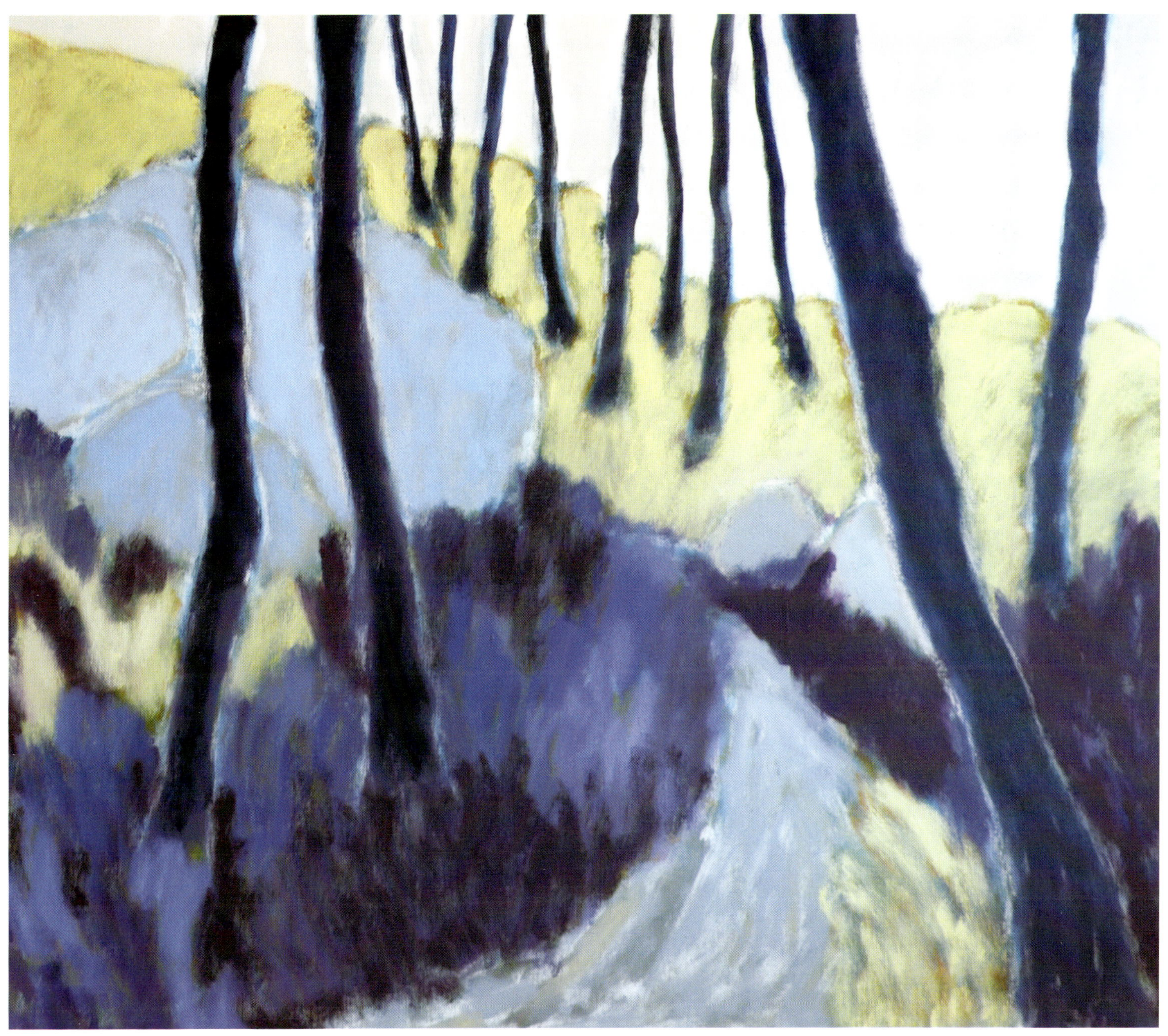

Forest near Lichtenberg, oil on canvas, 122x138 cm, 2010.

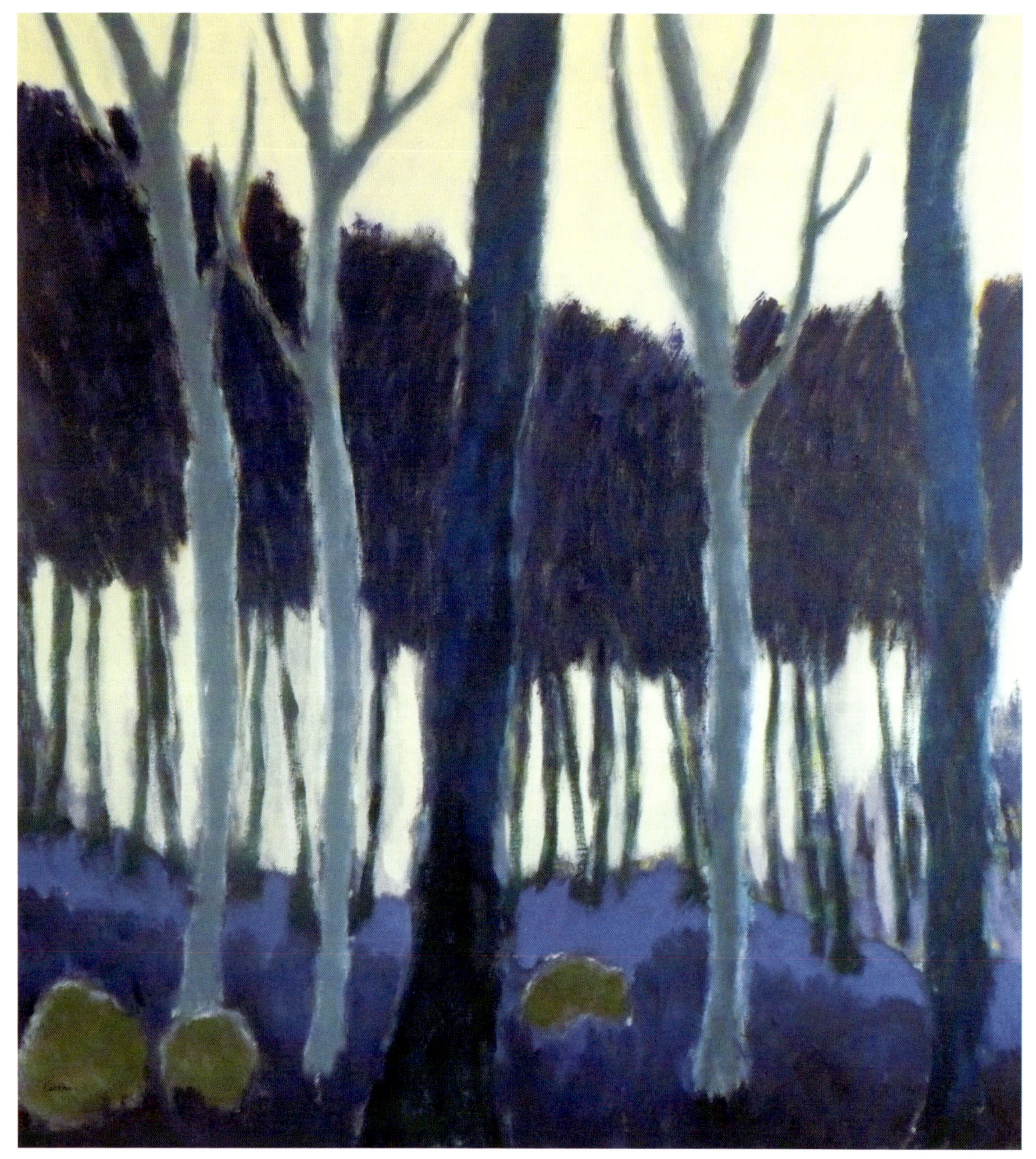

Forest's edge, Odenwald, oil on canvas, 152x138 cm, 2011.

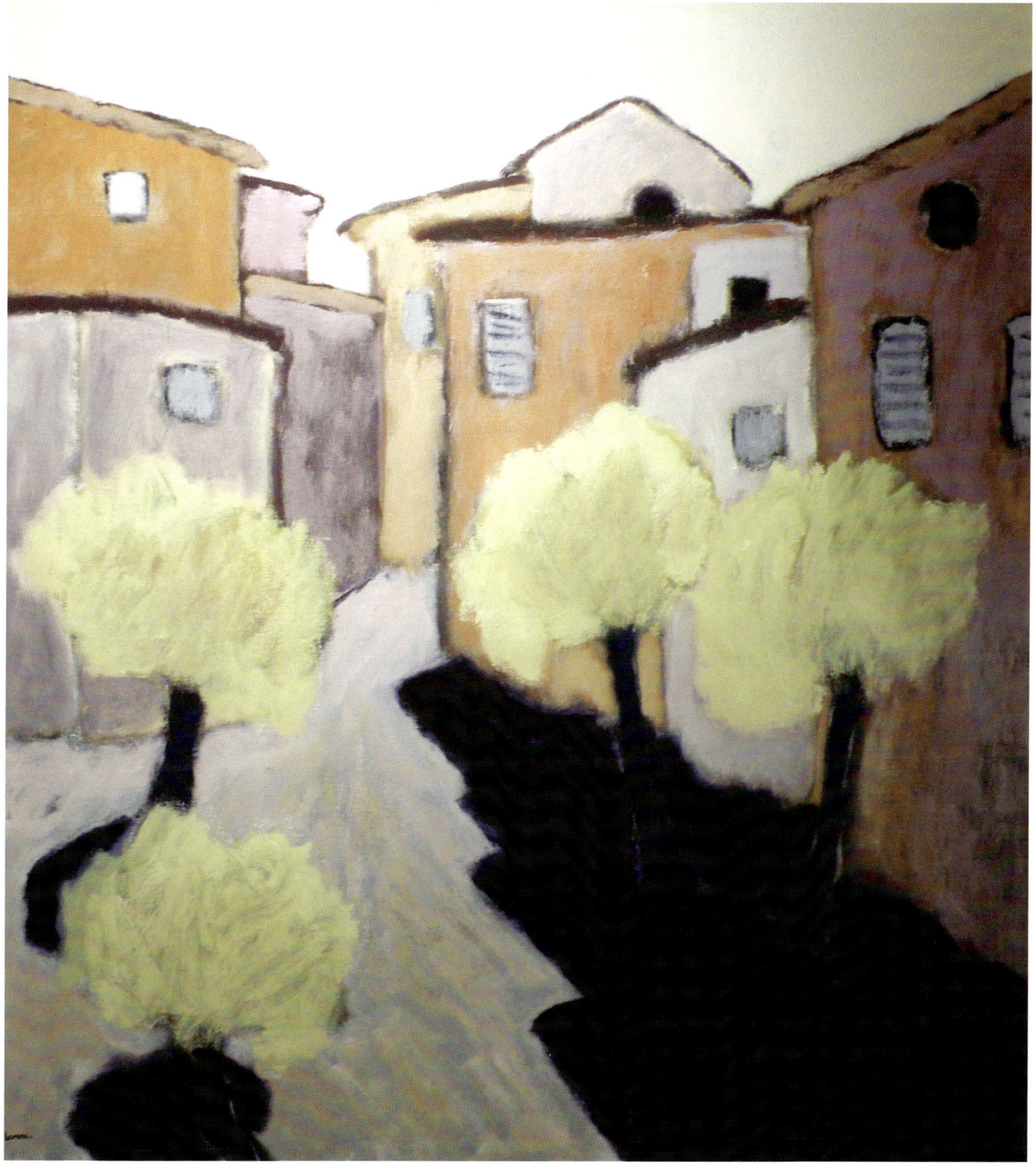

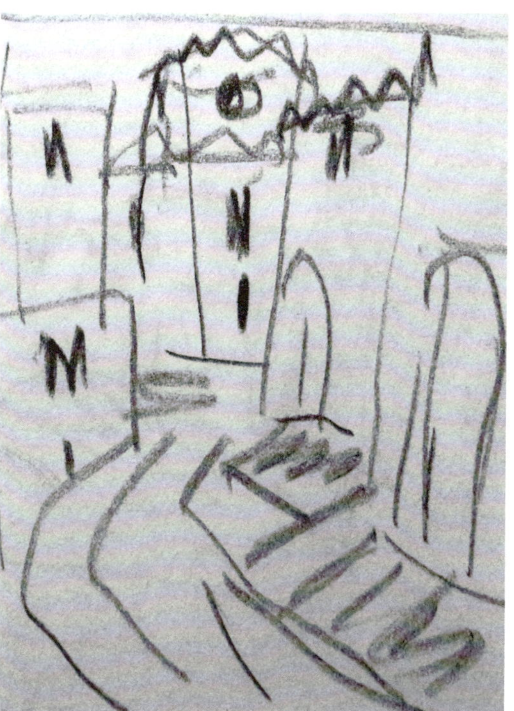

Street in Italy, oil on canvas, 138x122 cm, 2010. Private collection.

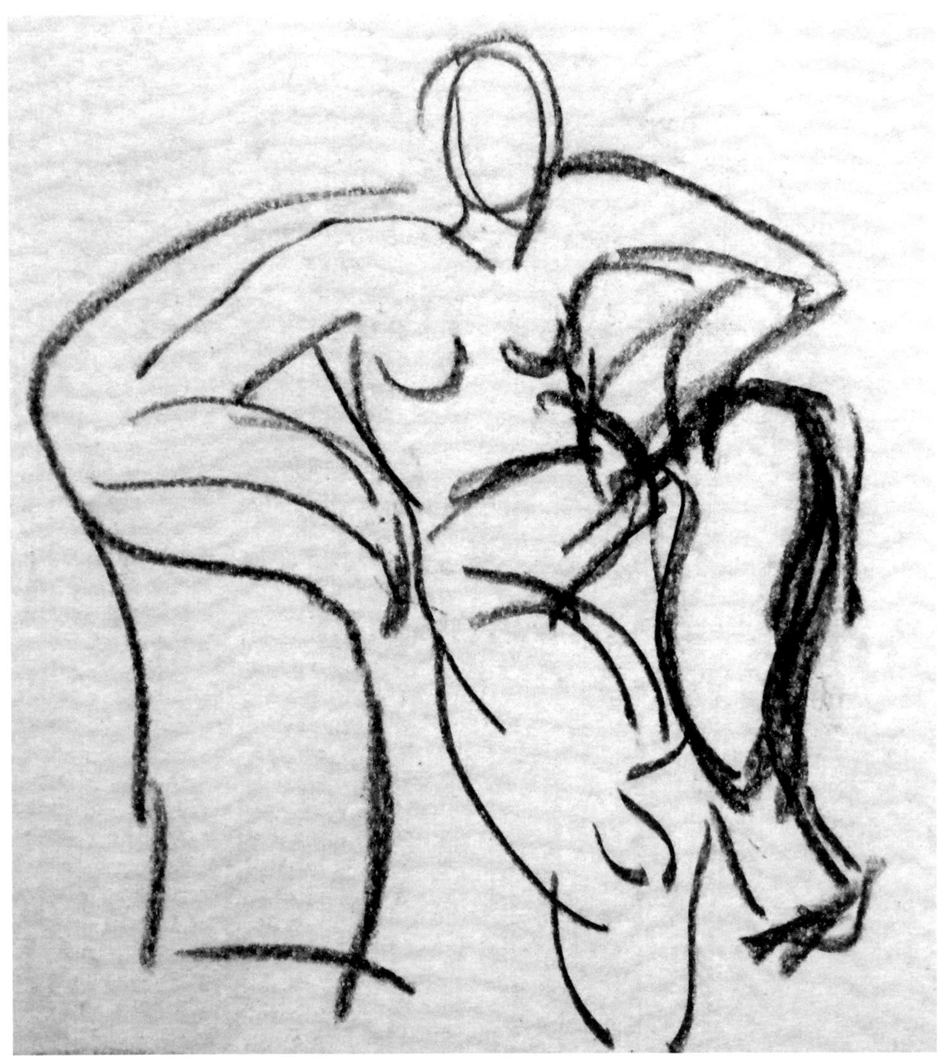

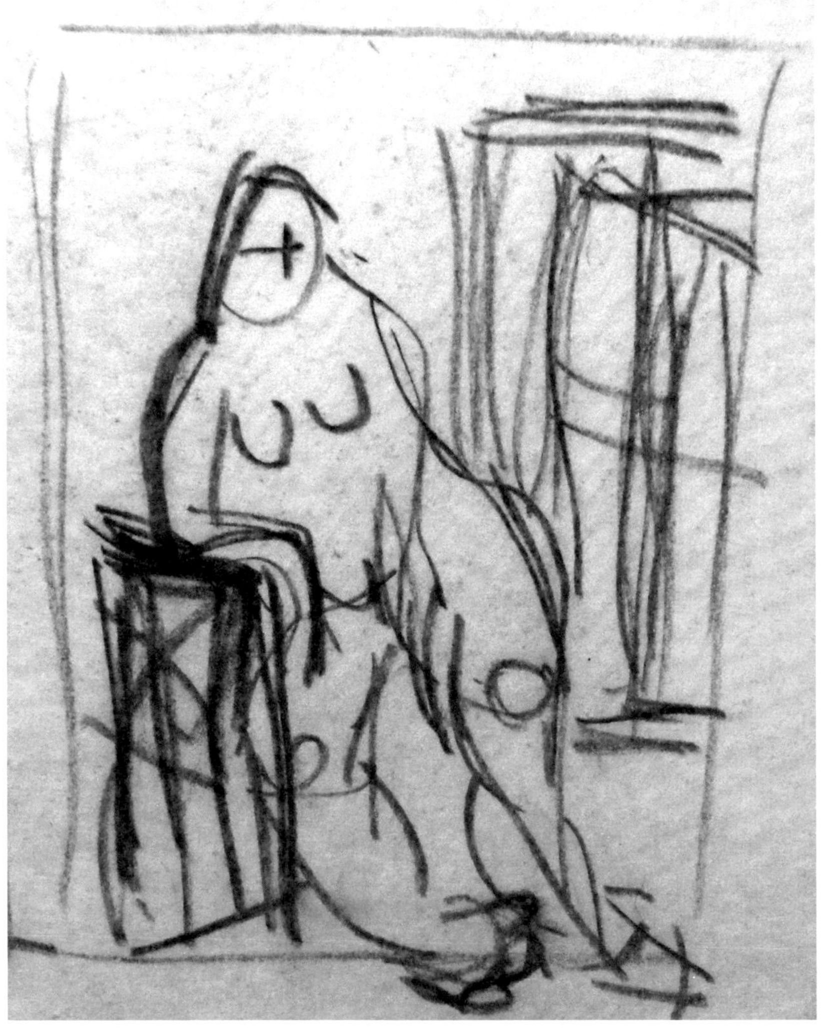

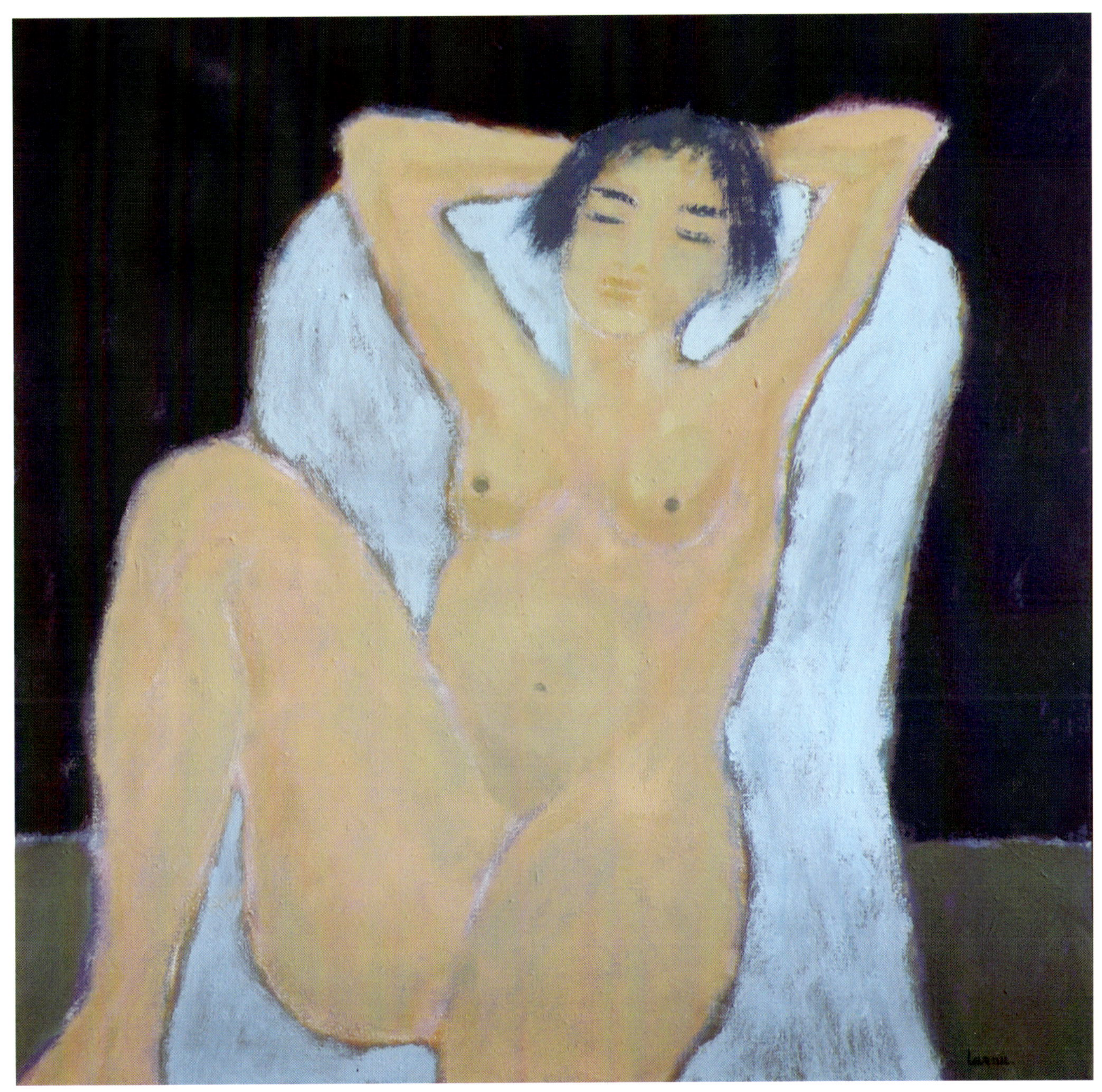

Nude reclining, oil on canvas, 92x92 cm, 2010.

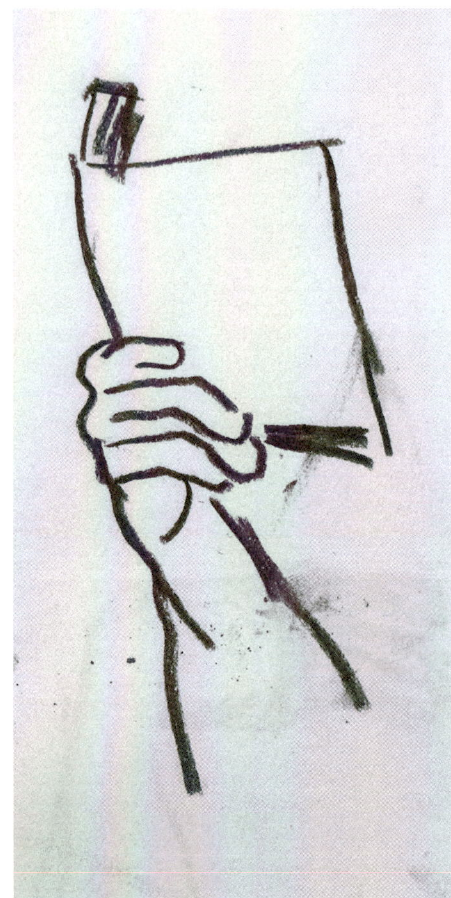

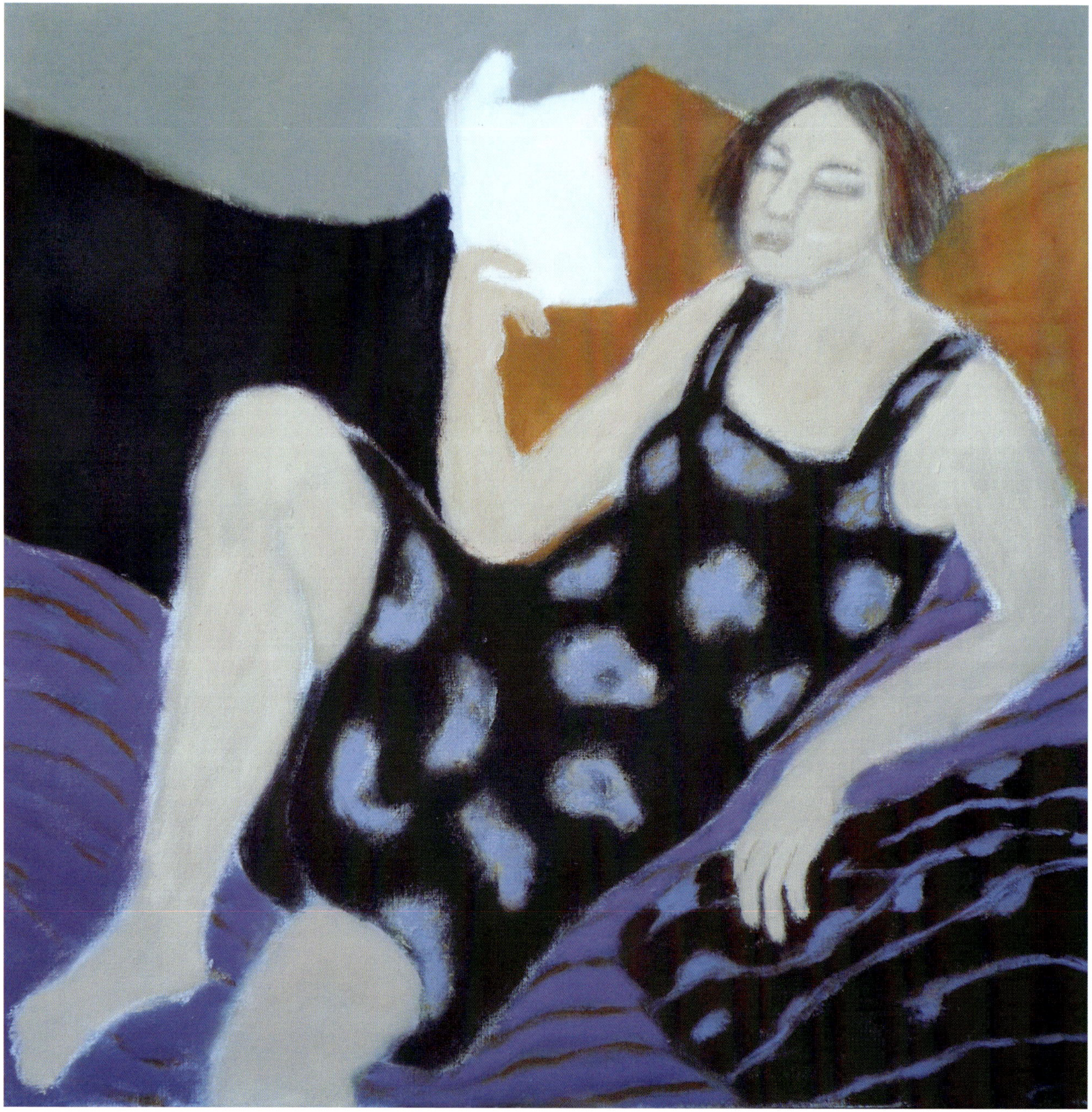

Reading VII, oil on canvas, 102x102 cm, 2010. Private collection.

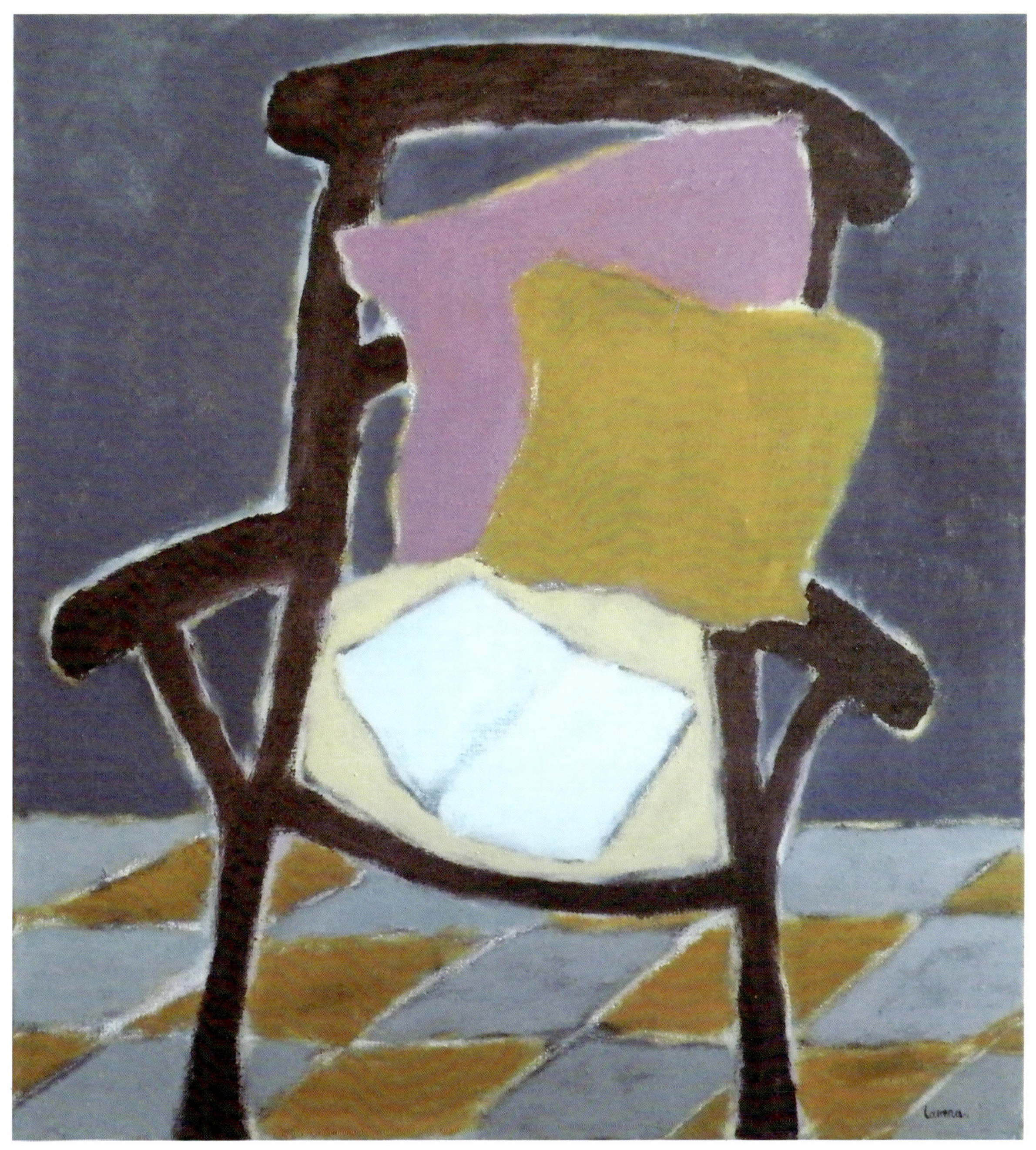

Chaise et livre, oil on canvas, 102x92 cm, 2010.

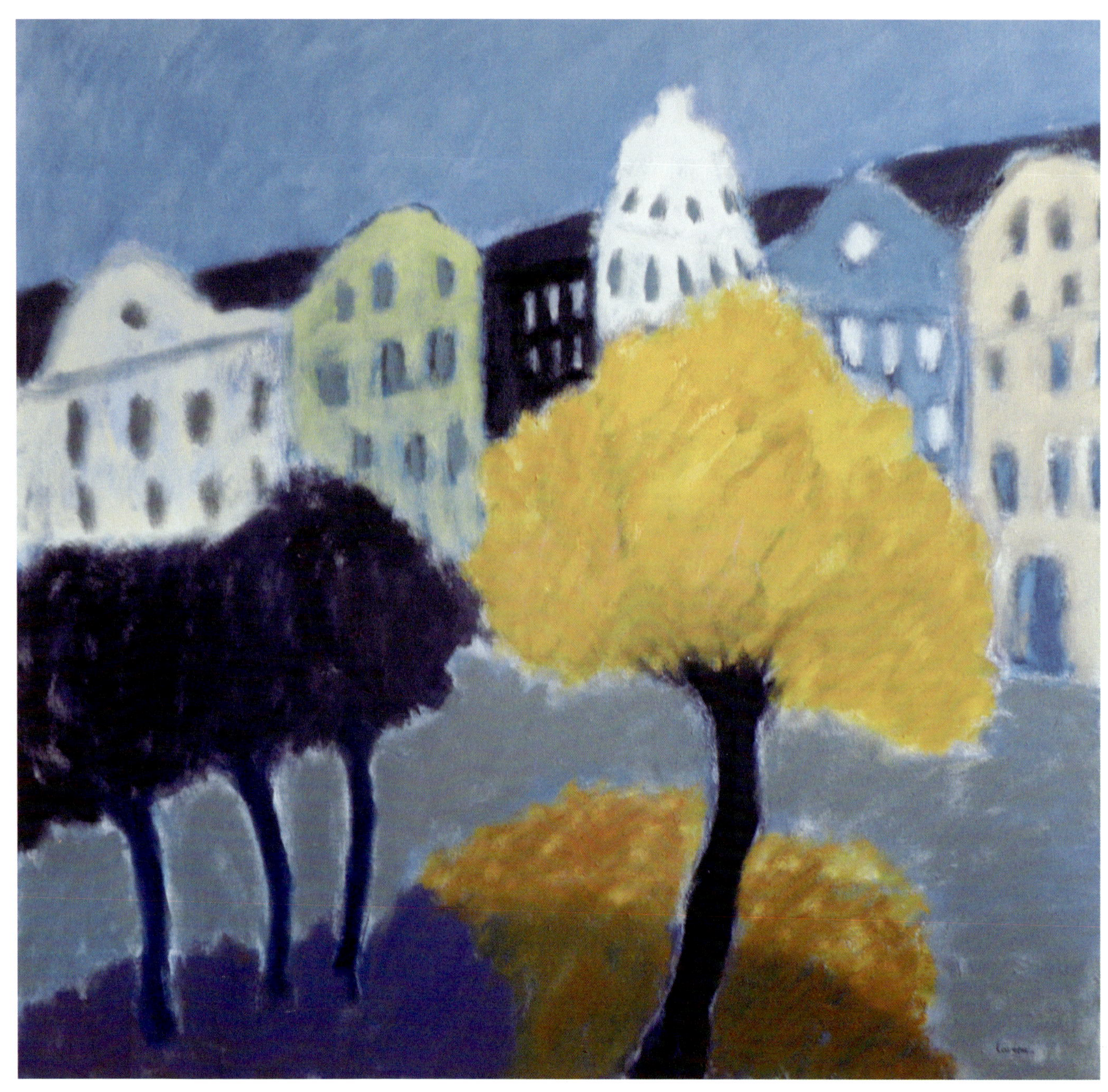

Leibnizstrasse Ecke Ku'damm, Berlin, oil on canvas, 117x117 cm, 2011.

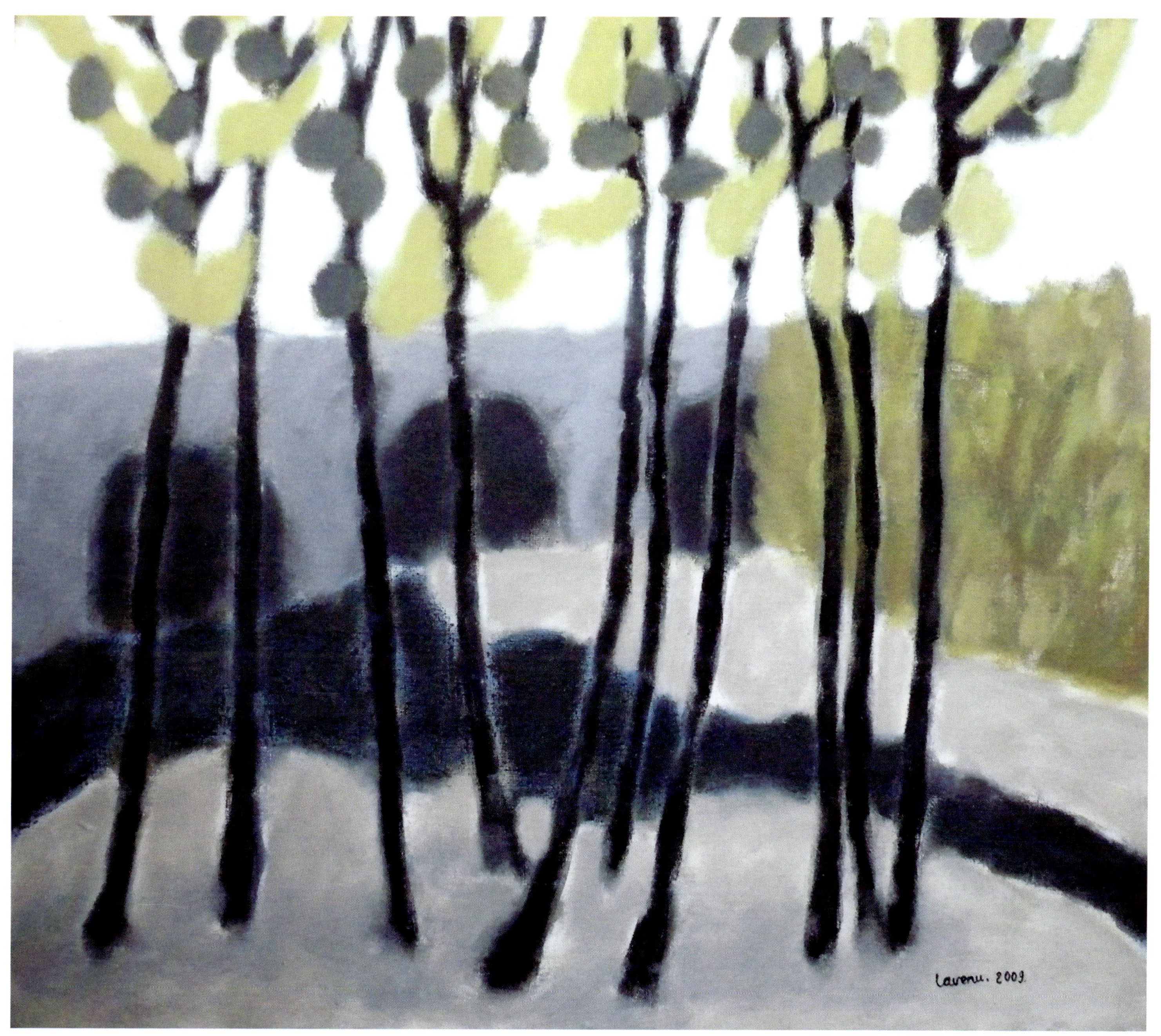

Spring near Chinon, oil on canvas, 92x102 cm, 2007-2009. Private collection.

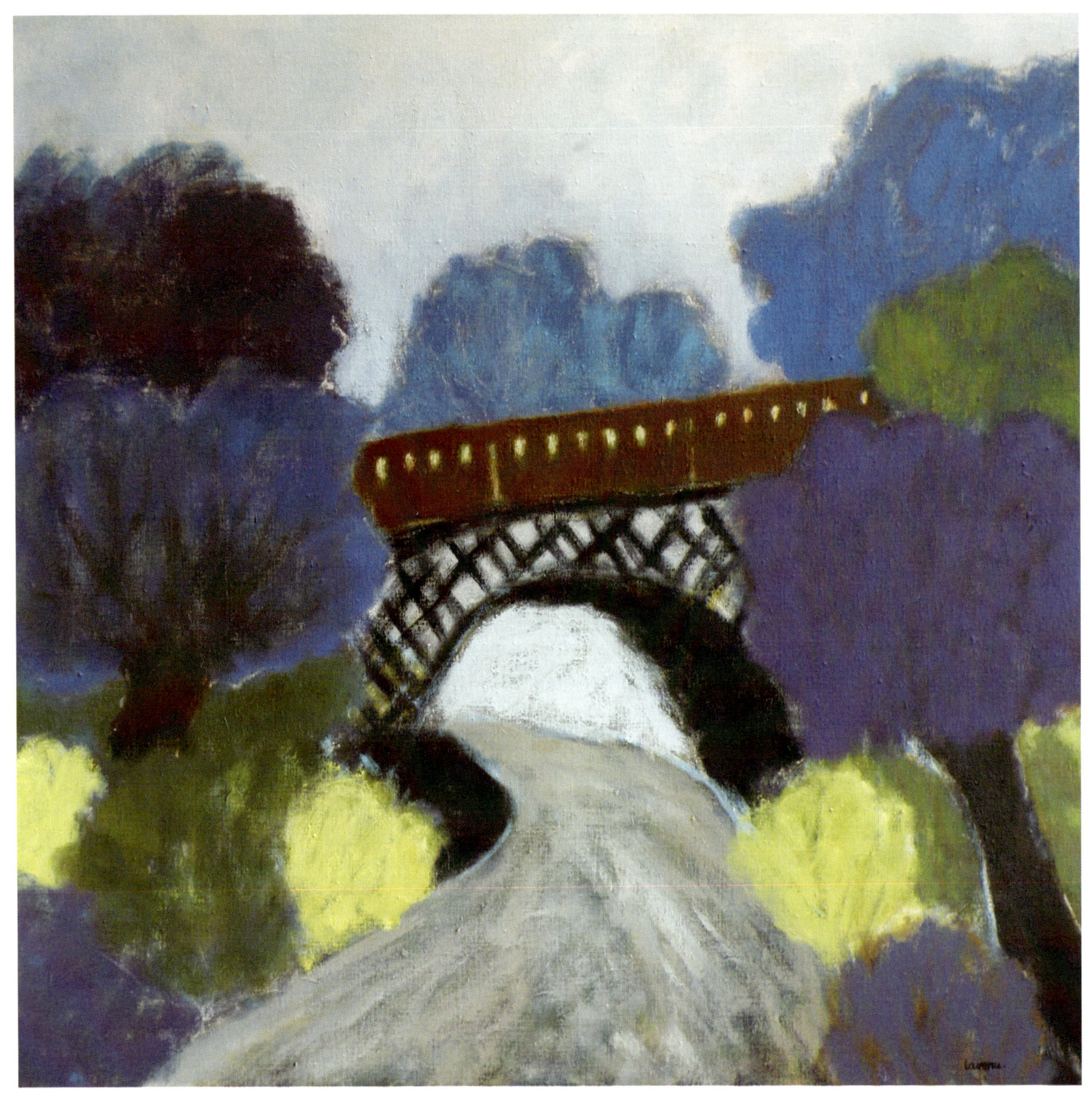

Siegmundshof Berlin, oil on canvas, 117x117 cm, 2011.

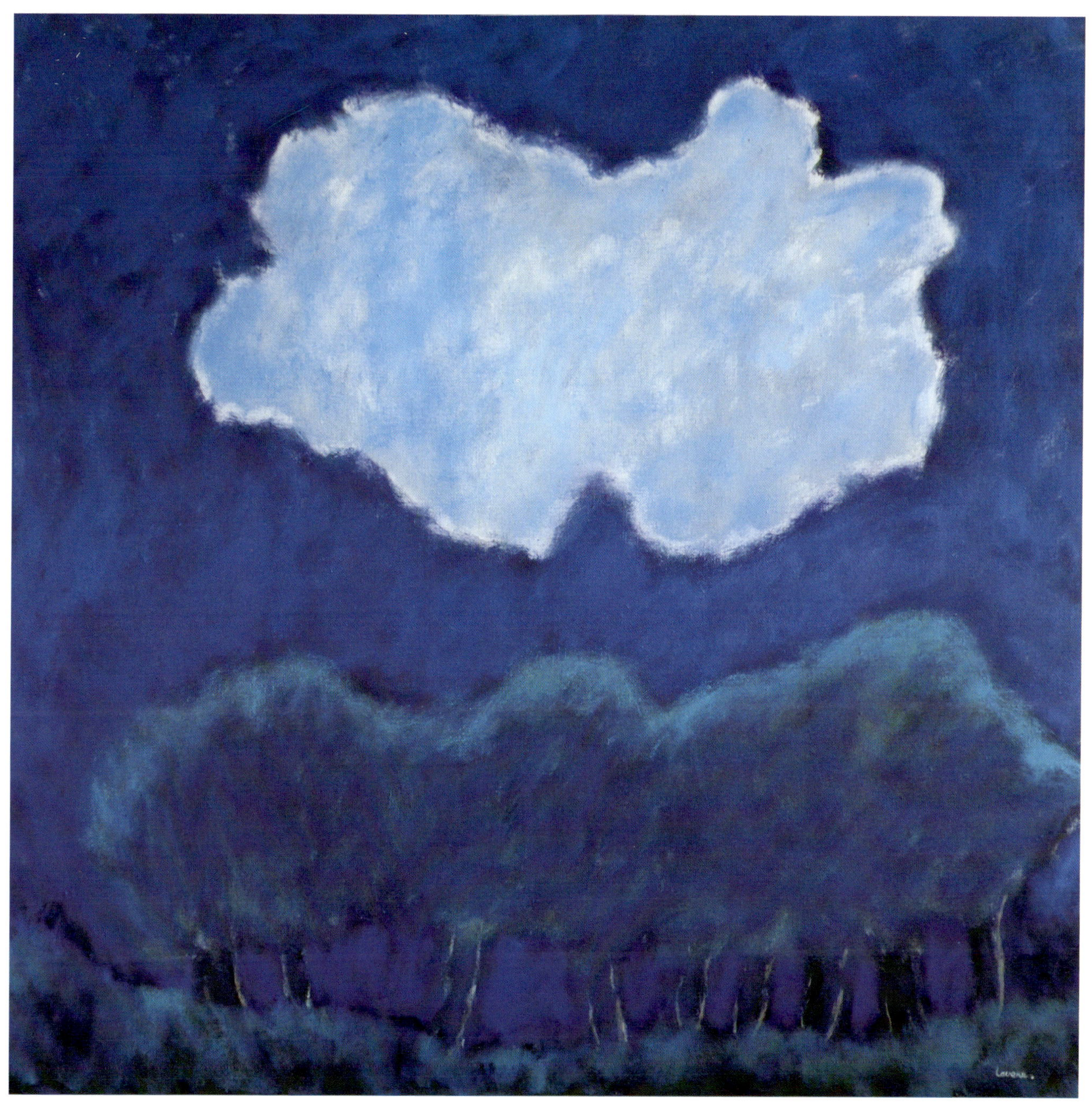

Twilight in Odenwald, oil on canvas, 117x117 cm, 2011. Private collection.

"After 26 years living in the US the vast open landscapes of California have become my subject matter and inspiration. I feel I have come full circle and finally at home in California."

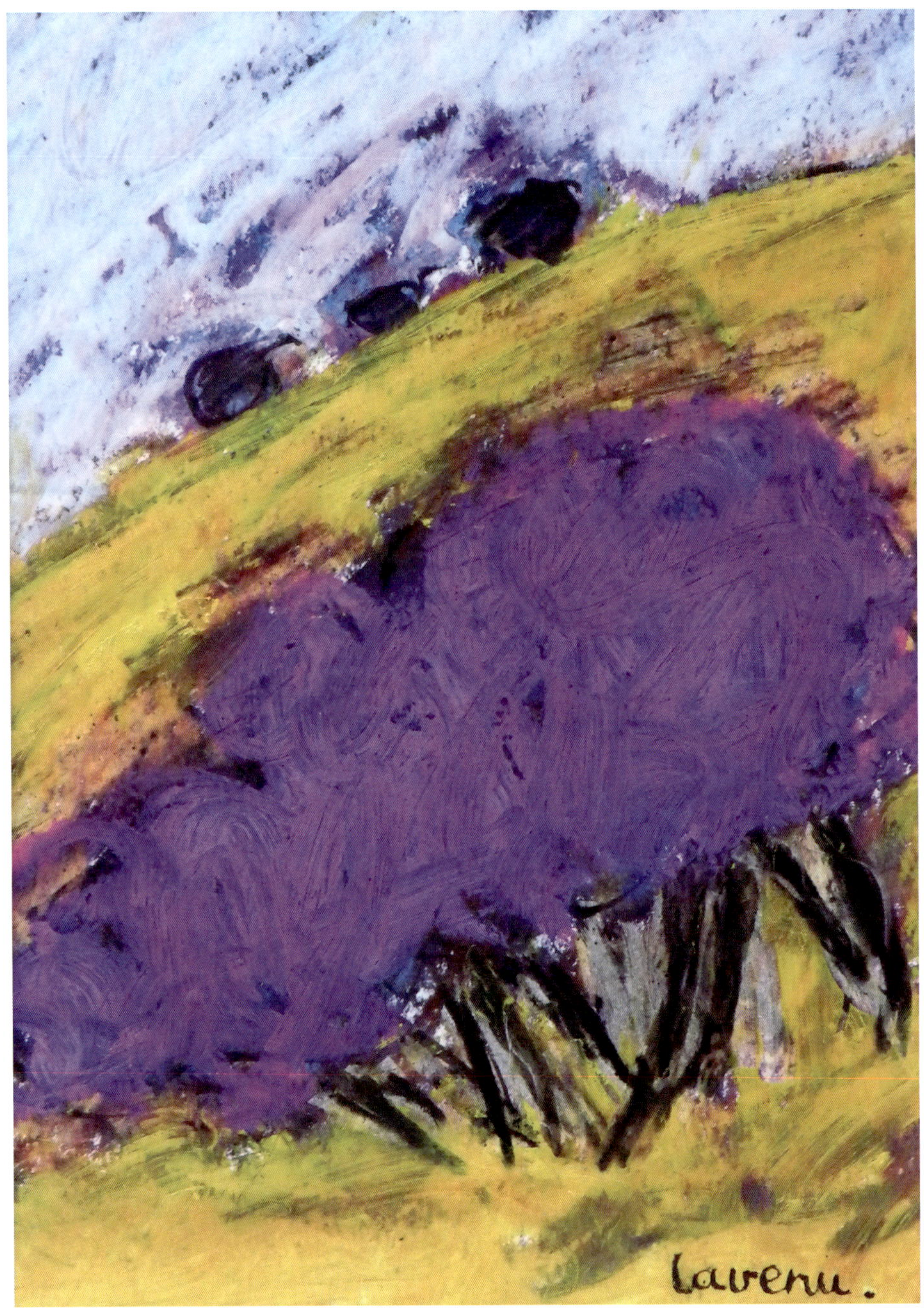

Arbres roses, oil pastel, 17x12 cm, 2011. Private collection.

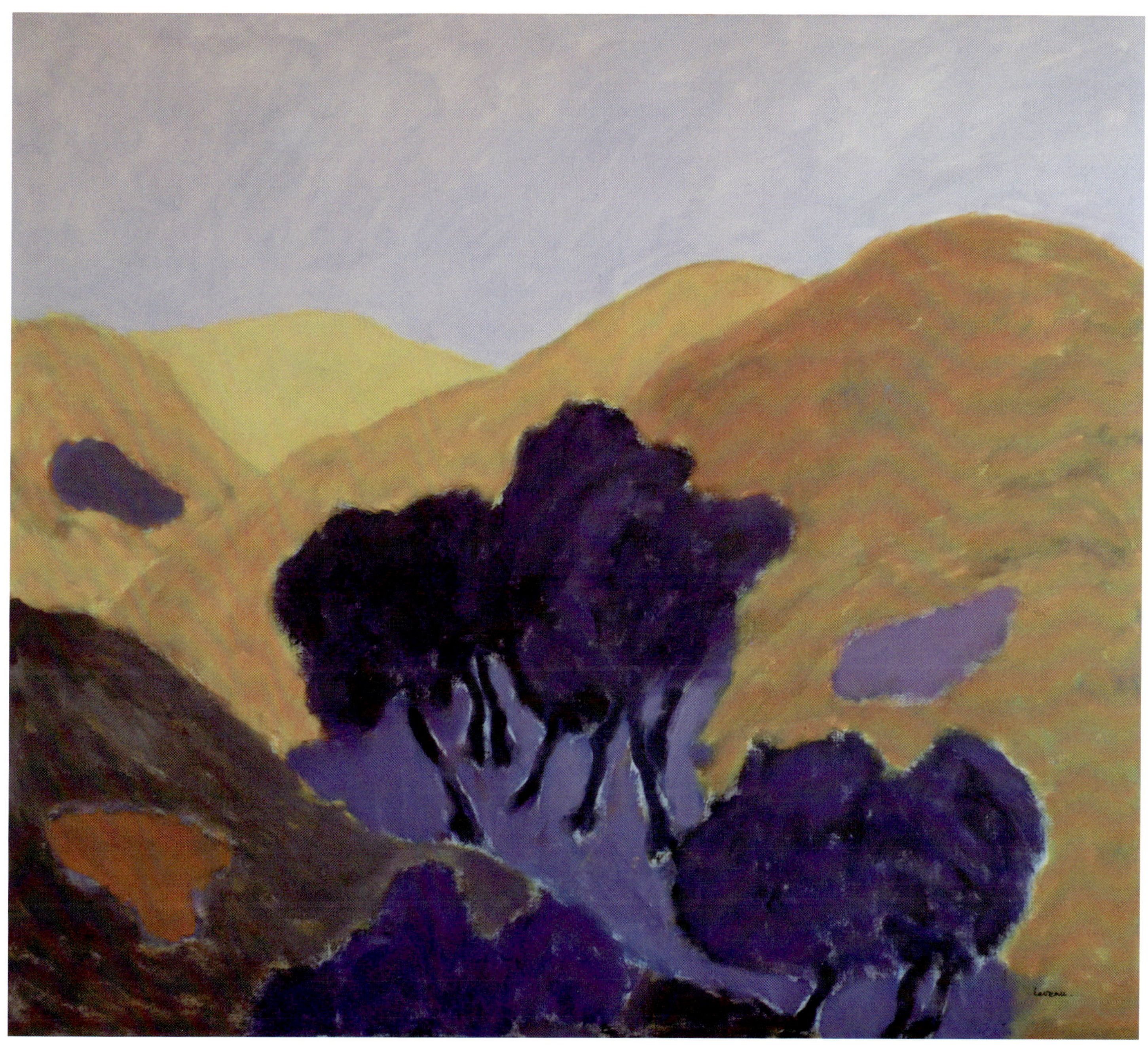

Pacheco Pass, oil on canvas, 138x152 cm, 2011.

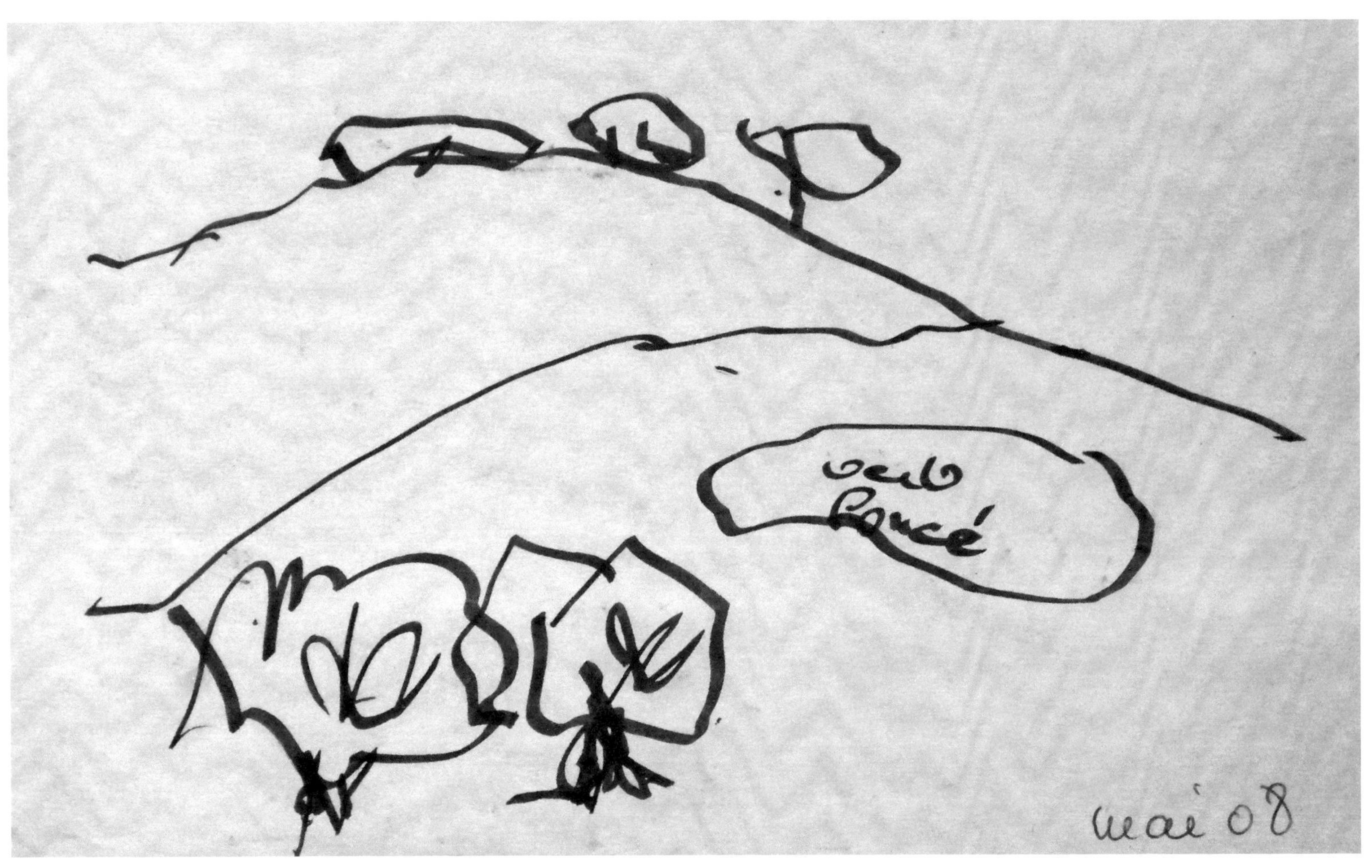
vert foncé
mai 08

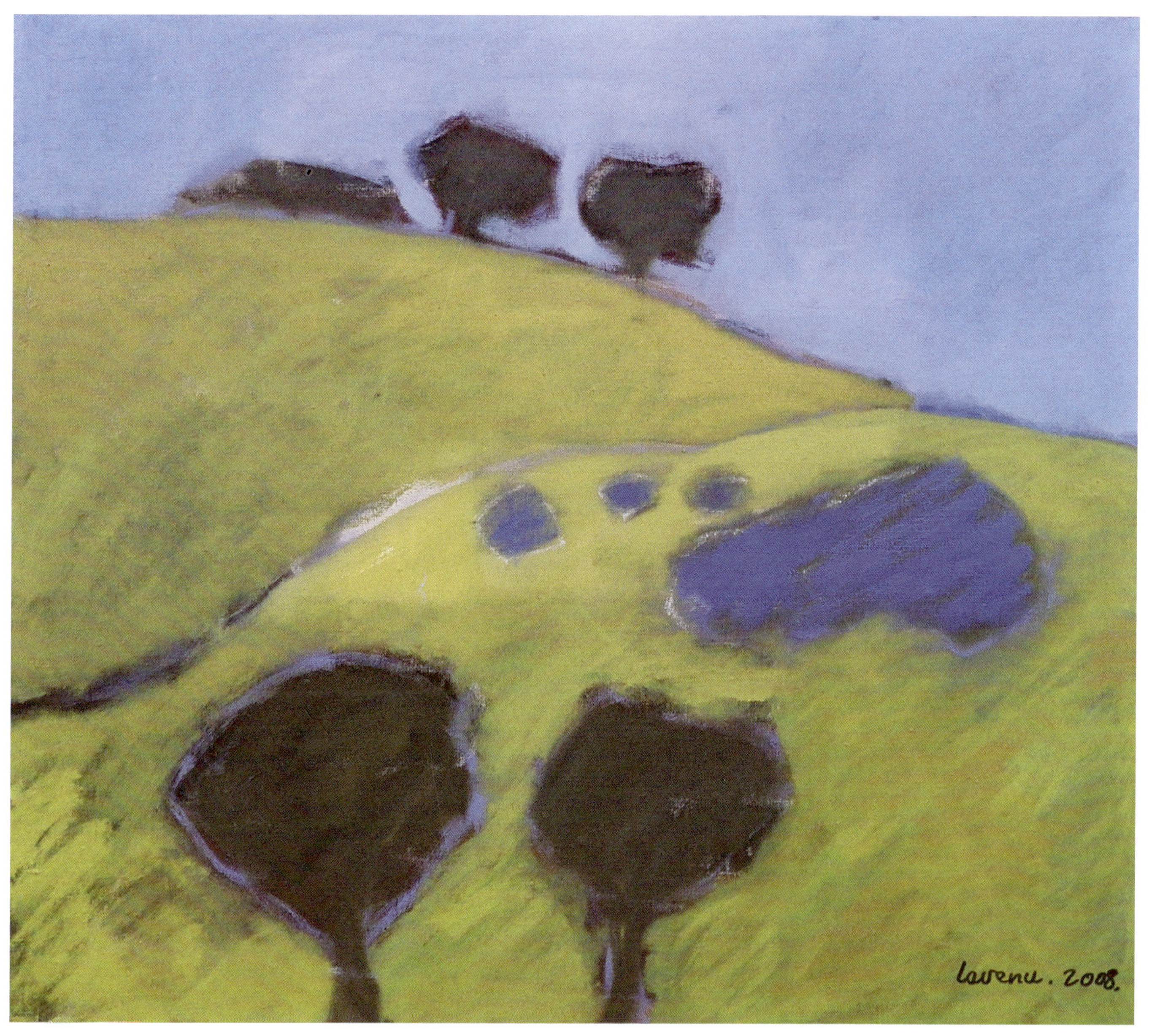

California landscape, spring, oil on canvas, 92x102 cm, 2008. Private collection.

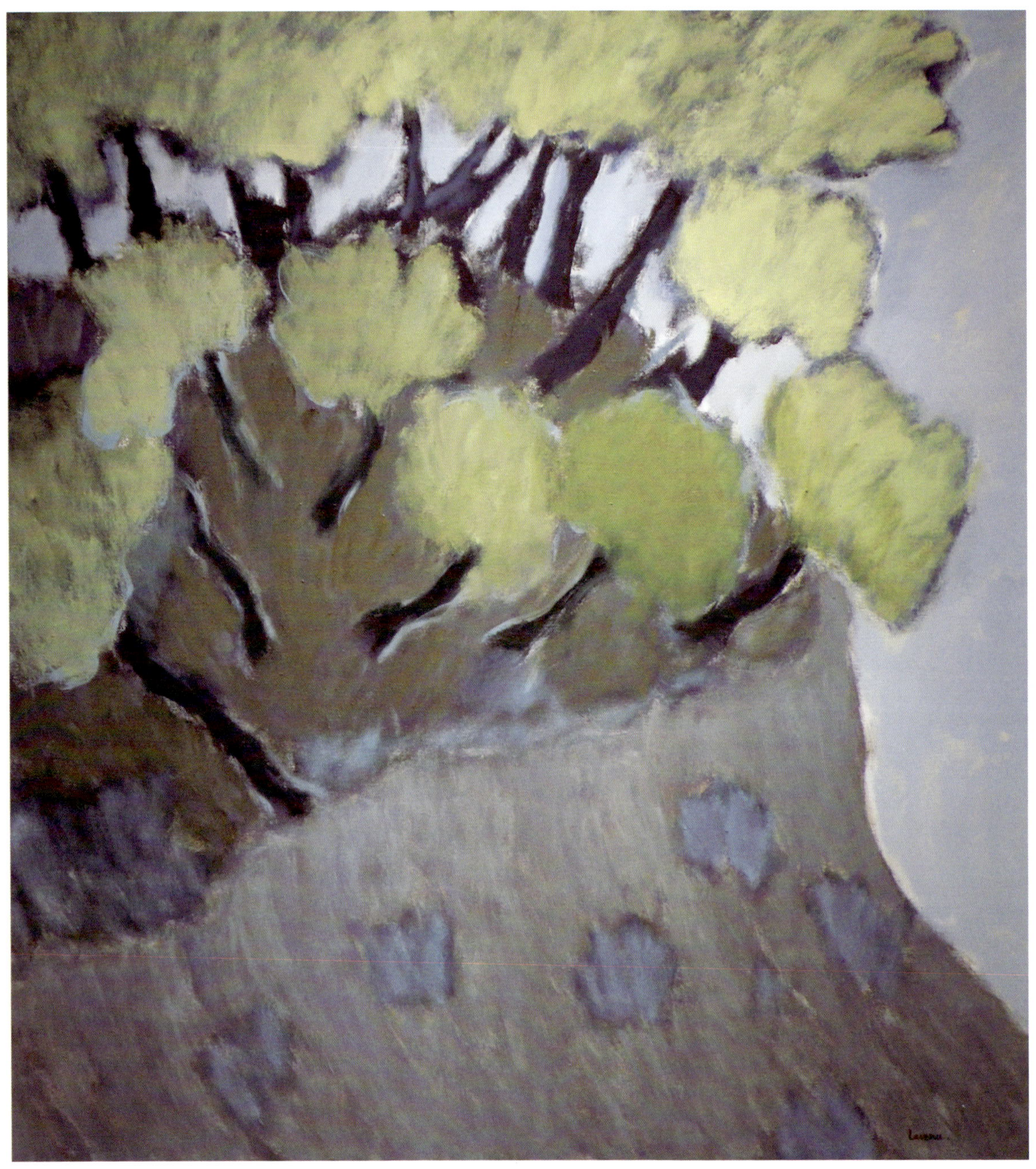

Muir Woods, oil on canvas, 138x122 cm, 2011. Private collection.

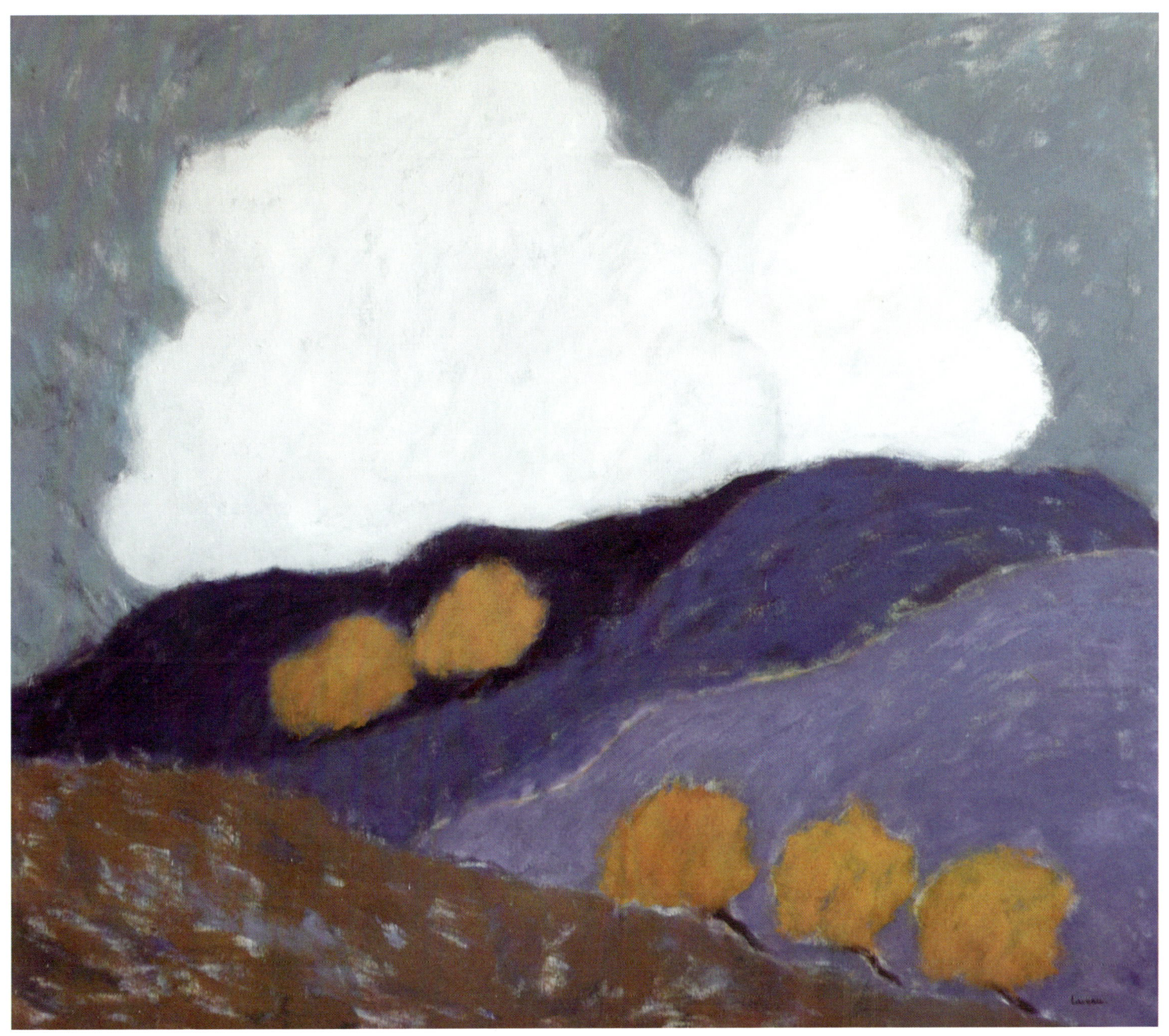

Before the storm, California, oil on canvas, 122x138 cm, 2011. Private collection.

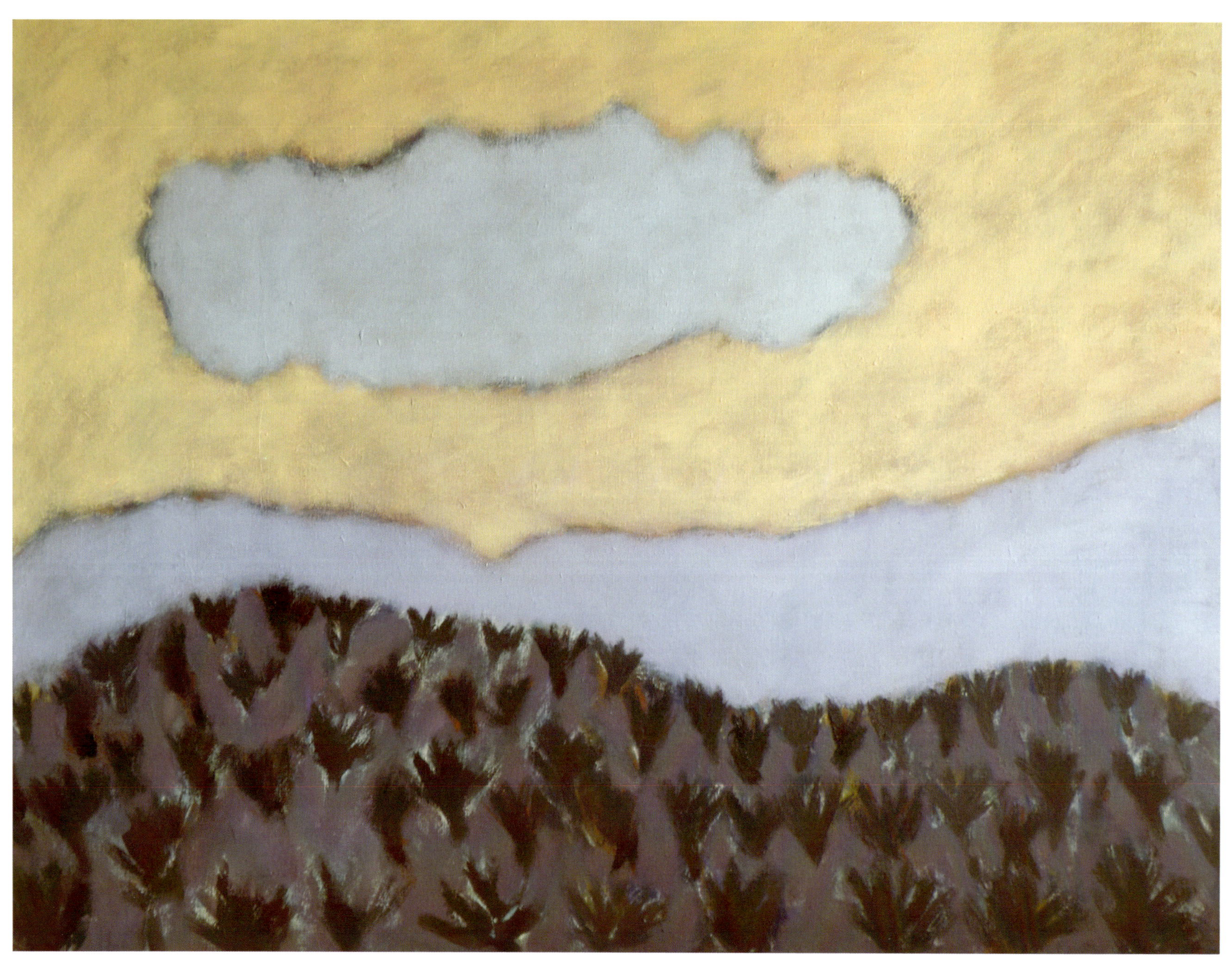

Almond trees in winter, California, oil on canvas, 112x142 cm, 2011. Private collection.

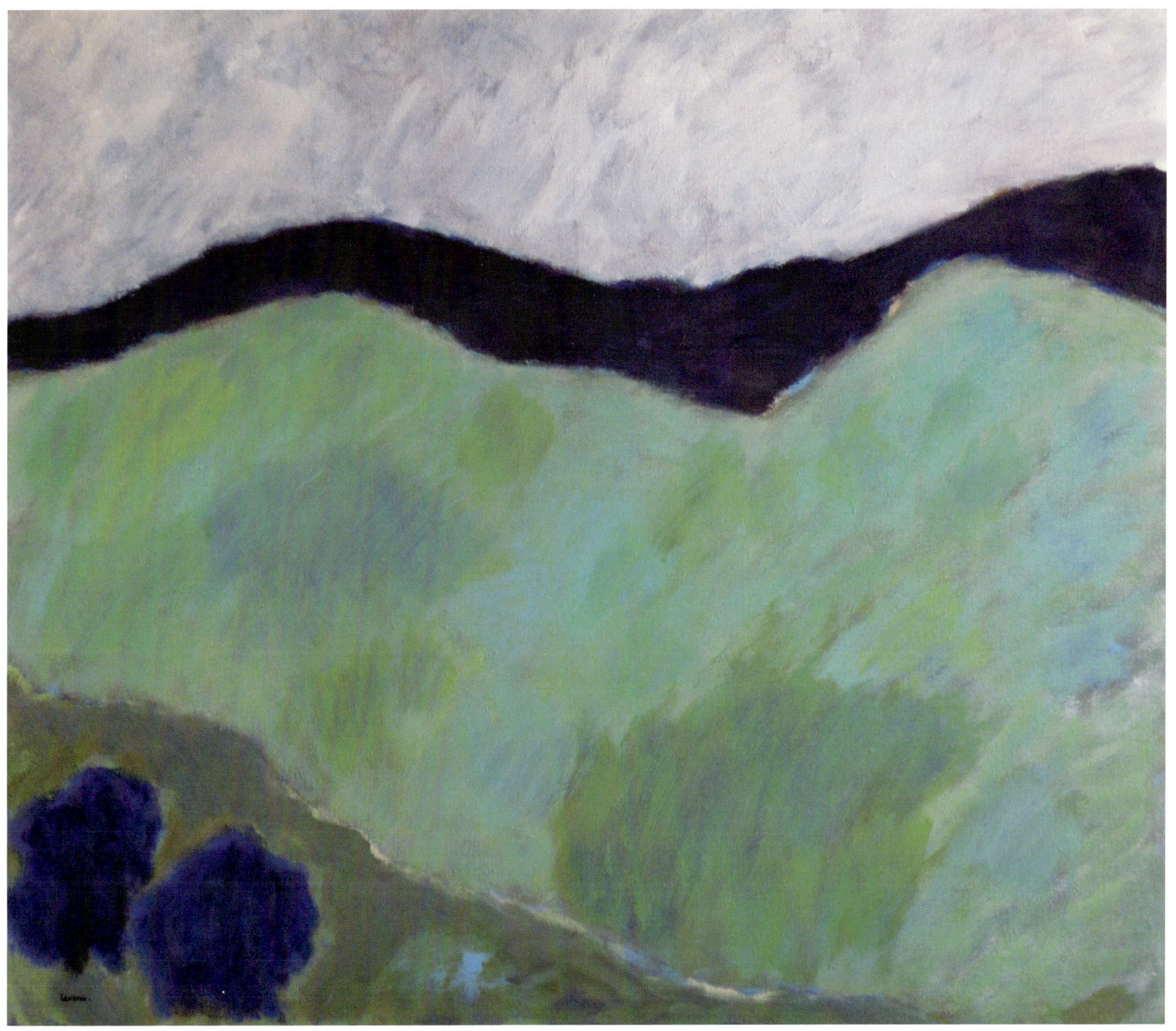

Road to Utah, oil on canvas, 122x138 cm, 2011.

Jacqueline Lavenu Studio & Gallery

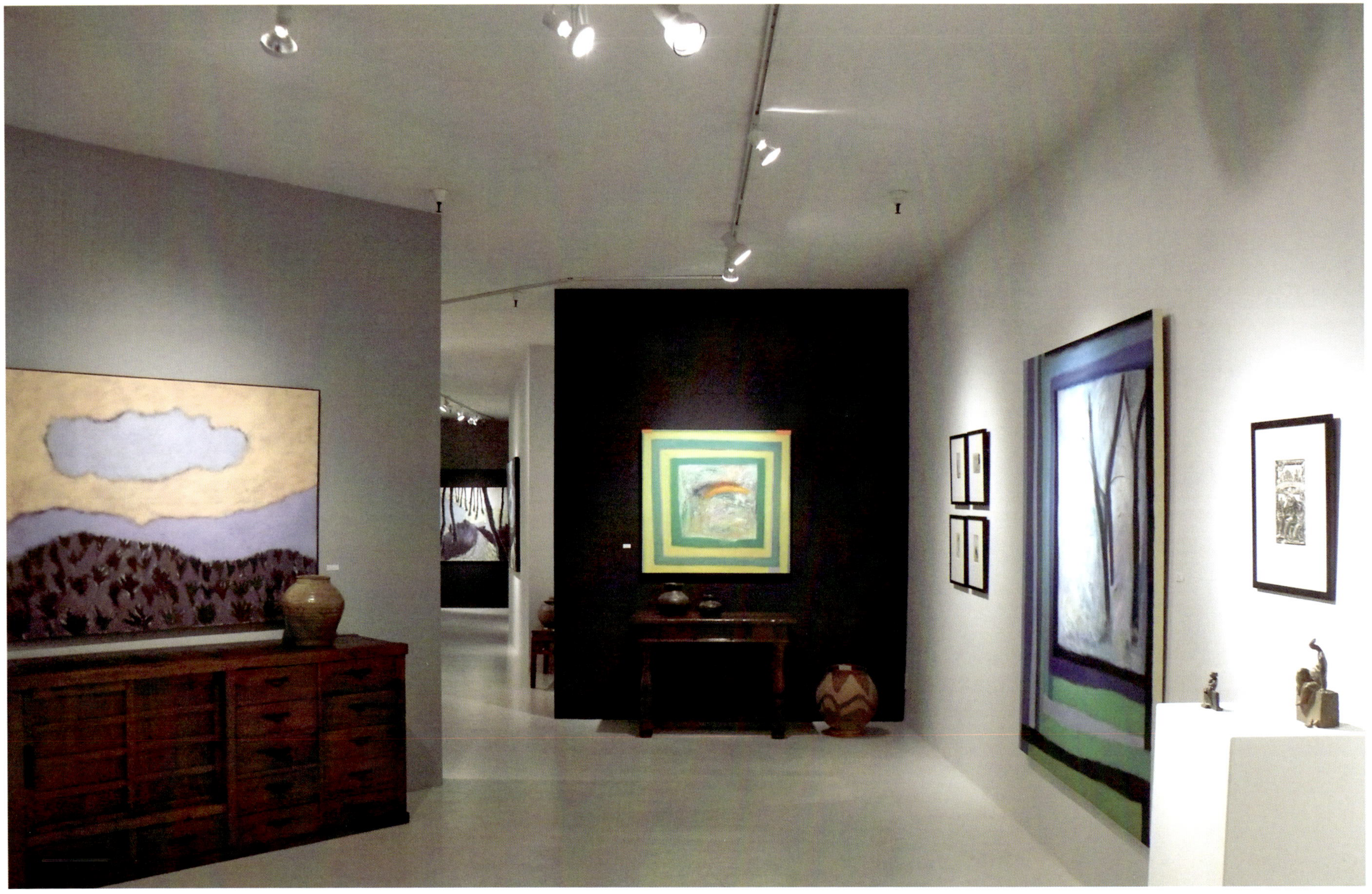

Jacqueline Lavenu Studio & Gallery. Works by Pia Stern, Igor Koutsenko, Albert Ultsch and Jacqueline Lavenu.
Japanese Merchant Tansu Chest and 17th Century Italian Writing Table with Nepalese, Japanese and Mexican ceramics.

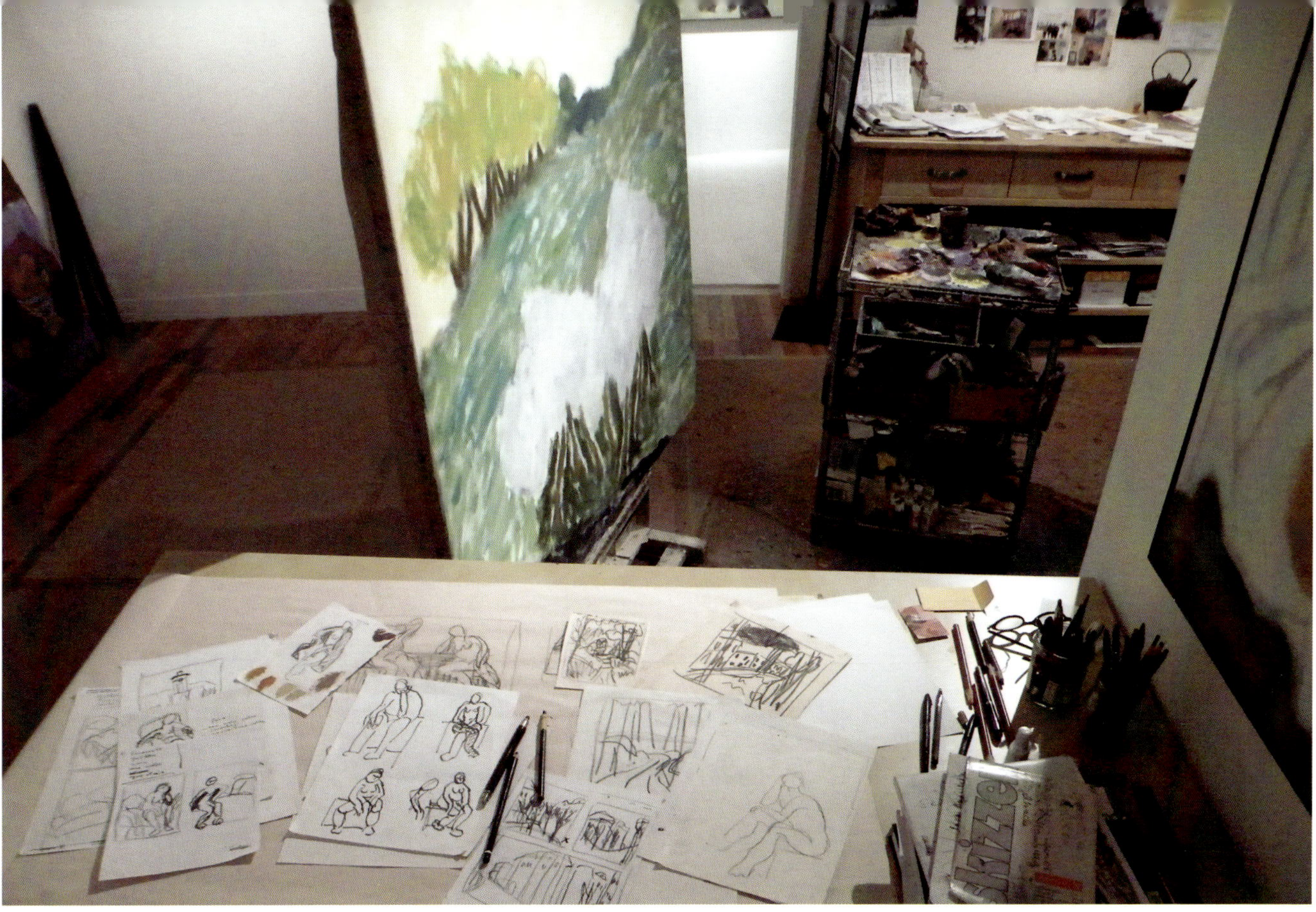

Jacqueline Lavenu Studio & Gallery opened its doors April 2010 in the Arts & Design building of San Diego's Little Italy and was the realization of Jacqueline's lifelong dream.

The main consideration for Jacqueline was to decide whether her work had reached a level of maturity to command a gallery all to itself. Having settled this in her mind Jacqueline has become her own gallerist and best representative for her work.

The idea to combine Art & Design was set many years ago: Art being such an essential part of our lives deserves to be presented as it would be seen in our homes. Color, composition and simplicity define Jacqueline's paintings. This same "Less is More" aesthetic she applies to her gallery. It is a place where one can sit, connect and absorb a serene ambiance. There is no pressure because the primary driver is not to sell but help people who are searching for beauty to bring into their homes.

The gallery is unique in that it brings together paintings and a few selected European and Asian antiques. This synthesis helps people imagine a painting in their home. Furthermore, since the focus is on the Art it also shows the primary role of a painting in any interior design project. That is it deserves to be selected first and furniture and accessories second.

The gallery speaks to a philosophy of "collecting" art. Jacqueline believes that the objective in owning art should not be that of "speculative investing"- with thoughts of appreciation in value. Rather Jacqueline views art as something that offers up an "experience"- an experience that should be brought into the home – one that will enrich, feed the soul, and elevate one's day to day life.

Jacqueline is not only interested in showcasing her own work – but also wants to promote other artists whose vision and work she feels is of quality, and complements her own: like Pia Stern, Igor Koutsenko, and sculptor Albert Ultsch. As Jacqueline puts it: "je ne cherche pas des peintres qui se vendent, je cherche à vendre des peintres que j'aime". (I am not looking for artists that sell. I am looking to sell artists I like).

Jacqueline Lavenu

Place of Birth:

Cherbourg, France

Education:

Art Academy, Le Mans, France.

Institute of Foreign Languages, Heidelberg, Germany.
Diploma in German Language.

Friedrich-Alexander Universität, Erlangen-Nürnberg, Germany.

Akademie der Bildenden Künste Nürnberg, Meisterschülerin (Master Student) with Professor Ernst Weil, Degree in Painting.

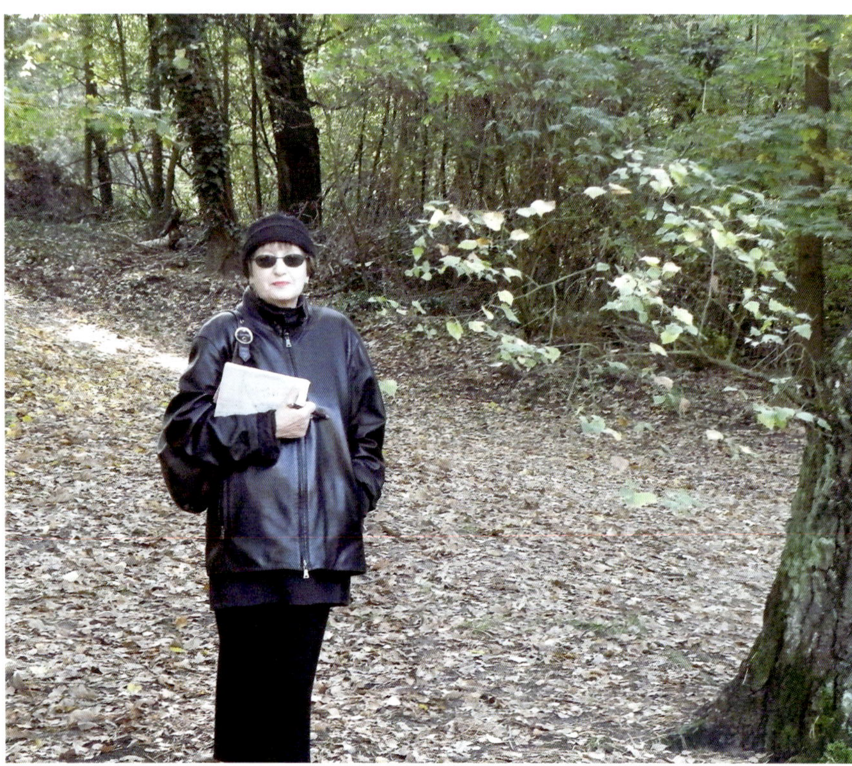

Jacqueline with sketchbook gathering inspiration, Germany, 2010.

Exhibitions

1973	Kunsthalle Nürnberg, Germany
	Bonn, Germany
1975	Pommersfelden Castle, Germany
	Bad Neustadt, Germany
	Grosse Kunstausstellung, Munich, Germany
1976	Contemporary Gallery, Dallas, Texas, USA
	Grosse Kunstausstellung, Haus der Kunst, Munich, Germany
1976/1980	Grosse Kunstausstellung, Haus der Kunst, Munich, Germany
1980	Gallery Lange, Berlin, Germany
	Max-Planck-Institut für Bildungsforschung, Berlin, Germany
1981	Grosse Kunstausstellung, Haus der Kunst, Munich, Germany
1982	Steigenberger, Berlin, Germany, Unter Schirmherrschaft von French Vice-Consul
1983	Bank für Handel und Industrie, Europa Center, Berlin, Germany
1984	Contemporary Gallery, Dallas, Texas, USA
1985	Gallery Davidson, Berlin, Germany
	Atelier, Berlin, Germany
1986-1988	San Diego Art Institute, San Diego, California, USA
1987	Palo Alto Medical Arts Foundation, Palo Alto, California, USA
1988	Hama Restaurant, Venice, California, USA
	Brushworks Gallery, San Diego, California, USA
	San Diego City Hall, San Diego, California, USA
1989-1998	Permanent exhibition in Gallery Davidson, Berlin, Germany
1996	Exhibit on the Island of Ibiza, Spain
1997/1998	Thidwicks Bookstore, Mission Hills, California, USA
1999/2000	Studio Exhibit, San Diego, California, USA
2000	Europa Center, Berlin, Germany
2001	Thidwicks Bookstore, San Francisco, California, USA
2002	Bread & Cie, San Diego, California, USA
2005	Roche-Bobois, La Jolla & Los Angeles, California, USA
2005	Studio Exhibit, San Diego, California, USA
2007	Bread & Cie, San Diego, California, USA
2008	Avenue5 Restaurant, San Diego, California, USA
2008	Gregory Matthew Inc., Scottsdale, Arizona, USA
2008-2010	Colibri Home, San Diego, California, USA
2009-2010	Studio Arts Gallery, San Diego, California, USA
2010-present	Jacqueline Lavenu Studio & Gallery, San Diego, California, USA